Wayne

Southwick

Grade 6

Springport Mich

1922

88

D1252155

AMERICAN SOLDIERS CELEBRATING THE FRENCH INDEPENDENCE DAY, PARIS, JULY 14, 1919

From a painting by J. F. Bouchor, Official Painter to the French Armies.

THE BEGINNER'S
AMERICAN HISTORY

BY

D. H. MONTGOMERY

AUTHOR OF THE LEADING FACTS OF HISTORY SERIES

NEW EDITION

GINN AND COMPANY

BOSTON · NEW YORK · CHICAGO · LONDON
ATLANTA · DALLAS · COLUMBUS · SAN FRANCISCO

THE LEADING FACTS OF HISTORY SERIES

BY D. H. MONTGOMERY

The Beginner's American History
(New Edition) (Biographies of
Eminent Americans)

An Elementary American History

The Leading Facts of American History
(New Revised Edition)

The Student's American History
(Revised Edition)

The Leading Facts of English History
(Revised Edition)

The Leading Facts of French History

The Athenæum Press

GINN AND COMPANY · PRO-
PRIETORS · BOSTON · U.S.A.

PREFATORY NOTE

THIS little book is intended by the writer as an introduction to his larger work entitled *The Leading Facts of American History*.

It is in no sense an abridgment of the larger history, but is practically an entirely new and distinct work.

Its object is to present clearly and accurately those facts and principles in the lives of some of the chief founders and builders of America which would be of interest and value to pupils beginning the study of our history. Throughout the book great care has been taken to relate only such incidents and anecdotes as are believed to rest on unexceptionable authority.

The words quoted literally in this book are enclosed in double quotation marks; those quoted in substance only are enclosed in single marks; while those attributed by the writer to different speakers have no marks.

In this edition the paging has been changed, but the numbering of the paragraphs remains the same.

DAVID H. MONTGOMERY.

CONTENTS

		PAGE
I.	COLUMBUS	1
II.	JOHN CABOT	14
III.	PONCE DE LEON, BALBOA, AND DE SOTO	19
IV.	SIR WALTER RALEIGH	22
V.	CAPTAIN JOHN SMITH	25
VI.	CAPTAIN HENRY HUDSON	36
VII.	CAPTAIN MYLES STANDISH	44
VIII.	LORD BALTIMORE	55
IX.	ROGER WILLIAMS	60
X.	KING PHILIP	66
XI.	WILLIAM PENN	76
XII.	GENERAL JAMES OGLETHORPE	84
XIII.	BENJAMIN FRANKLIN	89
XIV.	GEORGE WASHINGTON	103
XV.	DANIEL BOONE	132
XVI.	GENERAL JAMES ROBERTSON AND GOVERNOR JOHN SEVIER	140
XVII.	GENERAL GEORGE ROGERS CLARK	143
XVIII.	GENERAL RUFUS PUTNAM	150
XIX.	ELI WHITNEY	156
XX.	THOMAS JEFFERSON	162
XXI.	ROBERT FULTON	171
XXII.	GENERAL WILLIAM HENRY HARRISON	179
XXIII.	GENERAL ANDREW JACKSON	184
XXIV.	PROFESSOR MORSE	197
XXV.	GENERAL SAM HOUSTON	205
XXVI.	CAPTAIN ROBERT GRAY	209
XXVII.	CAPTAIN SUTTER	213
XXVIII.	ABRAHAM LINCOLN	222
XXIX.	SINCE THE CIVIL WAR — THE GREAT WAR	240
XXX.	A CHAPTER ON AMERICAN INVENTIONS	283
APPENDIX — A SHORT LIST OF BOOKS OF REFERENCE		i
INDEX		iii

LIST OF LARGE MAPS

PAGE

   I. Map illustrating Washington's Early Life . . . *facing*   106
  II. The Northern States in the Revolution . . . .   "   116
 III. The Southern States in the Revolution . . . .   "   124
 IV. The United States at the Close of the Revolution . . .   168
  V. The United States after the Purchase of Louisiana (1803)   169
 VI. The United States after the Purchase of Florida (1819) .   194
VII. The United States after the Acquisition of Texas (1845) .   208
VIII. The United States after the Acquisition of Oregon (1846)   211
 IX. The United States after the Acquisition of California and
       New Mexico (1848)   216
  X. The United States after the Gadsden Purchase (1853) . .   219
 XI. The United States after the Purchase of Alaska (1867).
       See Map of North America (giving a summary of the
       territorial growth of the United States) . . . *facing*   220
XII. Map of the World showing all the Possessions of the
       United States, including Islands . . . . . *facing*   244

NOTE. — In these maps it has been thought best to give the boundaries of the thirteen original states as they now exist; and to show the outlines of other states before they were organized and admitted.

LIST OF FULL-PAGE ILLUSTRATIONS

   I. American Soldiers in Paris (in colors) . . . . *Frontispiece*
  II. Liberty enlightening the World   43
 III. Indian Attack on a Settlement   73
 IV. "Yankee Doodle," or The Spirit of '76 . . . . *facing* 102
  V. Paul Revere's Ride . . . .   "   114
 VI. Battle of New Orleans . . . .   "   194
VII. Pershing's Victorious Army in Washington 277

THE BEGINNER'S AMERICAN HISTORY

I. CHRISTOPHER COLUMBUS

(1436–1506)[1]

1. Birth and boyhood of Columbus. * — Christopher Columbus,[2] the discoverer of America, was born at Genoa,[3] a seaport of Italy, more than four hundred and fifty years ago. His father was a wool-comber.[4] Christopher did not care to learn that trade, but wanted to become a sailor. Seeing the boy's strong liking for the sea, his father sent him to a school where he could

The paragraph headings, in heavy type, will be found useful for topical reference, and, if desired, as questions; by simply omitting these headings, the book may be used as a reader.

Teachers who wish a regular set of questions on each section will find them at the end of the section; see page 14. Difficult words are defined or pronounced at the bottom of the page where they first occur; reference to them will be found in the index.

[1] These enclosed dates under a name show, except when otherwise stated, the year of birth and death.

[2] Christopher Columbus (Kris'tof-er Ko-lum'bus).

[3] Genoa (Jen'o-ah); see map on page 15.

[4] Wool-comber: before wool can be spun into thread and woven into cloth, the tangled locks must be combed out straight and smooth; once this was all done by hand.

COLUMBUS AS A BOY

(From the statue in the Museum of Fine Arts, Boston.)

I

learn geography, map-drawing, and whatever else might help him to become, some day, commander of a vessel.

2. Columbus becomes a sailor. — When he was fourteen Columbus went to sea. In those days the Mediterranean[1] Sea swarmed with war-ships and pirates. Every sailor, no matter if he was but a boy, had to stand ready to fight his way from port to port.

In this exciting life, full of adventure and of danger, Columbus grew to manhood. The rough experiences he then had did much toward making him the brave, determined captain and explorer[2] that he afterwards became.

The light parts of this map show how much of the world was then well known; the white crosses show those countries of Eastern Asia of which something was known.

3. Columbus has a sea-fight; he goes to Lisbon. — According to some accounts, Columbus once had a desperate battle with a vessel off the coast of Portugal.[3] The fight lasted, it is said, all day. At length both vessels were found to be on fire. Columbus jumped from his blazing ship into the sea, and catching hold of a floating oar, managed, with its help, to swim to the shore, about six miles away.

[1] Mediterranean (Med′i-ter-rā′ne-an), the sea between Europe and Africa; it is shown on the map above, but not named.

[2] Explorer: one who explores or discovers new countries.

[3] Portugal is shown on the map on page 15.

He then went to the port of Lisbon.[1] There he
married the daughter of a famous sea captain. For a
long time after his marriage Columbus earned his living
partly by drawing maps, which he sold to commanders
of vessels visiting Lisbon, and partly by making voyages
to Africa, Iceland, and other countries.

4. What men then knew about the world. — The maps
which Columbus made and sold were very different from
those we now have. At that time not half of the world
had been discovered.[2] Europe, Asia, and a small part

This map shows how Columbus (not knowing that America lay in the way) hoped to
reach Asia and the East Indies by sailing west. The countries not then known are
shown covered with dark shading; for instance, nothing was then known of Africa
except the coast, and nothing at all of North and South America and Australia.

of Africa were the chief countries known. The maps of
Columbus may have shown the earth shaped like a ball;
but he supposed it to be much smaller than it really is.
No one then had sailed round the globe. No one then
knew what lands lay west of the broad Atlantic; for this
reason we should look in vain, on one of the maps drawn
by Columbus, for the great continents of North and
South America or for Australia or the Pacific Ocean.

[1] Lisbon; see map on page 15.   [2] See map on page 2.

5. The plan of Columbus for reaching the Indies by sailing west. — While living in Lisbon, Columbus made up his mind to try to do what no other man at that time dared attempt, — that was to cross the Atlantic Ocean He thought that, by doing so, he could get directly to Asia and the Indies, which, he believed, were opposite Portugal and Spain. If successful, he could open up a very profitable trade with the rich countries of the East, from which spices, drugs, and silk were brought to Europe. The people of Europe could not reach those countries directly by ships, because they had not then found their way round the southern point of Africa.

6. Columbus tries to get help in carrying out his plans. — Columbus was too poor to fit out even a single ship to undertake such a voyage as he had planned. He asked the king of Portugal to furnish some money or vessels toward it, but he received no encouragement. At length he determined to go to Spain and see if he could get help there.

On the southern coast of Spain there is a small port named Palos.[1] Within sight of the village of Palos, and within plain sight of the ocean, there was a convent,[2] — which is still standing, — called the Convent of Saint Mary.

One morning a tall, fine-looking man, leading a little boy by the hand, knocked at the door of this convent and begged for a piece of bread and a cup of water for the child. The man was Columbus, — whose wife was now dead, — and the boy was his son.

---

[1] Palos (Pä′lōs); see map on page 9.
[2] Convent: a house in which a number of people live who devote themselves to a religious life.

It chanced that the guardian of the convent noticed Columbus standing at the door. He liked his appearance, and coming up, began to talk with him. Columbus frankly told him what he was trying to do. The guardian of the convent listened with great interest; then he gave him a letter to a friend who, he thought, would help him to lay his plans before Ferdinand and Isabella,[1] the king and queen of Spain.

7. Columbus gets help for his great voyage. — Columbus left his son at the convent and set forward on his journey, full of bright hopes. But Ferdinand and Isabella could not then see him; and after waiting a long time, the traveller was

COLUMBUS BEGGING AT THE CONVENT

told that he might go before a number of learned men and tell them about his proposed voyage across the Atlantic.

After hearing what Columbus had to say, these men thought that it would be foolish to spend money in trying to reach the other side of the ocean.

People who heard what this captain from Lisbon wanted to do, began to think that he had lost his reason; and the boys in the streets laughed at him and called him crazy. Columbus waited for help seven years; he then made up his mind that he would wait

---

[1] Ferdinand (Fer'di-nand); Isabella (Iz-ah-bel'ah).

no longer. Just as he was about leaving Spain, Queen
Isabella, who had always felt interested in the brave
sailor, resolved to aid him. Two rich sea captains who
lived in Palos also decided to take part in the voyage.
With the assistance which Columbus now got he was
able to fit out three small vessels. He went in the
largest of the vessels — the only one which had an
entire deck — as admiral[1] or commander of the fleet.

8. Columbus sails. — Early on Friday morning, August
3, 1492, Columbus started from Palos to attempt to
cross that ocean which men then called the "Sea of
Darkness," — a name which showed how little they
knew of it, and how much they dreaded it.

We may be pretty sure that the guardian of the convent was one of those who watched the sailing of the
little fleet. From the upper windows of the convent he
could plainly see the vessels as they left the harbor of
Palos.

9. What happened on the first part of the voyage. — Columbus sailed first for the Canary Islands,[2] because from
there it would be a straight line, as he thought, across
to Japan and Asia.[3] He was obliged to stop at the
Canaries from August 12 to September 6, or more than
three weeks, in order to make a new rudder for one of
his vessels and to alter the sails of another.

At length all was ready, and he again set out on his
voyage toward the west. When the vessels got so far
out on the ocean that the sailors could no longer see
any of the islands, they were overcome with fear.
They made up their minds that they should never be

---

[1] Admiral (ad'mi-ral).

[2] Canaries (Ka-na'rez) ; see map on page 9.   [3] See map on page 3.

able to get back to Palos again. They were rough men, used to the sea, but now they bowed down their heads and cried like children. Columbus had hard work to quiet their fears and to encourage them to go forward with the voyage which they already wanted to give up.

10. What happened after they had been at sea many days. — For more than thirty days the three ships kept on their way toward the west. To the crew every day seemed a year. From sunrise to sunset nothing was to be seen but water and sky. At last the men began to think that they were sailing on an ocean which had no end. They whispered among themselves that Columbus had gone mad, and that if they kept on with him in command they should all be lost.

COLUMBUS REFUSES TO TURN BACK

Twice, indeed, there was a joyful cry of Land! land! but when they got nearer they saw that what they had thought was land was nothing but banks of clouds. Then some of the sailors said, Let us go to the admiral and tell him that we must turn back. What if he will not listen to us? asked others. Then we will throw him overboard, and say, when we reach Palos, that he fell into the sea and was drowned.

But when the crew went to Columbus and told him that they would go no further, he sternly ordered them to their work, declaring that, whatever might happen, he would not now give up the voyage.

11. Signs of land. — The very next day such certain signs of land were seen that the most faint-hearted took courage. The men had already noticed great flocks of land-birds flying toward the west, as if to guide them. Now some of the men on one vessel saw a branch of a thorn-bush float by. It was plain that it had not long been broken off from the bush, and it was full of red berries.

But one of the crew on the other vessel found something better even than the thorn-branch ; for he drew out of the water a carved walking-stick. Every one saw that such a stick must have been cut and carved by human hands. These two signs could not be doubted. The men now felt sure that they were approaching the shore, and what was more, that there were people living in that strange country.

12. Discovery of land. — That evening Columbus begged his crew to keep a sharp lookout, and he promised a velvet coat to the one who should first see land. All was now excitement, and no man closed his eyes in sleep that night.

Columbus himself stood on a high part of his ship, looking steadily toward the west. About ten o'clock he saw a moving light ; it seemed like a torch carried in a man's hand. He called to a companion and asked him if he could see anything of the kind ; yes, he, too, plainly saw the moving light ; but presently it disappeared.

Two hours after midnight a cannon was fired from the foremost vessel. It was the glad signal that the long-looked-for land was actually in sight. There it lay directly ahead, about six miles away.

Then Columbus gave the order to furl sails, and the three vessels came to a stop and waited for the dawn. When the sun rose on Friday, October 12, 1492, Columbus saw a beautiful island with many trees growing on it. That was his first sight of the New World.

13. Columbus lands on the island and names it; who lived on the island. — Attended by the captains of the other two vessels, and by a part of their crews, Columbus set

Map showing the direction in which Columbus sailed on his great voyage across the ocean.

out in a boat for the island. When they landed, all fell on their knees, kissed the ground for joy, and gave thanks to God. Columbus named the island San Salvador [1] and took possession of it, by right of discovery, for the king and queen of Spain.

He found that it was inhabited by a copper-colored people who spoke a language he could not understand. These people had never seen a ship or a white man before. They wore no clothing, but painted their bodies with bright colors. The Spaniards made them presents of strings of glass beads and red caps. In return they

[1] San Salvador (San Sal-va-dōr'): meaning the Holy Redeemer or Saviour

gave the Spaniards skeins of cotton yarn, tame parrots, and small ornaments of gold.

After staying here a short time Columbus set sail toward the south, in search of more land and in the hope of finding out where these people got their gold.

14. Columbus names the group of islands and their people. — As Columbus sailed on, he saw many islands in every

LANDING OF COLUMBUS

direction. He thought that they must be a part of the Indies which he was seeking. Since he had reached them by coming west from Spain, he called them the West Indies, and to the red men who lived on them he gave the name of Indians.

15. Columbus discovers two very large islands; his vessel is wrecked, and he returns to Spain in another. — In the course of the next six weeks, Columbus discovered the island of Cuba. At first he thought that it must be Japan, but afterward he came to the conclusion that it was not an island at all, but part of the mainland of Asia.

Next, he came to the island of Hayti,[1] or San Domingo.[2] Here his ship was wrecked. He took the timber of the wreck and built a fort on the shore. Leaving about forty of his crew in this fort, Columbus set sail for Palos in one of the two remaining vessels.

16. Columbus arrives at Palos; joy of the people; how Ferdinand and Isabella received him. — When the vessel of Columbus was seen entering the harbor of Palos, the whole village was wild with excitement. More than seven months had gone by since he sailed away from that port, and as nothing had been heard from him, many supposed that the vessels and all on board were lost. Now that they saw their friends and neighbors coming back, all was joy. The bells of the churches rang a merry peal of welcome; the people thronged the streets, shouting to each other that Columbus, the great navigator, had crossed the " Sea of Darkness " and had returned in safety.

The king and queen were then in the city of Barcelona,[3] a long distance from Palos. To that city Columbus now went. He entered it on horseback, attended by the proudest and richest noblemen of Spain. He brought with him six Indians from the West Indies. They were gaily painted and wore bright feathers in their hair. Then a number of men followed, carrying rare birds, plants, and gold and silver ornaments, all

[1] Hayti (Hă′ti).　　[2] San Domingo (San Dō-min′go); see map on page 12.
[3] Barcelona (Bar-se-lō′na); see map on page 9.

found in the New World. These were presents for the king and queen. Ferdinand and Isabella received Columbus with great honor. When he had told them the story of his wonderful voyage, they sank on their knees and gave praise to God; all who were present followed their example.

17. The last voyages of Columbus. — Columbus made three more voyages across the Atlantic. He discovered more islands near the coast of America, and he touched the coast of Central America and of South America, but that was all. He never set foot on any

The light parts of this map show how much of America Columbus discovered. (The long island is Cuba; the large one to the right is San Domingo.)

part of what is now the mainland of the United States; and he always thought that the land he had reached was part of Asia. He had found a new world, but he did not know it; all that he knew was how to get to it and how to show others the way.

18. Columbus in his old age. — The last days of this great man were very sorrowful. The king was disappointed because he brought back no gold to amount to anything. The Spanish governor of San Domingo hated Columbus, and when he landed at that island on one of his voyages, he arrested him and sent him back to Spain in chains. He was at once set at liberty; but he could not forget the insult. He kept the chains hanging on the wall of his room, and asked to have them buried with him.

Columbus was now an old man; his health was broken, he was poor, in debt, and without a home. Once he wrote to the king and queen saying, " I have not a hair upon me that is not gray, my body is weak, and all that was left to me . . . has been taken away and sold, even to the coat which I wore."

Not long after he had come back to Spain to stay, the queen died. Then Columbus felt that he had lost his best friend. He gave up hope and said, " I have done all that I could do; I leave the rest to God."

19. His death and burial. — Columbus died full of disappointment and sorrow, — perhaps it would not be too much to say that he died of a broken heart.

He was at first buried in Spain; then his body was taken up and carried to San Domingo, where he had wished to be buried. Whether it rests there to-day, or whether it was carried to Havana,[1] deposited in the cathedral or great church of that city, and was finally carried back to Spain,[2] no one can positively say. But wherever the grave of the great sailor may be, his memory will live in every heart capable of respecting a brave man; for he first dared to cross the " Sea of Darkness," and he discovered America.

[1] Havana (Ha-van'ah) : the capital of Cuba.

[2] At the close of the war of the United States with Spain what was believed to be the body of Columbus was taken from its tomb, in the Cathedral of Havana, and was carried back to Spain.

20. Summary. — In 1492 Christopher Columbus set sail from Spain to find a direct way across the Atlantic to Asia and the Indies. He did not get to Asia; but he did better : he discovered America. He died thinking that the new lands he had found were part of Asia; but by his daring voyage he first showed the people of Europe how to get to the New World.

When and where was Columbus born? What did he do when he was fourteen? What is said about his sea-fight? What did he do in Lisbon? How much of the world was then known? How did Columbus think he could reach Asia and the Indies? Why did he want to go there? What did he try to do in Portugal? Why did he go to Spain? Where did he first go in Spain? How did Columbus get help at last? When did he sail? What happened on the first part of the voyage? What happened after that? What is said about signs of land? What about the discovery of land? What did Columbus name the island? What did he find on it? What is said of other islands? What is said of the return of Columbus to Spain? What about the last voyages of Columbus? Did he ever land on any part of what is now the United States? What about his old age? What is said of his death and burial?

II. JOHN CABOT [1]

(Lived in England from 1472–1498)

21. John Cabot discovers the *continent* of North America. — At the time that Columbus set out on his first voyage across the Atlantic, in 1492, John Cabot, an Italian merchant, was living in the city of Bristol,[2] England. When the news reached that city that Columbus had discovered the West Indies, Cabot begged Henry the Seventh, king of England, to let him see if he could not find a shorter way to the Indies than that of Columbus. The king gave his consent; and in the spring of 1497

[1] Cabot (Cab'ot).   [2] See map on page 44.

John Cabot, with his son Sebastian,[1] who seems to have been born in Bristol, sailed from that port. They headed their vessels toward the northwest; by going in that

direction they hoped to get to those parts of Asia and the Spice Islands which were known to Europe, and which Columbus had failed to reach.

Map showing the city of Venice, Italy, where John Cabot had lived.

Early one bright morning toward the last of June, 1497, they saw land in the west. It was probably Cape Breton[2] Island, a part of Nova Scotia.[3] John Cabot named it "The Land First Seen." Up to this time Columbus had dis-covered nothing except the West India Islands; but John Cabot now saw the continent of North America. No civ-ilized man[4] had ever seen it before. There it lay, a great, lonely land, shaggy with for-ests, with not a house or a human being in sight.

22. John Cabot takes possession of the country for the king of England. — Cabot went on shore, with his son and

---

[1] Sebastian (Se-bast′yan).   [2] Breton (Brĕt′on).

[3] Nova Scotia (Nō′vah Sko′she-a).

[4] The Northmen: an uncivilized people of Norway and Denmark discovered the continent of North America about five hundred years before Cabot did. Nothing came of this discovery; and when Cabot sailed, no one seems to have known anything about what the Northmen had done so long before.

some of his crew. In the vast, silent wilderness they set up a large cross. Near to it they planted two flag-poles, and hoisted the English flag on one, and the flag of Venice,[1] the city where John Cabot had lived in Italy, on the other. Then they took possession of the land

for Henry the Seventh. It was in this way that the English came to consider that the eastern coast of North America was their property, although they did not begin to make settlements here until nearly a hundred years later.

23. John Cabot and his son return to Bristol. — After sailing about the Gulf of St. Lawrence without finding the passage

CABOT TAKING POSSESSION FOR ENGLAND

through to Asia for which they were looking, the voyagers returned to England.

The king was so pleased with what John Cabot had discovered that he made him a handsome present; and when the captain, richly dressed in silk, appeared in the street, the people of Bristol would "run after him like mad" and hurrah for the "Great Admiral," as they called him.

[1] Venice (Ven′is).

24. What the Cabots carried back to England from America. — The Cabots carried back to England some Indian traps for catching game and perhaps some wild turkeys, — an American bird the English had then never seen, but whose acquaintance they were not sorry to make. They also carried over the rib of a whale which they had found on the beach in Nova Scotia.

Near where the Cabots probably lived in Bristol there is a famous old church.[1] It was built long before the discovery of America, and Queen Elizabeth said that it was the most beautiful building of its kind in all England. In that church hangs the rib of a whale. It is believed to be the one the Cabots brought home with them. It reminds all who see it of that voyage in 1497 by which England got possession of a very large part of the continent of North America.

25. The second voyage of the Cabots; how they sailed along the eastern shores of North America. — About a year later, the Cabots set out on a second voyage to the west. They reached the gloomy cliffs of Labrador[2] on the northeastern coast of America, and they passed many immense icebergs. They saw numbers of Indians dressed in the skins of wild beasts, and polar bears as white as snow. These bears were great swimmers, and would dive into the sea and come up with a large fish in their claws. As it did not look to the Cabots as if the polar bears and the icebergs would guide them to the warm countries of Asia and the Spice Islands, they turned about and went south. They sailed along what is now the eastern coast of the United States for a very long distance; but, not finding any passage

---

[1] The church of St. Mary Redcliffe.   [2] Labrador (Lab'ra-dŏr).

through to the countries they were seeking, they returned to England.

The English now began to see what an immense extent of land they had found beyond the Atlantic.

Map showing how much of the continent of North America was discovered by the Cabots.

They could not tell, however, whether it was a continent by itself or a part of Asia. Like everybody in Europe, they called it the New World; but all that name really meant then was simply the New Lands across the sea.

26. How the New World came to be called America. — Not many years after this the New World received the name by which we now call it. An Italian navigator whose first name was Amerigo[1] made a voyage to it after it had been discovered by Columbus and the Cabots. He wrote an account of what he saw, and as this was the first printed description of the continent, it was named from him, AMERICA.

27. Summary. — In 1497 John Cabot and his son, Sebastian, from Bristol, England, discovered the mainland or continent of North America, and took possession of it for England. The next year they came over and sailed along the eastern coast of what is now the United States.

An Italian whose first name was Amerigo visited the

---

[1] Amerigo (A-ma-ree'go): his full name was Amerigo Vespucci (A-ma-ree'go Ves-poot'chee), or, as he wrote it in Latin, Americus Vespucius.

New World afterward and wrote the first account of the
mainland which was printed.   For this reason the whole
continent was named after him, AMERICA.

Who was John Cabot?   What did he try to do?   Who sailed with
him?   What land did they see?   Had Columbus ever seen it?   What
did Cabot do when he went on shore?   What is said of his return to
Bristol?   What did the Cabots carry back to England?   What is said
about the second voyage of the Cabots?   How did the New World
come to be called America?

III. PONCE DE LEON,[1] BALBOA,[2] AND
DE SOTO[3]

(Period of Discovery, 1513-1542)

**28. The magic fountain; Ponce de Leon discovers Florida;
Balboa discovers the Pacific Ocean.** — The Indians on the
West India Islands believed that there was a wonderful
fountain in a land to the west of them.   They said that
if an old man should bathe in its waters, they would
make him a boy again.   Ponce de Leon, a Spanish
soldier who was getting gray and wrinkled, set out to
find this magic fountain, for he thought that there was
more fun in being a boy than in growing old.

He did not find the fountain; and so his hair grew
grayer than ever and his wrinkles grew deeper.   But in
1513 he discovered a land bright with flowers, which he
named Florida.[4]   He took possession of it for Spain.

[1] Ponce de Leon (Pon'thay day Lā-ōn'), or, in English, Pons de Lee'on.
Many persons now prefer the English pronunciation of all these Spanish names.
[2] Balboa (Bal-bō'ah).   [3] De Soto (Dä So'to).
[4] Florida: this word means flowery; the name was given by the Spaniards
because they discovered the country on Easter Sunday, which they call Flowery
Easter.

The same year another Spaniard, named Balboa, set out to explore the Isthmus of Panama.[1] One day he climbed to the top of a very high hill, and discovered that vast ocean — the greatest of all the oceans of the globe — which we call the Pacific.

29. De Soto discovers the Mississippi. — Long after Balboa and Ponce de Leon were dead, a Spaniard named De Soto

landed in Florida and marched through the country in search of gold mines.

In the course of his long and weary wanderings, he came to a river more than a mile across. The Indians told him it was the Mississippi, or the Great River. In discovering it, De Soto had found the

DE SOTO'S FIRST VIEW OF THE MISSISSIPPI

largest river in North America; he had also found his own grave, for he died shortly afterward, and was secretly buried at midnight in its muddy waters.

30. The Spaniards build St. Augustine[2]; we buy Florida in 1819. — More than twenty years after the burial of De Soto, a Spanish soldier named Menendez[3] went to Florida and built a fort on the eastern coast.   This was

---

[1] Panama (Pan-a-mah').
[2] St. Augustine (Sănt Aw'gus-teen).   [3] Menendez (Ma-nen'deth).

in 1565. The fort became the centre of a settlement named St. Augustine. It is the oldest city built by white men, not only in what is now the United States, but in all North America.

In 1819, or more than two hundred and fifty years after St. Augustine was begun, Spain sold Florida to the United States.

OLD SPANISH GATEWAY AT ST. AUGUSTINE
(Called the " City Gate.")

31. Summary. — Ponce de Leon discovered Florida; another Spaniard, named Balboa, discovered the Pacific; still another, named De Soto, discovered the Mississippi. In 1565 the Spaniards began to build St. Augustine in Florida. It is the oldest city built by white men in the United States or, in fact, in all North America.

What is said about a magic fountain? What did Ponce de Leon do? What is said about Balboa? What is said about De Soto? What did Menendez do in Florida? What is said of St. Augustine?

IV. SIR WALTER RALEIGH [1]

(1552–1618)

32. Walter Raleigh sends two ships to America ; how the Indians received the Englishmen. — Although John Cabot discovered the continent of North America in 1497 and

SIR WALTER RALEIGH

took possession of the land for the English,[2] yet the English themselves did not try to settle here until nearly a hundred years later.

Then (1584) a young man named Walter Raleigh, who was a great favorite of Queen Elizabeth's, sent out two ships to America. The captains of these vessels landed on Roanoke [3] Island, on the coast of what is now the state of North Carolina. They found the island covered with tall red cedars and with vines thick with clusters of wild grapes. The Indians called this place the "Good Land." They were pleased to see the Englishmen, and they invited them to a great feast of roast turkey, venison,[4] melons, and nuts.

33. Queen Elizabeth names the country Virginia ; first settlers ; what they sent Walter Raleigh. — When the two

---

[1] Raleigh (Raw′li).   [2] See page 16.   [3] Roanoke (Ro-a-nōk′).
[4] Venison (ven′i-zon or ven′zon) : deer meat.

captains returned to England, Queen Elizabeth — the "Virgin Queen," as she was called — was delighted with what she heard of the "Good Land." She named it Virginia in honor of herself. She also gave Raleigh a title of honor. From that time he was no longer called plain Walter Raleigh or Mr. Raleigh, but Sir Walter Raleigh.

Sir Walter now (1585) shipped over emigrants[1] to settle in Virginia. They sent back to him, as a present, two famous American plants — one called Tobacco, the other the Potato. The queen had given Sir Walter a fine estate in Ireland, and he set out both the plants in his garden. The tobacco plant did not grow very well there, but the potato did; and after a time thousands of farmers began to raise that vegetable, not only in Ireland, but in England too. As far back as that time — or more than three hundred years ago — America was beginning to feed the people of the Old World.

34. The Virginia settlement destroyed. — Sir Walter spent immense sums of money on his settlement in Virginia, but it did not succeed. One of the settlers, named Dare, had a daughter born there. He named her Virginia Dare. She was the first English child born in America. But the little girl, with her father and mother and all the rest of the settlers, disappeared. It is supposed that

---

[1] Emigrants: persons who leave one country to go and settle in another. Thousands of emigrants from Europe now land in this country every month.

they were killed by the Indians or that they wandered away and starved to death; but all that we really know is that not one of them was ever seen again.

35. Last days of Sir Walter Raleigh. — After Queen Elizabeth died, King James the First became ruler of England. He accused Sir Walter of trying to take away his crown so as to make some one else ruler over the country. Sir Walter was sent to prison and kept there for many years.

THE FIRST PIPE OF TOBACCO
(Raleigh's servant thought his master was on fire.)

At last King James released him in order to send him to South America to get gold. When Sir Walter returned to London without any gold, the greedy king accused him of having disobeyed him because he had fought with some Spaniards. Raleigh was condemned to death and was beheaded.

But Sir Walter's attempt to settle Virginia led other Englishmen to try. Before he died they built a town, called Jamestown, on the coast. We shall presently read the history of that town. The English held Virginia from that time until it became part of the United States.

36. Summary. — Sir Walter Raleigh sent over men from England to explore the coast of America. Queen Elizabeth named the country they visited Virginia. Raleigh then shipped emigrants over to make a settlement. These emigrants sent him two American plants,

Tobacco and the Potato; in that way the people of Great Britain and Ireland came to like both. Sir Walter's settlement failed; but his example led other Englishmen to try to make one. Before he was beheaded they had succeeded.

What is said about Walter Raleigh? What is said about the Indians? What name did Queen Elizabeth give to the country? What did she do for Walter Raleigh? What did Sir Walter then do? What American plants did the emigrants send him? What did he do with those plants? What happened to the Virginia settlement? What is said of the last days of Sir Walter Raleigh? Did Sir Walter's attempt to settle Virginia do any good?

V. CAPTAIN JOHN SMITH

(1579–1631)

37. New and successful attempt to make a settlement in Virginia; Captain John Smith. — One of the leaders in the new expedition sent out to make a settlement in Virginia, while Raleigh was in prison, was Captain John Smith. He began life as a clerk in England. Not liking his work, he ran away and turned soldier. After many strange adventures, he was captured by the Turks and sold as a slave. His master, who was a Turk, riveted a heavy iron collar around his neck and set him to thrashing grain with a big wooden bat like a ball-club. One day the Turk rode up and struck his slave with his riding-whip. This was more than Smith could bear; he rushed at his master, and with one blow of his bat knocked his brains out. He then mounted the dead man's horse and escaped. After a time he got back to England; but as England seemed a little dull to Captain

Smith, he resolved to join some emigrants who were going to Virginia.

38. What happened to Captain Smith on the voyage; the landing at Jamestown; what the settlers wanted to do; Smith's plan. — On the way to America, Smith was accused of

CAPTAIN JOHN SMITH

plotting to murder the chief men among the emigrants so that he might make himself "King of Virginia." The accusation was false; but he was put in irons and kept a prisoner for the rest of the voyage.

In the spring of 1607 the emigrants reached Chesapeake [1] Bay, and sailed up a river which they named the James

in honor of King James the First, of England; when they landed they named the settlement Jamestown for the same reason. Here they built a log fort, and placed three or four small cannon on its walls. Most of the men who settled Jamestown came hoping to find mines of gold in Virginia, or else a way through to the Pacific Ocean and to the Indies,[2] which they thought could not be very far away. But Captain Smith

[1] Chesapeake (Ches'a-peek).

[2] These men (in case they failed to find gold in Virginia) were anxious to discover a short direct route to the East Indies, in order to open trade for the spices, drugs, silks, and pearls which were brought from those "rich countries of the East" to Europe. See Columbus, page 4, and Cabot, page 14.

wanted to help his countrymen to make homes here for themselves and their children.

39. Smith's trial and what came of it; how the settlers lived; the first English church; sickness; attempted desertion. — As soon as Captain Smith landed, he demanded to be tried by a jury[1] of twelve men. The trial took place. It was the first English court and the first English jury that ever sat in America. The captain proved his innocence and was set free. His chief accuser was condemned to pay him a large sum of money for damages. Smith generously gave this money to help the settlement.

As the weather was warm, the emigrants did not begin building log cabins at once, but slept on the ground, sheltered by boughs of trees. For a church they had an old tent, in which they met on Sunday. They were all members of the Church of England (or the Episcopal Church), and that tent was the first place of worship, that we know of, which was opened by Englishmen in America.

When the hot weather came, many fell sick. Soon the whole settlement was like a hospital. Sometimes three or four would die in one night. Captain Smith, though not well himself, did everything he could for those who needed his help.

When the sickness was over, some of the settlers

---

[1] Jury: a number of men, generally twelve, selected according to law to try a case in a court of law; in criminal cases they declare the person accused to be either guilty or not guilty.

were so discontented that they determined to seize the only vessel there was at Jamestown and to go back to England. Captain Smith turned the cannon of the fort against them. The deserters saw that if they tried to leave the harbor he would knock their vessel to pieces; so they came back. One of the leaders of these men was tried and shot; the other was sent to England in disgrace.

40. The Indians of Virginia. — When the Indians of America first met the white men, they were very friendly to them; but this did not last long, because often the whites treated the Indians very badly; in fact, the Spaniards made slaves of them and whipped many of them to death. But these were generally the Indians of the West Indies and South America; some of the tribes of North America, especially those in what is now New York State, were terribly fierce and a match for the Spaniards in cruelty.

The Indians at the east did not build cities, but lived in small villages. These villages were made up of huts, covered with the bark of trees. Such huts were called wigwams. The women did nearly all the work, such as building the wigwams and hoeing corn and tobacco. The men hunted and made war. Instead of guns, the Indians had bows and arrows. With these they could bring down a deer or a squirrel quite as well as a white man could now with a rifle. They had no iron, but made hatchets and knives out of sharp, flat stones. They never built roads, for they had no wagons, and at the east they did not use horses; but they could find their way with ease through the thickest forest. When they came to a river they swam across it, so they had no need of bridges. For boats they made canoes of birch bark. These canoes were almost as light as paper, yet they were very strong and handsome, and they

> floated on the river
> Like a yellow leaf in autumn,
> Like a yellow water-lily.[1]

In them they could go hundreds of miles quickly and silently. So every river and stream, throughout North America, became a roadway to the Indian.

41. Captain Smith goes in search of the Pacific; he is captured by Indians. — After that first long, hot summer was over, some of the settlers wished to explore the country and see if they could not find a short way through to the Pacific Ocean.[2]

CAPTAIN JOHN SMITH BEFORE POWHATAN

Captain Smith led the expedition. The Indians attacked them, killed three of the men, and took the captain prisoner. To amuse the Indians, Smith showed them his pocket compass. When the savages saw that the needle always pointed toward the north, they were greatly astonished; and, instead of killing their prisoner, they decided to take him to their chief. This

[1] Longfellow's *Hiawatha* (Hiawatha's Sailing). [2] See page 26.

chief was named Powhatan.[1]   He was a tall, grim-look-
ing old man, and he hated the settlers at Jamestown,
because he believed that they
had come to steal the land
from the Indians.

POCKET COMPASS

**42. Smith's life is saved by
Pocahontas[2]; her marriage to
John Rolfe.[3]** — Smith was
dragged into the chief's wigwam ; his head was laid on a
large, flat stone, and a tall
savage with a big club stood
ready to dash out his brains.   Just as Powhatan was
about to cry *"Strike !"* his daughter Pocahontas, a girl
of twelve or thirteen, ran up, and, putting her arms
around the prisoner's head, laid her own head on his —
now let the Indian with his uplifted club strike, if he dare.[4]

Instead of being angry with his daughter, Powhatan
promised her that he would spare Smith's life.   When
an Indian made such a promise as that he kept it, so
the captain knew that his head was safe.   Powhatan
released his prisoner and soon sent him back to Jamestown, and Pocahontas, followed by a number of Indians,
carried to the settlers presents of corn and venison.

Some years after this the Indian maiden married
John Rolfe, an Englishman who had come to Virginia.
They went to London, and Pocahontas died not far
from that city.   She left a son ; and from that son
came some noted Virginians.   One of them was John
Randolph.   He was a famous man in his day, and he

---

[1] Powhatan (Pow-ha-tan′).   [2] Pocahontas (Po-ka-hon′tas).
[3] Rolfe (Rolf).   [4] On Pocahontas, see List of Books in Appendix.

always spoke with pride of the Indian princess, as he called her.

43. Captain Smith is made governor of Jamestown; the gold-diggers; "Corn, or your life!" — More emigrants came over from England, and Captain Smith was now made governor of Jamestown. Some of the emigrants found some glittering earth which they thought was gold. Soon nearly every one was hard at work digging it. Smith laughed at them; but they insisted on loading a ship with the worthless stuff and sending it to London. That was the last that was heard of it.

The people had wasted their time digging this shining dirt when they should have been hoeing their gardens. Soon they began to be in great want of food. The captain started off with a party of men to buy corn of the Indians. The Indians contrived a cunning plot to kill the whole party. Smith luckily found it out; seizing the chief by the hair, he pressed the muzzle of a pistol against his heart and gave him his choice, — "Corn, or your life!" He got the corn, and plenty of it.

"CORN, OR YOUR LIFE!"

44. "He who will not work shall not eat." — Captain Smith then set part of the men to planting corn, so that they might raise what they needed. The rest of the settlers he took with him into the woods to chop down

trees and saw them into boards to send to England.
Many tried to escape from this labor; but Smith said,
Men who are able to dig for gold are able to chop; then
he made this rule: " He who will not work shall not
eat." Rather than lose his dinner, the laziest man now
took his axe and set off for the woods.

45. Captain Smith's cold-water cure. — But, though the
choppers worked, they grumbled. They liked to see the
chips fly and to hear the great trees "thunder as they
fell"; but the axe-handles raised blisters on their fingers.
These blisters made the men swear, so that commonly
one would hear "a loud oath" at every third stroke of
the axe. Smith said the swearing must be stopped.
He had each man's oaths numbered. When the day's
work was done, every offender was called up; his oaths
were counted; then he was told to hold up his right
hand, and a can of cold water was poured down his
sleeve for each oath. This new style of water-cure did
wonders; in a short time hardly an oath would be heard
in a whole week; it was just chop, chop, chop; and the
madder the men got, the more the chips would fly.[1]

**46. Captain Smith meets with an accident and goes back to
England; his return to America; his death.** — Captain Smith
had not been governor very long when he met with a
terrible accident. He was out in a boat, and a bag of
gunpowder he had with him exploded. He was so
badly hurt that he had to go back to England to get
proper treatment for his wounds.

He returned to America a number of years later,
explored the coast north of Virginia, and gave it the

[1] Smith tells this story himself in his *General History of Virginia:* see
Arber's Edition of Smith, *Complete Works*, page 439.

name of New England; but he never went back to Jamestown again. He died in London, and was buried in a famous old church in that city.[1]

47. What Captain Smith did for Virginia. — Captain John Smith was in Virginia less than three years; yet in that short time he did a great deal. First, he saved the settlers from starving, by making the Indians sell them corn. Next, by his courage, he saved them from the attacks of the savages. Lastly, he taught them how to work. Had it not been for him, the people of Jamestown would probably have lost all heart and gone back to England. He insisted on their staying; and so, through him, the English got their first real foothold in America. But this was not all; he wrote two books on Virginia, describing the soil, the trees,

A SETTLER'S LOG CABIN

the animals, and the Indians. He also made some excellent maps of Virginia and of New England. These books and maps taught the English people many things about this country, and were a great help to those who wished to emigrate to America. For these reasons, Captain Smith has rightfully been called the "Father of Virginia."

48. Negro slaves sent to Virginia; tobacco. — About ten years after Captain Smith left Jamestown, the commander of a Dutch ship brought a number of negro

[1] The church of St. Sepulchre: it is not very far from St. Paul's Cathedral.

slaves to Virginia (1619) and sold them to the settlers.
That was the beginning of slavery in this country. Later,
when other English settlements had been made, they
bought slaves; and so, after a time, every settlement
north as well as south owned more or less negroes. The
people of Virginia employed most of their slaves in
raising tobacco. They sold this in England; and, as it
generally brought a good price, many of the planters[1]
became quite rich.

**49. Bacon's war against Governor Berkeley[2]; Jamestown
burned.** — Long after Captain Smith was in his grave,
Sir William Berkeley was made governor of Virginia
by the king of England. Governor Berkeley treated
the people very badly. At last a young planter named
Bacon raised a small army and marched against the
governor, who was in Jamestown. The governor, finding that he had few friends to fight for him, made haste
to get out of the place. Bacon then entered it with his
men; but as he knew that, if necessary, the king would
send soldiers from England to aid the governor in getting it back, he set fire to the place and burned it. It
was never built up again, and only a crumbling church-
tower and a few gravestones can now be seen where
Jamestown once stood. Those ruins mark the first
English town settled in America.

**50. What happened later in Virginia; the Revolution;
Washington; four presidents.** — But though Jamestown
was destroyed, Virginia kept growing in strength and
wealth. What was better still, the country grew in
the number of its great men. The king of England

---

[1] Planter: a person who owns a plantation or large farm at the South; it is
cultivated by laborers living on it; once these laborers were generally negro
slaves.   [2] Berkeley (Berk'lï).

continued to rule America until, in 1776, many of the people of Virginia demanded that independence should be declared. The great war of the Revolution overthrew the king's power and made us free. The military leader of that war was a Virginia planter named George Washington.

After we had gained the victory and peace was made, we chose presidents to govern the country. Four out of five of our first presidents, beginning with Washington, came from Virginia. For this reason that state has sometimes been called the "Mother of Presidents."

51. Summary. — In 1607 Captain John Smith, with a number of other emigrants, made the first lasting settlement built by Englishmen in America. Through Captain Smith's energy and courage, Jamestown, Virginia, took firm root. Virginia was the first state to demand the independence of America, and Washington, who was a Virginian, led the war of the Revolution by which that independence was gained.

What can you tell about Captain John Smith before he went to Virginia? What happened to him on his way to Virginia? What is said about the landing of the settlers in Virginia? What did they want to do? What did Captain Smith want to do? What is said about Captain Smith's trial? What is said about the church in Jamestown? What happened to the settlers? What did some of them try to do? Who stopped them? Tell what you can about the Indians. What kind of houses did they live in? Did they have guns? Did they have iron hatchets and knives? Did they have horses and wagons? What kind of boats did they have? What happened to Captain Smith when he went in search of the Pacific? What did Pocahontas do? What is said about her afterward? What about the gold-diggers? How did Captain Smith get corn? What did he make the settlers do? What is said about Captain Smith's cold-water cure? Why did Captain Smith go back to England? What three things did he do for Virginia? What is said about his books and maps? What is said of negro slaves? What is said about tobacco? What is said about Governor Berkeley and Mr. Bacon? What happened to Jamestown? What did the war of the Revolution do? Who was its great military leader? Why is Virginia sometimes called the "Mother of Presidents"?

VI. CAPTAIN HENRY HUDSON

(Voyages from 1607 to 1611)

52. Captain Hudson tries to find a northwest passage to China and the Indies. — When Captain John Smith sailed for Virginia, he left in London a friend, named Henry Hudson, who had the name of being one of the best sea-captains in England.

Map showing how Captain Hudson hoped to reach Asia by sailing northwest from England.

While Smith was in Jamestown, a company of London merchants sent out Captain Hudson to try to discover a passage to China and the Indies.[1] When he left England, he sailed to the northwest, hoping that he could find a way open to the Pacific across the North Pole or not far below it.[2]

He knew that if he found such a passage, it would be much shorter than a voyage round the globe further south; because, as any one can see, it is not nearly so far round the top of an apple, near the stem, as it is round the middle.

[1] On the Indies and other countries of the far East, see page 4, and Note 2 on page 26.

[2] See John Cabot's attempt to find a northwest passage to Asia, on page 15.

Hudson could not find the passage he was looking for; but he saw mountains of ice, and he went nearer to the North Pole than any one had ever done before.

53. The Dutch hire Captain Hudson; he sails for America. — The Dutch people in Holland had heard of Hudson's voyage, and a company of merchants of that country hired the brave sailor to see if he could find a passage to Asia by sailing to the northeast.

He set out from the port of Amsterdam,[1] in 1609, in a vessel named the *Half Moon*. After he had gone quite a long distance, the sailors got so tired of seeing nothing but fog and ice that they refused to go any further.

Then Captain Hudson turned his ship about and sailed for the coast of North America. He did that because his friend, Captain Smith of Virginia, had sent him a letter, with a map, which made him think that he could find such a passage as he wanted north of Chesapeake Bay.

54. Captain Hudson reaches America and finds the "Great River." — Hudson got to Chesapeake Bay; but the weather was so stormy that he thought it would not be safe to enter it. He therefore sailed northward along the coast. In September, 1609, he entered a beautiful bay, formed by the spreading out of a noble river. At that point the stream is more than a mile wide, and he called it the "Great River." On the eastern side of it, not far from its mouth, there is a long, narrow island: the Indians of that day called it Manhattan Island.[2]

---

[1] See map on page 44.
[2] Manhattan (Man-hat'tan).

**55. The tides in the " Great River ";
Captain Hudson begins to sail up the
stream.** — One of the remarkable things
about the river which Hudson had
discovered is that it has hardly any
current, and the tide from the ocean
moves up for more than a hundred
and fifty miles. If no fresh water
ran in from the hills, still the sea
would fill the channel for a long distance, and so make a kind of salt-
water river of it. Hudson noticed
how salt it was, and that, perhaps,
made him think that he had at last
actually found a passage which would
lead him through from the Atlantic
to the Pacific. He was delighted
with all he saw, and said, " This is
as beautiful a land as one can tread
upon." Soon he began to sail up the
stream, wondering what he should see
and whether he should come out on an
ocean which would take him to Asia.

**56. Hudson's voyage on the " Great
River " ; his feast with the Indians.** — At
first he drifted along, carried by the
tide, under the shadow of a great
natural wall of rock. That wall,
which we now call the Palisades,[1] is

[1] Palisades: this name is given to the wall of rock
on the Hudson, because, when seen near by, it somewhat resembles a palisade, or high fence made of stakes
or posts set close together, upright in the ground.

from four hundred to six hundred feet high; it extends for nearly twenty miles along the western shore of the river.

Then, some distance further up, Captain Hudson came to a place where the river winds its way through great forest-covered hills, called the Highlands. At the end of the fifth day he came to a point on the eastern bank above the Highlands, where the city of Hudson now stands. Here an old Indian chief invited him to go ashore. Hudson had found the Indians, as he says, "very loving"; so he thought he would accept the invitation. The savages made a great feast for the captain. They gave him not only roast pigeons, but also a roast dog, which they cooked specially for him: they wanted he should have the very best.

CAPTAIN HUDSON ON THE GREAT RIVER

These Indians had never seen a white man before. They thought that the English captain, in his bright scarlet coat trimmed with gold lace, had come down from the sky to visit them. What puzzled them, however, was that he had such a pale face instead of having a red one like themselves.

At the end of the feast Hudson rose to go, but the Indians begged him to stay all night. Then one of them got up, gathered all the arrows, broke them to pieces, and threw them into the fire, in order to show the captain that he need not be afraid to stay with them.

57. Captain Hudson reaches the end of his voyage and turns back; trouble with the Indians. — But Captain Hudson made up his mind that he must now go on with his voyage. He went back to his ship and kept on up the river until he had reached a point about a hundred and fifty miles from its mouth. Here the city of Albany now stands. He found that the water was growing shallow, and he feared that if the *Half Moon* went further she would get aground. It was clear to him, too, that wherever the river might lead, he was not likely to find it a short way through to China.

On the way down stream a thievish Indian, who had come out in a canoe, managed to steal something from the ship. One of the crew chanced to see the Indian as he was slyly slipping off; picking up a gun he fired and killed him. After that Hudson's men had several fights with the Indians.

58. Hudson returns to Europe; the " Great River " is called by his name; his death. — Early in October the captain set sail for Europe. Ever since that time the beautiful river which he explored has been called the Hudson, in his honor.

The next year Captain Hudson made another voyage, and entered that immense bay in the northern part of America which we now know as Hudson Bay. There he got into trouble with his men. Some of them seized him and set him adrift, with a few others, in an open boat. Nothing more was ever heard of the brave English sailor. The bay which bears his name is probably his grave.

59. The Dutch take possession of the land on the Hudson and call it New Netherland; how New Netherland became New York. — As soon as the Dutch in Holland heard that Captain Hudson had found a country where the Indians had plenty of rich furs to sell, they sent out people to trade with them. Holland is sometimes called the Netherlands; that is, the Low Lands. When the Dutch took possession of the country on the Hudson (1614), they gave it the name of New Netherland,[1] for the same reason that the English called one part of their possessions in America New England. In the course of a few years the Dutch built (1615) a fort and some log cabins on the lower end of Manhattan Island. After a time they named this little settlement New Amsterdam, in remembrance of the port of Amsterdam in Holland from which Hudson sailed.

After the Dutch had held the country of New Netherland about fifty years, the English (1664) seized it. They changed its name to New York, in honor of the Duke of York, who was brother to the king. The English also changed the name of New Amsterdam to that of New York City.

60. The New York "Sons of Liberty" in the Revolution; what Henry Hudson would say of the city now. — More than a hundred years after this the young men of New York, the "Sons of Liberty," as they called themselves, made ready with the "Sons of Liberty" in other states to do their full part, under the lead of General Washington, in the great war of the Revolution, — that war by which we gained our freedom from the rule of the king of England, and became the United States of America.

[1] New Netherland: this is often incorrectly printed New Netherlands.

The silent harbor where Henry Hudson saw a few Indian canoes is now one of the busiest seaports in the world. The great statue of Liberty stands at its entrance.[1] To it fleets of ships and steamers are constantly coming from all parts of the globe; from it other fleets of vessels are constantly going. If Captain Hudson could see the river which bears his name, and Manhattan Island now covered with miles of buildings which make the largest and wealthiest city in America, he would say: There is no need of my looking any further for the riches of China and the Indies, for I have found them here.

61. Summary. — In 1609 Henry Hudson, an English sea-captain, then in the employ of the Dutch, discovered the river now called by his name. The Dutch took possession of the country on the river, named it New Netherland, and built a small settlement on Manhattan Island. Many years later the English seized the country and named it New York. The settlement on Manhattan Island then became New York City. It is now the largest and wealthiest city in the United States and one of the greatest seaports for shipping and trade in the world.

Who was Henry Hudson? What did he try to find? What did the Dutch hire him to do? Where did he go? What did he call the river he discovered? What is said about that river? Tell what you can of Hudson's voyage up the river. What is said about the Indians? Why did Hudson turn back? What did he do then? What is the river he discovered called now? What happened to Captain Hudson the next year? What did the Dutch do? What did they name the country? Why? What did they build there on Manhattan Island? Who seized New Netherland? What name did they give it? What is said of the "Sons of Liberty"? What would Hudson say if he could see New York City now?

[1] In her right hand Liberty holds a torch to guide vessels at night.

LIBERTY ENLIGHTENING THE WORLD

(A statue in the harbor of New York City, given to the American people by the people of France.)

VII. CAPTAIN MYLES[1] STANDISH

(1584-1656)

62. The English Pilgrims in Holland ; why they left England.
— When the news of Henry Hudson's discovery of
the Hudson River reached Holland, many Englishmen

were living in the
Dutch city of
Leyden.[2] These
people were
mostly farmers
who had fled from
Scrooby[3] and
neighboring vil-
lages in the north-
east of England.
They called them-
selves Pilgrims, because they were wanderers from their
old homes.

The Pilgrims left England because King James
would not let them hold their religious meetings in
peace. He thought, as all kings then did, that everybody in England should belong to the same church and
worship God in the same way that he did.[4] He was

---

[1] Myles (Miles) : Standish himself wrote it Myles.

[2] Leyden (Lī′den) ; see map on this page.

[3] Scrooby (Skroo′bĭ) ; see map on this page.

[4] There were some people in England who thought much as the Pilgrims
did in regard to religion, but who did not then leave the Church of England
(as the Pilgrims left it). They were called Puritans because they insisted on
making certain changes in the English mode of worship, wishing, as they said,
to *purify* it. Many Puritans came to New England with Governor Winthrop
in 1630; after they settled in America they established independent churches
like the Pilgrims.

afraid that if people were allowed to go to whatever church they thought best, it would lead to disputes and quarrels, which would end by breaking his kingdom to pieces. Quite a number of Englishmen, seeing that they could not have religious liberty at home, escaped with their wives and children to Holland; for there the Dutch were willing to let them have such a church as they wanted.

63. Why the Pilgrims wished to leave Holland and go to America. — But the Pilgrims were not contented in Holland. They saw that, if they stayed in that country, their children would grow up to be more Dutch than English. They saw, too, that they could not hope to get land in Holland. They resolved, therefore, to go to America, where they could get farms for nothing, and where their children would never forget the English language or the good old English customs and laws. In the wilderness they could not only enjoy entire religious freedom, but they could build up a settlement which would certainly be their own.

64. The Pilgrims, with Captain Myles Standish, sail for England and then for America; they reach Cape Cod and choose a governor there. — In 1620 a company of Pilgrims sailed for England on their way to America. Captain Myles Standish, an English soldier, who had fought in Holland, joined them. He did not belong to the Pilgrim church, but he had become a great friend to those who did.

About a hundred of these people sailed from Plymouth,[1] England, for the New World, in the ship *Mayflower*. Many of those who went were children and young people. The Pilgrims had a long, rough passage across

[1] Plymouth (Plim'uth).

the Atlantic. Toward the last of November (1620) they saw land. It was Cape Cod, that narrow strip of sand, more than sixty miles long, which looks like an

arm bent at the elbow, with a hand bent like a half-clenched fist.

Finding that it would be difficult to go further, the Pilgrims decided to land and explore the cape; so the *Mayflower* entered Cape Cod Harbor, inside the half-shut fist, and then came to anchor.

Before they landed, the Pilgrims held a meeting in the cabin, and drew up an agreement in writing for the government of the settlement. They signed the agreement, and then chose John Carver governor.

65. Wash-day ; what Standish and his men found on the cape. — On the first Monday after they had reached the cape, all the women went on shore to wash, and so Monday has been kept as wash-day in New England ever since. Shortly after that, Captain Myles Standish, with a number of men, started off to see the country. They found some Indian corn buried in the sand ; and a little further on a young man named William Bradford, who afterward became governor, stepped into an Indian deer-trap. It jerked him up by the leg in a way that must have made even the soberest Pilgrim smile.

66. **Captain Standish and his men set sail in a boat for a blue hill in the west, and find Plymouth Rock; Plymouth Harbor; landing from the *Mayflower*.** — On clear days the people on board the *Mayflower*, anchored in Cape Cod Harbor, could see a blue hill, on the mainland, in the west, about forty miles away. To that blue hill Standish and some others determined to go. Taking a sailboat, they started off. A few days later they passed the hill which the Indians called Manomet,[1] and entered a fine harbor. There, on December 21, 1620, — the shortest day in the year, — they landed on that famous stone which is now known all over the world as Plymouth Rock.

THE LANDING AT PLYMOUTH

Standish, with the others, went back to the *Mayflower* with a good report. They had found just what they wanted, — an excellent harbor where ships from England could come in; a brook of nice drinking-water; and last of all, a piece of land that was nearly free from trees, so that nothing would hinder their planting corn early in the spring. Captain John Smith of Virginia[2] had been there before them, and had named the place Plymouth on his map of New England. The Pilgrims liked the name, and so made up their minds to keep it. The

[1] Manomet (Man'o-met).   [2] See page 32.

Mayflower soon sailed for Plymouth, and the Pilgrims set to work to build the log cabins of their little settlement.

67. Sickness and Death. — During that winter nearly half the Pilgrims died. Captain Standish showed himself to be as good a nurse as he was a soldier. He, with Governor Carver and their minister, Elder Brewster, cooked, washed, waited on the sick, and did everything that kind hearts and willing hands could do, to help their suffering friends. But the men who had begun to build houses had to stop that work to dig graves. When these graves were filled, they were smoothed down flat, so that no prowling Indian should count them and see how few white men there were left.

"WELCOME! WELCOME!"

68. Samoset,[1] Squanto,[2] and Massasoit[3] visit the Pilgrims. — One day in the spring the Pilgrims were startled at seeing an Indian walk boldly into their little settlement. He cried out in good English, "Welcome! welcome!" This visitor was named Samoset; he had met some sailors years before, and had learned a few English words from them.

[1] Samoset (Sam'o-set).   [2] Squanto (Skwon'to).   [3] Massasoit (Mas'sa-soit).

The next time Samoset came he brought with him another Indian, whose name was Squanto. Squanto was the only one left of the tribe that had once lived at Plymouth. All the rest had died of a dreadful sickness, or plague. He had been stolen by some sailors, and carried to England; there he had learned the language. After his return he had joined an Indian tribe that lived about thirty miles further west. The chief of that tribe was named Massasoit; and Squanto said that he was coming directly to visit the Pilgrims.

In about an hour Massasoit, with some sixty warriors, appeared on a hill just outside the settlement. The Indians had painted their faces in their very gayest style — black, red, and yellow. If paint could make them handsome, they were determined to look their best.

69. Massasoit and Governor Carver make a treaty of friendship; how Thanksgiving was kept; what Squanto did for the Pilgrims. — Captain Standish, attended by a guard of honor, went out and brought the chief to Governor Carver. Then Massasoit and the governor made a solemn promise or treaty, in which they agreed that the Indians of his tribe and the Pilgrims should live like friends and brothers, doing all they could to help each other. That promise was kept for more than fifty years; it was never broken until long after the two men who made it were in their graves.

When the Pilgrims had their first Thanksgiving, they invited Massasoit and his men to come and share it. The Indians brought venison and other good things; there were plenty of wild turkeys roasted; and so they all sat down together to a great dinner, and had a merry time in the wilderness.

Squanto was of great help to the Pilgrims. He showed them how to catch eels, where to go fishing, when to plant their corn, and how to put a fish in every hill to make the corn grow faster.

After a while he came to live with the Pilgrims. He liked them so much that, when the poor fellow died, he begged Governor Bradford to pray that he might go to the white man's heaven.

70. Canonicus[1] **dares Governor Bradford to fight ; the palisade ; the fort and meeting-house.** — West of where Massasoit lived, there were some Indians on the shore of Narragansett Bay,[2] in what is now Rhode Island. Their chief was named Canonicus, and he was no friend to Massasoit or to the Pilgrims. Canonicus thought he could frighten the white men away ; so he sent a bundle of sharp, new arrows, tied round with a rattlesnake skin, to Governor Bradford : that meant that he dared the governor and his men to come out and fight. Governor Bradford threw away the arrows, and then filled the snake-skin up to the mouth with powder and ball. This was sent back to Canonicus. When he saw it, he was afraid to touch it, for he knew that Myles

1 Canonicus (Ka-non′i-kus).
2 Narragansett (Nar′a-gan′set) ; see map on page 62.

Standish's bullets could whistle louder and cut deeper than his Indian arrows.

But though the Pilgrims did not believe that Canonicus would attack them, they thought it best to build a very high, strong fence, called a palisade, round the town.

They also built a log fort on one of the hills, and used the lower part of the fort for a church. Every Sunday all the people, with Captain Standish at the head, marched to their meeting-house, where a man stood on guard outside. Each Pilgrim carried his gun, and set it down near him. With one ear he listened sharply to the preacher; with the other he listened just as sharply for the cry, Indians! Indians! But the Indians never came.

THE PALISADE BUILT ROUND PLYMOUTH

71. The new settlers; trouble with the Indians in their neighborhood; Captain Standish's fight with the savages. — By and by more emigrants came from England and settled about twenty-five miles north of Plymouth, at a place which is now called Weymouth. The Indians in that neighborhood did not like these new settlers, and they made up their minds to come upon them suddenly and murder them.

Governor Bradford sent Captain Standish, with a few men, to see how great the danger was. He found the Indians very bold. One of them came up to him, whetting a long knife. He held it up, to show how sharp it was, and then patting it, he said, " By and by, it shall eat, but not speak." Presently another Indian came up. He was a big fellow, much larger and stronger than Standish. He, too, had a long knife, as keen as a razor. "Ah," said he to Standish, "so this is the mighty captain the white men have sent to destroy us! He is a little man; let him go and work with the women."[1]

The captain's blood was on fire with rage; but he said not a word. His time had not yet come. The next day the Pilgrims and the Indians met in a log cabin. Standish made a sign to one of his men, and he shut the door fast. Then the captain sprang like a tiger at the big savage who had laughed at him, and snatching his long knife from him, he plunged it into his heart.

A hand-to-hand fight followed between the white men and

| MYLES STANDISH'S KETTLE, SWORD, AND PEWTER DISH | COPY OF MYLES STANDISH'S SIGNATURE |

the Indians. The Pilgrims gained the victory, and carried back the head of the Indian chief in triumph to Plymouth. Captain Standish's bold action saved both of the English settlements from destruction.

72. What else Myles Standish did; his death. — But Standish did more things for the Pilgrims than fight

[1] See Longfellow's poem, *The Courtship of Miles Standish*. This quotation is truthful in its rendering of the *spirit* of the words used by the Indian in his insulting speech to Standish; it should be understood, however, that the poem does not always adhere closely either to the chronology or to the exact facts of history.

for them; for he went to England, bought goods for them, and borrowed money to help them.

He lived to be an old man. At his death he left, among other things, three well-worn Bibles and three good guns. In those days, the men who read the Bible most were those who fought the hardest.

Near Plymouth there is a high hill called Captain's Hill. That was where Standish made his home during the last part of his life. A granite monument, over a hundred feet high, stands on top of the hill. On it is a statue of the brave captain looking toward the sea. He was one of the makers of America.

73. Governor John Winthrop founds[1] Boston. — Ten years after the Pilgrims landed at Plymouth, a large company of English people under the leadership of Governor John Winthrop came to New England. They were called Puritans[2]; they, too, were seeking that religious freedom which was denied them in the old country. One of the vessels which brought over these new settlers was named the *Mayflower*. She may have been the very ship which in 1620 brought the Pilgrims to these shores.

Governor Winthrop's company named the place where they settled Boston, in grateful remembrance of the beautiful old city of Boston,[3] England, from which some of the chief emigrants came. The new settlement was

---

[1] Founds: begins to build.

[2] On the Puritans see note on page 44. The Puritans were determined to find some place where they could worship God in the way they thought right; but they had no intention of giving those who thought different from them the liberty of worshipping God in a manner unlike theirs. When such people came later and tried to settle among the New England Puritans, the Puritans compelled them to move on.

[3] Boston, England; see map on page 44.

called the Massachusetts Bay[1] Colony,[2] Massachusetts being the Indian name for the Blue Hills, near Boston. The Plymouth Colony was now often called the Old Colony, because it had been settled first. After many years, these two colonies were united, and still later they became the state of Massachusetts.

74. How other New England colonies grew up ; the Revolution. — By the time Governor Winthrop arrived English settlements had been made in Maine, New Hampshire, and later (1724), in the country which afterward became the state of Vermont. Connecticut and Rhode Island were first settled by emigrants who went from Massachusetts.

When the Revolution broke out, the people throughout New England took up arms in defence of their rights. The first blood of the war was shed on the soil of Massachusetts, near Boston.

75. Summary. — The Pilgrims landed at Plymouth, New England, in 1620. One of the chief men who came with them was Captain Myles Standish. Had it not been for his help, the Indians might have destroyed the settlement. In 1630 Governor John Winthrop, with a large company of Puritan emigrants from England, settled Boston. Near Boston the first battle of the Revolution was fought.

Why did some Englishmen in Holland call themselves Pilgrims? Why had they left England ? Why did they now wish to go to America? Who was Myles Standish ? From what place in England, and in what ship, did the Pilgrims sail ? What land did they first see

[1] Massachusetts Bay ; see map on page 62.

[2] Colony : here a company of settlers who came to America from England, and who were subject to the king of England, as all the English settlers of America were until the Revolution.

in America ? What did they do at Cape Cod Harbor ? What did the
Pilgrims do on the Cape ? Where did they land on December 21,
1620 ? What happened during the winter ? What is said of Samoset ?
What is said about Squanto ? What is said about Massasoit ? What
did Massasoit and Governor Carver do ? What is said about the first
Thanksgiving ? What is said about Canonicus and Governor Bradford ? What did the Pilgrims build to protect them from the Indians ?
What is said about Weymouth ? What did Myles Standish do there ?
What else did Myles Standish do besides fight ? What is said of his
death ? What did Governor John Winthrop do ? What did the people
of New England do in the Revolution ? Where was the first blood
shed ?

VIII. LORD BALTIMORE

(1580-1632)

**76. Lord Baltimore's settlement in Newfoundland; how
Catholics were then treated in England.** — While Captain
Myles Standish was helping build up Plymouth, Lord
Baltimore, an English nobleman, was trying to make a
settlement on the cold, foggy island of Newfoundland.

Lord Baltimore had been brought up a Protestant, but
had become a Catholic. At that time Catholics were
treated very cruelly in England. They were ordered by
law to attend the Church of England. They did not like
that church any better than the Pilgrims did; but if they
failed to attend it, they had to take their choice between
paying a large sum of money or going to prison.

Lord Baltimore hoped to make a home for himself and
for other English Catholics in the wilderness of Newfoundland, where there would be no one to trouble them.
But the unfortunate settlers were fairly frozen out. They
had winter a good share of the year, and fog all of it.
They could raise nothing, because, as one man said, the
soil was either rock or swamp : the rock was as hard as

iron ; the swamp was so deep that you could not touch bottom with a ten-foot pole.

77. The king of England gives Lord Baltimore part of Virginia, and names it Maryland ; what Lord Baltimore paid for it. — King Charles the First, of England, was a good friend to Lord Baltimore ; and when the settlement in Newfoundland was given up, he made him a present of an immense three-cornered piece of land in America. This piece was cut out of Virginia, north of the Potomac [1] River.

The king's wife, who was called Queen Mary, was a French Catholic.   In her honor, Charles named the country he had given Lord Baltimore, Mary Land, or Maryland.   He could not have chosen a better name,

because Maryland was to be a shelter for many English people who believed in the same religion that the queen did.

All that Lord Baltimore was to pay for Maryland, with its twelve thousand square miles of land and water, was two Indian ar-

PART OF WINDSOR CASTLE

rows.   These he agreed to send every spring to the royal palace of Windsor [2] Castle, near London.

The arrows would be worth nothing whatever to the king ; but they were sent as a kind of yearly rent. They showed that, though Lord Baltimore had the use of Maryland, and could do pretty much as he pleased with it, still the king did not give up all control of it.

[1] Potomac (Po-to′mak) ; see map, page 124.   [2] Windsor (Win′zor).

In Virginia and in New England the king had granted all land to companies of persons, and he had been particular to tell them just what they must or must not do; but he gave Maryland to one man only. More than this, he promised to let Lord Baltimore have his own way in everything, so long as he made no laws in Maryland which should be contrary to the laws of England. So Lord Baltimore had greater privileges than any other holder of land in America at that time.

78. **Lord Baltimore dies; his son sends emigrants to Maryland; the landing; the Indians; St. Mary's.** — Lord Baltimore died before he could get ready to come to America.

THE LANDING IN MARYLAND

His eldest son then became Lord Baltimore. He sent over a number of emigrants; part of them were Catholics, and part were Protestants: all of them were to have equal rights in Maryland. In the spring of 1634 these people landed on a little island near the mouth of the Potomac River. There they cut down a tree and made a large cross of it; then, kneeling round that cross, they all joined in prayer to God for their safe journey.

A little later they landed on the shore of the river. There they met some Indians. Under a huge mulberry tree they bargained with the Indians for a place to build a town, and paid for the land in hatchets, knives, and beads.

The Indians were greatly astonished at the size of the ship in which the white men came. They thought that it was made like their canoes, and that it was simply the trunk of a tree hollowed out. They wondered where the English could have found a tree big enough to make it.

The emigrants named their settlement St. Mary's, because they had landed on a day kept sacred to the

Virgin Mary.[1] The Indians gave up one of their largest wigwams to Father White, one of the priests who had come over, and he made a church of it. It was the first English Catholic church which was opened in America.

The Indians and the settlers lived and worked together, side by side. The red men showed the emigrants how to hunt in the forest, and the Indian women taught the white women how to make hominy,[2] and to bake johnny-cake [3] before the open fire.

79. Maryland the home of religious liberty. — Maryland was different from the other English colonies in America, because there, and there only, every Christian, whether Catholic or Protestant, had the right to worship God in his own way.   In that humble little village of St. Mary's,

---

[1] March 25 : Annunciation or Lady Day.

[2] Hominy : corn hulled, broken, and boiled.

[3] Johnny-cake : a kind of bread made of Indian meal.

made up of thirty or forty log huts and wigwams in the woods, "religious liberty had its only home in the wide world." [1]

But more than this, Lord Baltimore generously invited people who had been driven out of the other settlements on account of their religion[2] to come and live in Maryland. He gave a hearty welcome to all, whether they thought as he did or not. Thus he showed that he was a noble man by nature as well as a nobleman by name.

80. Maryland falls into trouble; the city of Baltimore built. — But this happy state of things did not last long. Some of the people of Virginia were very angry because the king had given Lord Baltimore part of what they thought was their land. They quarrelled with the new settlers and made them a great deal of trouble.

Then worse things happened. Men went to Maryland and undertook to drive out the Catholics. In some cases they acted in a very shameful manner toward Lord Baltimore and his friends; among other things, they put Father White in irons and sent him back to England as a prisoner. Lord Baltimore had spent a great deal of money in building up the settlement, but his right to the land was taken away from him for a time, and all who dared to defend him were badly treated.

St. Mary's never grew to be much of a place, but not quite a hundred years after the English landed there a new and beautiful city was begun (1729) in Maryland. It was named Baltimore, in honor of that Lord Baltimore who sent out the first emigrants. When the

[1] That is, "religious liberty" for all Christians. We shall see when we come to read about the settlement which Roger Williams made in Rhode Island in 1636 that he gave entire religious liberty to all classes of men.

[2] See Note 2 on the Puritans on page 53.

Revolutionary War broke out, the citizens of Baltimore showed that they were not a bit behind the other colonies of America in their spirit of independence.

81. Summary. — King Charles the First of England gave Lord Baltimore, an English Catholic, a part of Virginia and named it Maryland, in honor of his wife, Queen Mary. A company of emigrants came out to Maryland in 1634. It was the first settlement in America in which all Christian people had entire liberty to worship God in whatever way they thought right. That liberty they owed to Lord Baltimore.

Who was Lord Baltimore, and what did he try to do in Newfoundland? How were Catholics then treated in England? What did the king of England give Lord Baltimore in America? What did the king name the country? What was Lord Baltimore to pay for Maryland? What did the king promise Lord Baltimore? What did Lord Baltimore's son do? When and where did the emigrants land? What did they call the place? What is said about the Indians? Of what was Maryland the home? Why did some of the people of Virginia trouble them? What is said of the city of Baltimore? What is said of the Revolution?

IX. ROGER WILLIAMS

(1600-1684)

82. Roger Williams comes to Boston ; he preaches in Salem and in Plymouth ; his friendship for the Indians. — Shortly after Governor John Winthrop and his company settled Boston,[1] a young minister named Roger Williams came over from England to join them.

Mr. Williams soon became a great friend to the Indians, and while he preached at Salem,[2] near Boston, and at Plymouth, he came to know many of them. He

[1] See page 53.   [2] Salem (Sā′lem).

took pains to learn their language, and he spent a great deal of time talking with the chief Massasoit[1] and his men, in their dirty, smoky wigwams. He made the savages feel that, as he said, his whole heart's desire was to do them good. For this reason they were always glad to see him and ready to help him. A time came, as we shall presently see, when they were able to do quite as much for him as he could do for them.

83. Who owned the greater part of America? what the king of England thought; what Roger Williams thought and said. — The company that had settled Boston held the land by permission of the king of England. He considered that most

THE CHURCH IN WHICH ROGER WILLIAMS
PREACHED IN SALEM
(It is still standing.)

of the land in America belonged to him, because John Cabot[2] had discovered it.

But Roger Williams said that the king had no right to the land unless he bought it of the Indians, who were living here when the English came.

Now the people of Massachusetts were always quite willing to pay the Indians a fair price for whatever land they wanted; but many of them were afraid to have Mr. Williams preach and write as he did. They believed that if they allowed him to go on speaking out so boldly

[1] See page 48.   [2] See page 15.

against the king, the English monarch would get so
angry that he would take away Massachusetts from
them and give it to a new company. In that case,

Map showing Roger Williams's route from
Salem to Mount Hope.

those who had settled here
would lose everything.
For this reason the people
of Boston tried to make
the young minister agree
to keep silent on this subject.

**84. A constable is sent
to arrest Roger Williams;
he escapes to the woods, and
goes to Mount Hope.** — But
Mr. Williams was not one
of the kind to keep silent.
Then the chief men of
Boston sent a constable down to Salem, with orders to
seize him and send him back to England. When he
heard that the constable was after
him, Mr. Williams slipped quietly out
of his house and escaped to the
woods.

There was a heavy depth of snow
on the ground; but the young man
made up his mind that he would go
to his old friend Massasoit, and ask
him to help him in his trouble.

Striking fire with flint and
steel. The sparks were
caught on some old, half-
burnt rag, and were then
blown to a blaze.

Massasoit lived near Mount Hope,
in what is now Rhode Island, about eighty miles southwest from Salem. There were no roads through the
woods, and it was a long, dreary journey to make on

foot; but Mr. Williams did not hesitate. He took a hatchet to chop fire-wood, a flint and steel to strike fire with, — for in those days people had no matches, — and, last of all, a pocket compass to aid him in finding his way through the thick forest.

All day he waded wearily on through the deep snow, only stopping now and then to rest or to look at his compass and make sure that he was going in the right direction. At night he would gather wood enough to make a little fire to warm himself or to melt some snow for drink. Then he would cut down a few boughs for a bed, or if he was lucky enough to find a large, hollow tree, he would creep into that. There he would fall asleep, while listening to the howling of the wind or to the fiercer howling of the hungry wolves prowling about the woods.

At length, after much suffering from cold and want of food, he managed to reach Massasoit's wigwam. There the big-hearted Indian chief gave him a warm welcome. He took him into his poor cabin and kept him till spring — there was no board bill to pay. All the Indians liked the young minister, and even Canonicus,[1] that savage chief of a neighboring tribe, who had dared Governor Bradford to fight, said that he "loved him as his own son."

85. Roger Williams at Seekonk[2]; "What cheer, friend?" — When the warm days came, in the spring of 1636, Mr. Williams began building a log hut for himself at Seekonk, on the east bank of the Seekonk River. But he was told that his cabin stood on ground owned by the people of Massachusetts; so he, with a few friends

---

[1] Canonicus; see page 50. [2] Seekonk (See′konk).

who had joined him, took a canoe and paddled down stream to find a new place to build.

"What cheer, friend? what cheer?" shouted some Indians who were standing on a rock on the western bank of the river. That was the Indian way of saying: How do you do? and just then Roger Williams was right glad to hear it. He landed on what is now called "What Cheer Rock," [1] and had a talk with the red men.

"WHAT CHEER, FRIEND?"

They told him that there was a fine spring of water round the point of land a little further down. He went there, and liked the spot so much that he decided to stay. His friend Canonicus owned the land, and he gladly let him have what he needed. Roger Williams believed that a kind Providence had guided him to this pleasant place, and for this reason he named it PROVIDENCE.

Providence was the first settlement made in America which set its doors wide open to every one who wished to come and live there. Not only all Christians, but Jews, and even men who went to no church whatever, could

[1] "What Cheer Rock" is on the east side of the city of Providence.

go there and be at peace.[1] This great and good work
was done by Roger Williams. Providence grew in time
to be the chief city in the state of Rhode Island. When
the Revolution began, every man and boy in the state,
from sixteen to sixty, stood ready to fight for liberty.

86. Summary. — Roger Williams, a young minister of
Salem, Massachusetts, declared that the Indians, and
not the king of England, owned the land in America.
The governor of Massachusetts was afraid that if Mr.
Williams kept on saying these things, the king would

here of it and would take
away the land held by the
people of Boston and the other
settlements. He therefore
sent a constable to arrest the
young minister and put him
on board a ship going back to
England. When Mr. Williams
knew this, he fled to the Indian chief, Massasoit. In
1636 Roger Williams began building Providence. Providence was the first settlement in America which offered
a home to all men without asking them anything whatever about their religious belief.

Who was Roger Williams? What is said about him and the
Indians? Who did Mr. Williams think first owned the land in
America? How did many of the people of Massachusetts feel about
Mr. Williams? What did the chief men of Boston do? What did
Mr. Williams do? Describe his journey to Mount Hope. What did
Massasoit do for Mr. Williams? What did Mr. Williams do at See-
konk? What happened after that? Why did he name the settle-
ment Providence? What is said of Providence? What about the
Revolution?

[1] See Note 1 on page 59.

X. KING PHILIP

(Time of the Indian War, 1675-1676)

87. Death of Massasoit; Wamsutta[1] and Philip; Wamsutta's sudden death. — When the Indian chief Massasoit[2] died, the people of Plymouth lost one of their best friends. Massasoit left two sons, one named Wamsutta, who became chief in his father's place, and the other called Philip. They both lived near Mount Hope, in Rhode Island.

The governor of Plymouth heard that Wamsutta was stirring up the Indians to make war on the whites, and he sent for the Indian chief to come to him and give an account of himself. Wamsutta went, but on his way back he suddenly fell sick, and soon after he reached home he died. His young wife was a woman who was thought a great deal of by her tribe, and she told them that she felt sure the white people had poisoned her husband in order to get rid of him. This was not true, but the Indians believed it.

88. Philip becomes chief; why he hated the white men; how the white men had got possession of the Indian lands. — Philip now became chief. He called himself "King Philip." His palace was a wigwam made of bark. On great occasions he wore a bright red blanket and a kind of crown made of a broad belt ornamented with shells. King Philip hated the white people because, in the first place, he believed that they had murdered his brother; and next, because he saw that they were

---

[1] Wamsutta (Wam-sut'ta).
[2] Massasoit; see page 48.

growing stronger in numbers every year, while the Indians were becoming weaker.

When the Pilgrims landed at Plymouth, Massasoit, Philip's father, held all the country from Cape Cod back to the eastern shores of Narragansett Bay: that is, a strip about thirty miles wide. The white settlers bought a small piece of this land. After a while they bought more, and so they kept on, until in about fifty years they got nearly all of what Massasoit's tribe had once owned. The Indians had nothing left but two

THE BELT WHICH KING PHILIP WORE FOR A CROWN

little necks of land, which were nearly surrounded by the waters of Narragansett Bay. Here they felt that they were shut up almost like prisoners, and that the white men watched everything that they did.

89. How King Philip felt; signs of the coming war; the "Praying Indians"; the murder. — King Philip was a very proud man — quite as proud, in fact, as the king of England. He could not bear to see his people losing power. He said to himself, If the Indians do not rise and drive out the white men, then the white men will certainly drive out the Indians. Most of the Indians now had guns, and could use them quite as well as the whites could; so Philip thought that it was best to fight.

The settlers felt that the war was coming. Some of them fancied that they saw the figure of an Indian bow in the clouds. Others said that they heard sounds like guns fired off in the air, and horsemen riding furiously up and down in the sky, as if getting ready for battle.

But though many Indians now hated the white settlers, this was not true of all. A minister, named John Eliot, had persuaded some of the red men near Boston

to give up their religion, and to try to live like the white people. These were called " Praying Indians." One of them who knew King Philip well told the settlers that Philip's warriors were grinding their hatchets sharp for war. Soon afterward this " Praying Indian" was found murdered. The white people accused three of Philip's men of having killed him. They were tried, found guilty, and hanged.

90. Beginning of the war at Swansea[1]; burning of Brookfield. — Then Philip's warriors began the war in the summer of 1675. Some white settlers were going home from church in the town of Swansea, Massachusetts ; they had been to pray that there might be no fighting. As they walked along, talking together,

---

[1] Swansea (Swon'ze).

two guns were fired out of the bushes. One of the white men fell dead in the road, and another was badly hurt.

The shots were fired by Indians. This was the way they always fought when they could. They were not cowards ; but they did not come out and fight boldly, but would fire from behind trees and rocks. Fre-quently a white man would be killed without even seeing who shot him.

At first the fighting was mainly in those villages of Plymouth Colony which were nearest Narragansett Bay ; then it spread to the valley of the Connecticut River and the neighbor-hood. Deerfield, Springfield, Brook-field,[1] Groton,[2] and many other places

INDIAN ATTACK ON A VILLAGE

in Massachusetts were attacked. The Indians would creep up stealthily in the night, burn the houses, carry off the women and children prisoners if they could, kill the rest of the inhabitants, take their scalps home and hang them up in their wigwams.

[1] See map on page 68.
[2] Groton (Graw'ton).

At Brookfield the settlers left their houses, and gathered in one strong house for defence. The Indians burned all the houses but that one, and did their best to burn that, too. They dipped rags in brimstone, — such as we make matches of, — fastened them to the points of their arrows, set fire to them, and then shot the blazing arrows into the shingles of the roof. When the Indians saw that the shingles had caught, and were beginning to flame up, they danced for joy, and roared like wild bulls. But the men in the house managed to put out the fire on the roof. Then the savages got a cart, filled it with hay, set it on fire, and pushed it up against the house. This time they thought that they should certainly burn the white people out; but just then a heavy

COLONEL GOFFE'S BRAVE LEADERSHIP

shower came up, and put out the fire. A little later, some white soldiers marched into the village, and saved the people in the house.

91. The fight at Hadley; what Colonel [1] Goffe [2] did. — At Hadley, the people were in the meeting-house when the

---

[1] Colonel (kur'nel) : the chief officer of a regiment of soldiers.
[2] Goffe (Goff) ; see List of Books in Appendix.

terrible Indian war-whoop[1] rang through the village. The savages drove back those who dared to go out against them, and it seemed as if the village must be destroyed. Suddenly a white-haired old man, sword in hand, appeared among the settlers. No one knew who he was; but he called to them to follow him, as a captain calls to his men, and they obeyed him. The astonished Indians turned and ran. When all was over, the whites looked for their brave leader, but he was gone; they never saw him again. Many thought that he was an angel who had been sent to save them. But the angel was Colonel Goffe, an Englishman, one of the judges who, during a great war in England, had sentenced King Charles the First to death. He had escaped to America; and, luckily for the people of Hadley, he was hiding in the house of a friend in that village when the Indians attacked it.

92. How a woman drove off an Indian. — In this dreadful war with the savages there were times when even the women had to fight for their lives. In one case a woman had been left in a house with two young children. She heard a noise at the window, and looking up, saw an Indian trying to raise the sash. Quick as thought, she clapped the two little children under two large brass kettles which stood near. Then, seizing a shovelful of red-hot coals from the open fire, she stood ready, and just as the Indian thrust his head into the room, she dashed the coals right into his face and eyes. With a yell of agony the Indian let go his hold, dropped to the ground as though he had been shot, and ran howling to the woods.

[1] War-whoop (war-hoop): a very loud, shrill cry made by the Indians when engaged in war, or as a shout of alarm.

93. The great swamp fight ; burning the Indian wigwams ; what the Chief Canonchet [1] said. — During the summer and autumn of 1675 the Indians on the west side of Narragansett Bay [2] took no open part in King Philip's War. But the next winter the white people found that these Indians were secretly receiving and sheltering the savages who had been wounded in fighting for that noted chief. For that reason the settlers determined to raise a large force and attack them. The Indians had gathered in a fort on an island in a swamp. This fort was a very difficult place to reach. It was built of the trunks of trees set upright in the ground. It was so strong that the savages felt quite safe.

Starting very early in the morning, the attacking party waded fifteen miles through deep snow. Many of them had their hands and feet badly frozen. One of the chief men in leading the attack was Captain Benjamin Church of Plymouth ; he was a very brave soldier, and knew all about Indian life and Indian fighting. In the battle, he was struck by two bullets, and so badly wounded that he could not move a step further ; but he made one of his men hold him up, and shouted to his soldiers to go ahead. The fight was a desperate one, but at length the fort was taken. The attacking party lost more than two hundred and fifty men in killed and wounded ; the Indians lost as many as a thousand.

After the battle was over, Captain Church begged the men not to burn the wigwams inside the fort, for there were a great number of old men and women and little Indian children in the wigwams. But the men were very mad against the savages, and would not listen

[1] Canonchet (Kä-non'chet).   [2] See map on page 68.

INDIAN ATTACK ON A
SETTLEMENT

(The building on the right is
a block-house, or fort made
of hewn logs. These block-
houses were built as places
of refuge for the settlers,
in case of an attack on the
town by the Indians.)

73

to him. They set the wigwams on fire, and burned
many of these poor creatures to death.

Canonchet, the chief of the tribe, was taken prisoner.
The settlers told him they would spare his life if he
would try to make peace. " No," said he, "we will all
fight to the last man rather than become slaves to the
white men." He was then told that he must be shot.
" I like it well," said he. " I wish to die before my
heart becomes soft, or I say anything unworthy of
myself."

**94. Philip's wife and son are taken prisoners ; Philip is
shot ; end of the war.** — The next summer Captain Church,
with a lot of " brisk Bridgewater lads," chased King
Philip. and his men, and took many of the Indians
prisoners. Among those then taken captive were King
Philip's wife and his little boy. When Philip heard
of it he cried out, " My heart breaks ; now I am ready
to die." He had good reason for saying so. It was
the custom in England to sell such prisoners of war
as slaves. Following this custom, the Massachusetts
settlers took this boy, the grandson of that Massasoit[1]
who had helped them when they were poor and weak,
and sold him with his mother. They were sent to the
Bermuda Islands,[2] and there worked to death under the
hot sun and the lash of the slave-driver's whip.

Not long after that, King Philip himself was shot.
He had been hunted like a wild beast from place to
place. At last he had come back to see his old home
at Mount Hope[3] once more. There Captain Church

[1] See page 48.

[2] Bermuda (Ber-mu'dah) : the Bermuda Islands are in the Atlantic, north of
the West India Islands and east of South Carolina ; they belong to Great Britain.

[3] See map on page 62.

found him; there the Indian warrior was shot. His head and hands were cut off, — as was then done in England in such cases, — and his head was carried to Plymouth and set up on a pole. It stood there twenty years.

King Philip's death brought the war to an end. It had lasted a little over a year; that is, from the early summer of 1675 to the latter part of the summer of 1676. In that short time the Indians had killed between five and six hundred white settlers, and had burned thirteen villages to ashes, besides partly burning a great many more. The

DEATH OF KING PHILIP

war cost so much money that many people were made poor by it; but the strength of the Indians was broken; and they never dared to trouble the people of Southern New England again.

95. Summary. — In 1675 King Philip began a great Indian war against the people of Southeastern New England. His object was to kill off the white settlers, and get back the land for the Indians. He did kill a large number, and he destroyed many villages; but in the end the white men gained the victory. Philip's wife and child were sold as slaves, and he was shot. The Indians never attempted another war in this part of the country.

Who was Wamsutta? What happened to him? Who was "King Philip"? Why did he hate the white men? What did he say to himself? What is said about the "Praying Indians"? What happened to one of them? What was done with three of Philip's men? Where and how did the war begin? To what part of the country did it spread? Tell about the Indian attack on Brookfield. What happened at Hadley? Tell how a woman drove off an Indian. Tell all you can about the Great Swamp Fight. What is said about Canonchet? What is said of King Philip's wife and son? What happened to King Philip himself? What is said about the war?

XI. WILLIAM PENN

(1644-1718)

96. King Charles the Second gives William Penn a great piece of land, and names it Pennsylvania. — King Charles the Second of England owed a large sum of money to a young Englishman named William Penn. The king was fond of pleasure, and he spent so much money on himself and his friends that he had none left to pay his just debts. Penn knew this; so he told His Majesty that if he would give him a piece of wild land in America, he would ask nothing more.

Charles was very glad to settle the account so easily. He therefore gave Penn a great territory[1] north of Maryland[2] and west of the Delaware River. This

[1] Territory: any very large extent of land.
[2] See map on page 79.

territory was nearly as large as England. The king
named it Pennsylvania, a word which means Penn's
Woods. At that time the land was not thought to be
worth much. No one then had discovered the fact
that beneath Penn's Woods there were immense mines
of coal and iron,
which would one
day be of greater
value than all the
riches of the king
of England.

97. William Penn's
religion ; what he
wanted to do with
his American land. —
Penn belonged to
a religious society
called the Society
of Friends ; to-day
they are generally
spoken of as Quak-
ers. They are a
people who try to
find out what is

WILLIAM PENN RECEIVING THE GRANT OF
PENNSYLVANIA FROM CHARLES II

right by asking their own hearts. They believe in
showing no more signs of respect to one man than to
another, and at that time they would not take off their
hats even to the king himself.

Penn wanted the land which had been given him
here as a place where the Friends or Quakers might
go and settle. A little later the whole of what is
now the state of New Jersey was bought by Penn

and other Quakers for the same purpose. We have seen [1] that neither the Pilgrims nor the Catholics had any real peace in England. The Quakers suffered even more still; for oftentimes they were cruelly whipped and thrown into dark and dirty prisons, where many died of the bad treatment they received. William Penn himself had been shut up in jail four times on account of his religion; and though he was no longer in such danger, because the king was his friend, yet he wanted to provide a safe place for others who were not so well off as he was.

WILLIAM PENN

98. **Penn sends out emigrants to Pennsylvania; he gets ready to go himself; his conversation with the king.** — Penn accordingly sent out a number of people who were anxious to settle in Pennsylvania. The next year, 1682, he made ready to sail, himself, with a hundred more emigrants. Just before he started, he called on the king in his palace in London. The king was fond of

[1] See pages 44 and 55.

joking, and he said to Penn that he should never expect to see him again, for he thought that the Indians would be sure to catch such a good-looking young man as Penn was and eat him. 'But, Friend Charles,' said Penn, 'I mean to buy the land of the Indians, so they will rather keep on good terms with me than eat me.' 'Buy their lands!' exclaimed the king. 'Why, is not the whole of America mine?' 'Certainly not,' answered Penn. 'What!' replied the king; 'did n't my people discover it?[1] and so have n't I the right to it?' 'Well, Friend Charles,' said Penn, 'suppose a canoe, full of Indians, should cross the sea and they should discover England, would that make it theirs? Would you give up the country to them?' The king did not know what to say to this; it was a new way of looking at the matter. He probably said to himself, These Quakers are a strange people; they seem to think that even American savages have rights which should be respected.

99. **Penn founds[2] the city of Philadelphia; his treaty[3] with the Indians; his visit to them; how the Indians and the Quakers got on together.** — When William Penn reached America, in 1682, he sailed up the broad and beautiful Delaware River, for nearly a hundred miles. There he stopped, and resolved to build a city on its banks. He

[1] Referring to the discovery of the American continent by the Cabots, sent out by Henry the Seventh of England, see page 15.
[2] Founds: begins to build. [3] Treaty: an agreement; and see page 49.

gave the place the Bible name of Philadelphia,[1] or the City of Brotherly Love, because he hoped that all of its citizens would live together like brothers. The streets were named from the trees then growing on the land, and so to-day many are still called Walnut, Pine, Cedar, Vine, and so on.

PENN AND THE INDIANS

Penn said, "We intend to sit down lovingly among the Indians." On that account, he held a great meeting with them, under a wide-spreading elm. The tree stood in what is now a part of Philadelphia.[2] Here

[1] See Revelation i. 11 and iii. 7.

[2] The "Treaty Elm," as it was called, stood in what is now Kensington, a district which is included within the bounds of Philadelphia. The tree is no longer standing.

Penn and the red men made a treaty, or agreement, by which they promised each other that they would live together as friends as long as the water should run in the rivers, or the sun shine in the sky.

Nearly a hundred years later, while the Revolutionary War was going on, the British army took possession of the city. It was cold, winter weather, and the men wanted fire-wood; but the English general thought so much of William Penn that he set a guard of soldiers round the great elm, to prevent any one from chopping it down.

Not long after the great meeting under the elm, Penn visited some of the savages in their wigwams. They treated him to a dinner — or shall we say a lunch? — of roasted acorns. After their feast, some of the young savages began to run and leap about, to show the Englishman what they could do. When Penn was in college at Oxford he had been fond of doing such things himself. The sight of the Indian boys made him feel like a boy again; so he sprang up from the ground, and beat them all at hop, skip, and jump. This completely won the hearts of the red men.

From that time, for sixty years, the Pennsylvania settlers and the Indians were fast friends. The Indians said, "The Quakers are honest men; they do no harm; they are welcome to come here." In New England there had been, as we have seen,[1] a terrible war with the savages, but in Pennsylvania no Indian ever shed a drop of Quaker blood.

100. How Philadelphia grew; what was done there in the Revolution; William Penn's last years and death. — Philadelphia grew quite fast. William Penn let the people

[1] See page 68.

have land very cheap, and he said to them, "You shall be governed by laws of your own making." Even after Philadelphia became a good-sized town, it had no poorhouse, for none was needed ; everybody seemed to be able to take care of himself.

WILLIAM PENN IN PRISON

When the Revolution began, the people of Pennsylvania and of the country north and south of it sent men to Philadelphia to decide what should be done. This meeting was called the Congress. It was held in the old State House, a building which is still standing ; and in 1776 Congress declared the United States of America independent of England. In the war, the people of Delaware and New Jersey fought side by side with those of Pennsylvania.

William Penn spent a great deal of money in helping Philadelphia and other settlements. After he returned to England he was put in prison for debt, by a rascally fellow he had employed. He did not owe the money, and he proved that the man who said that he did was no better than a thief. Penn was released from prison ; but his long confinement in jail had broken his health down. When he died the Indians of Pennsylvania sent his widow some beautiful furs, in remembrance of their

"Brother Penn," as they called him. They said that the furs were to make her a cloak, "to protect her while passing through this thorny wilderness without her guide."

About twenty-five miles west of London, on a country road within sight of the towers of Windsor Castle,[1] there stands a Friends' meeting-house, or Quaker church.[2] In the yard back of the meeting-house, William Penn lies buried. For a hundred years or more, there was no mark of any kind to show where he rests; but now a small stone bearing his name points out the grave of the founder of the great state of Pennsylvania.

101. Summary. — Charles the Second, king of England, owed William Penn, a young English Quaker, a large sum of money. In order to settle the debt, the king gave him a great piece of land in America, and named it Pennsylvania, or Penn's Woods. Penn wished to make a home for Quakers in America; and in 1682 he came over, and began building the city of Philadelphia. When the Revolution broke out, men were sent from all parts of the country to Philadelphia, to hold a meeting called the Congress. In 1776, Congress declared the United States independent.

To whom did King Charles the Second owe a large sum of money? How did he pay his debt? What did the king name the country? What does the name mean? What valuable mines have been found there? What is said about the Friends or Quakers? What did Penn want the land here for? How were the Quakers then treated in England? What did Penn do in 1682? Tell what the king said to Penn and what Penn replied. What city did Penn begin to build here? What does Philadelphia mean? What did Penn and the Indians do? What did the English general do about the great elm in the Revolution? Tell about Penn's dinner with the Indians. Did the Indians trouble the Quakers? What is said of the growth of Philadelphia? What was done there in the Revolution? Tell what you can about Penn's last days. Where is he buried?

---

[1] Windsor Castle; see page 56.   [2] It is known as Jordan's meeting-house.

XII. GENERAL JAMES OGLETHORPE[1]

(1696-1785)

102. The twelve English colonies in America; General Oglethorpe makes a settlement in Georgia. — We have seen[2] that the first real colony or settlement made in America by the English was in Virginia in 1607. By the beginning of 1733, or in about a hundred and twenty-five years, eleven more had been made, or twelve in all. They stretched along the seacoast, from the farthest coast of Maine to the northern boundary of Florida, which was then owned by the Spaniards.[3]

The two colonies farthest south were North Carolina and South Carolina. In 1733 James Oglethorpe, a brave English soldier, who afterward became General Oglethorpe, came over here to make a new settlement. This new one, which made thirteen[4] in all, was called Georgia in honor of King George the Second, who gave a piece of land for it, on the seacoast, below South Carolina.

103. What it was that led General Oglethorpe to make this new settlement. — General Oglethorpe had a friend in England who was cast into prison for debt. There the unfortunate man was so cruelly treated that he fell sick and died, leaving his family in great distress.

---

[1] Oglethorpe (Ō'gel-thorp).   [2] See page 26.

[3] Because the Spaniards had settled it in 1565; see page 20.

[4] These thirteen colonies or settlements were: First, the four New England colonies (New Hampshire, Massachusetts, Connecticut, and Rhode Island; Maine was then part of Massachusetts, and Vermont was claimed by both New Hampshire and New York). Secondly, four middle colonies (New York, New Jersey, Pennsylvania, with Delaware). Thirdly, five southern colonies (Maryland, Virginia, North Carolina, South Carolina, and Georgia).

The General felt the death of his friend so much that he set to work to find out how other poor debtors lived in the London prisons. He soon saw that great numbers of them suffered terribly. The prisons were crowded and filthy. The men shut up in them were ragged and dirty ; some of them were fastened with heavy chains ; and a good many actually died of starvation.

General Oglethorpe could not bear to see strong men killed off in this manner. He thought if the best of them — those who were honest and willing to work — could have the chance given them of earning their living, that they would soon do as well as any men. It was to help them that he persuaded the king to give the land of Georgia.

104. Building the city of Savannah ; what the people of Charleston, South Carolina, did ; a busy settlement ; the alligators. — General Oglethorpe took thirty-five families to America in 1733. They settled on a bank of the Savannah [1] River, about twenty miles from the sea. The General laid out a town with broad, straight, handsome streets, and with many small squares or parks. He called the settlement Savannah, from the Indian name of the river on which it stands.

[1] Savannah (Sa-van'ah).

The people of Charleston, South Carolina, were glad to have some English neighbors south of them that would help them fight the Spaniards of Florida, who hated the English, and wanted to drive them out. They gave the newcomers a hundred head of cattle, a drove of hogs, and twenty barrels of rice.

The emigrants set to work with a will, cutting down the forest trees, building houses, and planting gardens. There were no idlers to be seen at Savannah: even the children found something to do that was helpful.

LAYING OUT THE CITY OF SAVANNAH

Nothing disturbed the people but the alligators. They climbed up the bank from the river to see what was going on. But the boys soon taught them not to be too curious. When one monster was found impudently prowling round the town, they thumped him with sticks till they fairly beat the life out of him. Soon the alligators decided not to pay any more visits to the settlers.

105. Arrival of some German emigrants; "Ebenezer"[1]; "blazing" trees. — After a time, some German Protestants, who had been cruelly driven out of their native land on account of their religion, came to Georgia. General Oglethorpe gave them a hearty welcome. He

1 Ebenezer (Eb-e-ne′zer).

had bought land of the Indians, and so there was plenty of room for all. The Germans went up the river, and then went back a number of miles into the woods; there they picked out a place for a town. They called their settlement by the Bible name of Ebenezer,[1] which means "The Lord hath helped us."

There were no roads through the forests, so the new settlers "blazed" the trees; that is, they chopped a piece of bark off, so that they could find their way through the thick woods when they wanted to go to Savannah. Every tree so marked stood like a guide-post; it showed the traveller

THE "BLAZED" TREES

which way to go until he came in sight of the next one.

106. Trying to make silk; the queen's American dress. — The settlers hoped to be able to get large quantities of silk to send to England, because the mulberry tree grows wild in Georgia, and its leaves are the favorite food of the silkworm.[2] At first it seemed as if the

---

[1] See 1 Samuel vii. 12.   [2] Silkworm: a kind of caterpillar which spins a fine, soft thread of which silk is made.

plan would be successful, and General Oglethorpe took over some Georgia silk as a present to the queen of England. She had a handsome dress made of it for her birthday; it was the first American silk dress ever worn by an English queen. But after a while it was found that silk could not be produced in Georgia as well as it could in Italy and France, and so in time cotton came to be raised instead.

107. Keeping out the Spaniards; Georgia powder at Bunker Hill; General Oglethorpe in his old age. — The people of Georgia did a good work in keeping out the Spaniards, who were trying to get possession of the part of the country north of Florida. Later, like the settlers in North Carolina and South Carolina, they did their full share in helping to make America independent of the rule of the king of England. When the war of the Revolution began, the king had a lot of powder stored in Savannah. The people broke into the building, rolled out the kegs, and carried them off. Part of the powder they kept for themselves, and part they seem to have sent to Massachusetts; so that it is quite likely that the men who fought at Bunker Hill may have loaded their guns with some of the powder given them by their friends in Savannah. In that case the king got it back, but in a somewhat different way from what he expected.

General Oglethorpe spent the closing years of his life in England. He lived to a very great age. Up to the last, he had eyes as bright and keen as a boy's. After the Revolution was over, the king made a treaty, or agreement, by which he promised to let the United States of America live in peace. General Oglethorpe was able to read that treaty without spectacles. He had lived to see the colony of Georgia which he had settled become a free and independent state.

108. Summary. — In 1733 General James Oglethorpe brought over a number of emigrants from England, and settled Savannah, Georgia. Georgia was the thirteenth English colony; it was the last one established in this country. General Oglethorpe lived to see it become one of the United States of America.

At the beginning of 1733 how many English colonies were there in America? Who was General Oglethorpe? What did he do? Why was the new settlement called Georgia? Tell what happened to a friend of General Oglethorpe's. What did he wish to do for the poor debtors? What is said about the settlement of Savannah? What is said about the German emigrants and Ebenezer? What is said about raising silk? What good work did the people of Georgia do? What is said about Georgia powder in the Revolution? What is said of General Oglethorpe in old age?

XIII. BENJAMIN FRANKLIN

(1706–1790)

109. Growth of Philàdelphia; what a young printer was doing for it. — By the year 1733, when the people of Savannah [1] were building their first log cabins, Philadelphia [2] had grown to be the largest city in this country, — though it would take more than seventy such cities to make one as great as Philadelphia now is.

Next to William Penn,[3] the person who did the most for Philadelphia was a young man who had gone from Boston to make his home among the Quakers. He lived in a

---

[1] See page 85.   [2] See page 79.   [3] See page 76.

small house near the market.   On a board over the door he had painted his name and business; here it is:

110. Franklin's newspaper and almanac[1]; how he worked; standing before kings. — Franklin was then publishing a small newspaper, called the *Pennsylvania Gazette*.[2] To-day we print newspapers by steam at the rate of two or three hundred a minute; but Franklin, standing in his shirt-sleeves at a little press, printed his with his own hands.   It was hard work, as you could see by the drops of sweat that stood on his forehead; and it was slow as well as hard.   The young man not only wrote himself most of what he printed in his paper, but he often made his own ink; sometimes he even made his own type.[3] When he got out of paper he would take a wheelbarrow, go out and buy a load, and wheel it home.   To-day there are more than three hundred

FRANKLIN WHEELING A LOAD OF PAPER

[1] Almanac (al′mă-nak).   [2] Gazette (ga-zet′): a newspaper.
   [3] Type: the raised metal letters used in printing are made by melting lead and some other metals together and pouring the mixture into molds.

newspapers printed in Philadelphia; then there were only two, and Franklin's was the better of those two.

Besides this paper he published an almanac, which thousands of people bought. In it he printed such sayings as these: "*He who would thrive*[1] *must rise at five,*" and "*If you want a thing well done, do it yourself.*" But Franklin was not contented with simply printing these sayings, for he practised them as well.

FRANKLIN PRINTING HIS NEWSPAPER

Sometimes his friends would ask him why he began work so early in the morning, and kept at it so many hours. He would laugh, and tell them that his father used to repeat to him this saying of Solomon's: "*Seest thou a man diligent in his business? he shall stand before kings; he shall not stand before mean men.*"[2]

At that time the young printer never actually expected to stand in the presence of a king; but years later he met with five; and one of them, his friend, the king of France, gave him his picture set round with diamonds.

---

[1] Thrive: to get on in business, to prosper.　　[2] See Proverbs xxii. 29.

111. Franklin's boyhood; making tallow candles; he is apprenticed[1] **to his brother; how he managed to save money to buy books.** — Franklin's father was a poor man with a large family. He lived in Boston, and made soap and candles. Benjamin went to school two years; then, when he was ten years old, his father set him to work in his factory, and he never went to school again. He was now kept busy filling the candle-molds with melted tallow, cutting off the ends of the wicks, and running errands. But the boy did not like this kind of work;

A TYPE
(The letter B.)

and, as he was very fond of books, his father put him in a printing office. This office was carried on by James Franklin, one of Benjamin's brothers. James Franklin paid a small sum of money each week for Benjamin's board; but the boy told him that if he would let him have half the money to use as he liked, he would board himself. James was glad to do this. Benjamin then gave up eating meat, and, while the others went out to dinner, he would stay in the printing office and eat a boiled potato, or perhaps a handful of raisins. In this way he saved up a number of coppers every week; and when he got enough laid by he would buy a book.

But James Franklin was not only a mean man, but a hot-tempered one; and when he got angry with his young apprentice, he would beat and knock him about. At length the lad, who was now seventeen,

---

[1] Apprenticed: bound by a written agreement to learn the trade of a master, who is bound by the same agreement to teach the trade. In Franklin's time an apprentice had to bind himself to serve seven years, and in most ways he was entirely under the control of his master.

made up his mind that he would run away, and go to New York.

112. Young Franklin runs away; he goes to New York, and then to Philadelphia. — Young Franklin sold some of his books, and with the money paid his passage to New York by a sailing vessel, — for in those days there were no steamboats or railroads in America. When he got to New York, he could not find work, so he decided to go on to Philadelphia.

He started to walk across New Jersey to Burlington on the Delaware River, a distance of about fifty miles; there he hoped to get a sailboat going down the river to Philadelphia. Shortly after he set out, it began to rain hard, and the lad was soon wet to the skin and splashed all over with red mud; but he kept on until noon; then took a rest; and on the third day he reached Burlington and got passage down the river.

113. Franklin's Sunday walk in Philadelphia; the rolls; Miss Read; the Quaker meeting-house. — Franklin landed in Philadelphia on Sunday morning (1723). He was tired and hungry; he had but a single dollar in the world. As he walked along, he saw a bakeshop open. He went in and bought three great, puffy rolls for a penny [1] each. Then he started up Market Street, where he was one day to have his newspaper office. He had

---

[1] Penny: an English coin worth two cents.

a roll like a small loaf of bread tucked under each arm; and he was eating the other as though it tasted good to him. As he passed a house, he noticed a nice-looking young woman who saw him. She seemed to want

FRANKLIN'S FIRST DAY IN PHILADELPHIA

to laugh; and well she might, for Franklin appeared like a youthful tramp who had been robbing a baker's shop. The young woman was Miss Deborah[1] Read. A number of years later Franklin married her. He always said that he could not have got a better wife.

Franklin kept on in his walk until he came to the Delaware. He took a hearty drink of river water to settle his breakfast, and then gave away the two rolls he had under his arm to a poor woman with a child. On his way back from the river, he followed a number

of people to a Quaker meeting-house. At the meeting no one spoke. Franklin was tired out, and, not having any preacher to keep him awake, he soon fell asleep, and

[1] Deborah (Deb'o-rah).

slept till the meeting was over. He says, "This was the first house I was in, or slept in, in Philadelphia."

114. Franklin finds work; he goes back to Boston on a visit; he learns to stoop. — The next day the young man found some work in a printing office. Six months afterward he decided to go back to Boston to see his friends. He started on his journey with a good suit of clothes, a silver watch, and a well-filled purse.

While in Boston, Franklin went to call on a minister who had written a little book[1] which he had been very fond of reading. As he was coming away from the minister's house, he had to go through a low passage-way under a large beam. "Stoop! stoop!" cried

STOOP! STOOP!

out the gentleman; but Franklin did not understand him, and so hit his head a sharp knock against the beam. "Ah," said his friend, as he saw him rubbing his head, "you are young, and have the world before you; *stoop* as you go through it, and you will miss many hard thumps." Franklin says that this sensible advice, which was thus beat into his head, was of great use afterward; in fact, he learned then how to stoop to conquer.

[1] The name of this book, written by the Rev. Cotton Mather, was *Essays to do Good.*

115. Franklin returns to Philadelphia ; he goes to London ; water against beer. — Franklin soon went back to Philadelphia. The governor of Pennsylvania then persuaded him to go to London, telling him that he would help him to get a printing-press and type to start a newspaper in Philadelphia.

When Franklin reached London, he found that the governor was one of those men who promise great things, but do nothing. Instead of buying a press, Franklin had to go to work in a printing office to earn his bread. He stayed in London more than a year. At the office where he worked, the men were great beer drinkers. One of his companions bought six pints a day. He began with a pint before breakfast ; then took another pint at breakfast ; then a pint between breakfast and dinner ; then a pint at dinner ; then a pint in the afternoon ; and, last of all, a pint after he had done work. Franklin drank nothing but water. The others laughed at him, and nicknamed him the "Water-American" ; but, after a while, they had to confess that he was stronger than they were who drank so much strong beer.

The fact was that Franklin could beat them, both at work and at play. When they went out for a bath in the Thames,[1] they found that their "Water-American" could swim like a fish ; and he so astonished them that a rich Londoner tried to persuade him to start a swimming school to teach his sons ; but Franklin had stayed in England long enough, and he now decided to go back to Philadelphia.

[1] Thames (Tĕms). London, the largest city in the world, is situated on both sides of the river Thames, about fifty miles from its mouth.

116. Franklin sets up his newspaper; "sawdust pudding."
— After his return to America, Franklin labored so diligently that he was soon able to set up a newspaper of his own. He tried to make it a good one. But some people thought that he spoke his mind too freely. They complained of this to him, and gave him to understand that if he did not make his paper to please them, they would stop taking it or advertising in it.

Franklin heard what they had to say, and then invited them all to come and have supper with him. They went, expecting a feast, but they found nothing on the table but two dishes of corn-meal mush and a big pitcher of cold water. That kind of mush was then eaten only by very poor people; and because it was yellow and coarse, it was nicknamed " sawdust pudding."

Franklin gave everybody a heaping plateful; and then, filling his own, he made a hearty supper of it. The others tried to eat, but could not. After Franklin had finished his supper, he looked up and said quietly, " My friends, any one who can live on 'sawdust pudding' and cold water, as I can, does not need much help from others." After that, no one went to the young printer with complaints about his paper. Franklin, as we have seen,[1] had learned to stoop; but he certainly did not mean to go stooping through life.

117. Franklin's plan of life; what he did for Philadelphia.
— Not many young men can see their own faults, but Franklin could see his. More than that, he tried hard to get rid of them. He kept a little book in which he wrote down his faults. If he wasted half an hour of time or a shilling of money, or said anything that he

[1] See page 95.

had better not have said, he wrote it down in his book.
He carried that book in his pocket all his life, and he
studied it as a boy at school studies a hard lesson. By
it, he learned three things, — first, to do the right thing ;
next, to do it at the right time ; last of all, to do it in
the right way.

As he was never tired of helping himself to get
upward and onward, so, too, he was never tired of helping others. He started the first public library in Philadelphia, which was also the first in America. He set
on foot the first fire-engine company and the first military company in that city. He got the people to pave
the muddy streets with stone ; he helped to build the
first academy, — now called the University of Pennsylvania, — and he also helped to build the first hospital.

118. Franklin's experiments [1] **with electricity ; the wonderful bottle ; the picture of the king of England.** — While doing
these things and publishing his paper besides, Franklin
found time to make experiments with electricity. Very
little was then known about this wonderful power ; but a
Dutchman, living in the city of Leyden [2] in Holland,
had discovered a way of bottling it up in what is called
a Leyden Jar. Franklin had one of these jars, and he
was never tired of seeing what new and strange thing
he could do with it.

He contrived a picture of the king of England with
a movable gilt crown on his head. Then he connected
the crown by a long wire with the Leyden jar. When

---

[1] Experiments: here an experiment is a trial made to discover something
unknown. Franklin made these experiments, or trials, with electricity and with
thunder clouds in order to find out what he could about them.

[2] Leyden (Li´den) ; see map on page 44.

he wanted some fun, he would dare any one to go up to the picture and take off the king's crown. Why, that's easy enough, a man would say; and would walk up and seize the crown. But no sooner had he touched it than he would get an electric shock which would make his fingers tingle as they never tingled before. With a loud Oh! Oh! he would let go of the crown, and start back in utter astonishment, not knowing what had hurt him.

119. The electrical kite. — But Franklin's greatest experiment was made one day in sober earnest, with a kite. He believed that the electricity in the bottle, or Leyden jar, was the same thing as the lightning we see in a thunderstorm. He knew well enough how to get an electric spark from the jar, for with such a spark he had once killed a turkey for dinner; but how could he get a spark from a cloud in the sky?

He thought about it for a long time; then he made a kite out of a silk handkerchief, and fastened a sharp iron

point to the upright stick of the kite.   One day, when
a thunderstorm was seen coming up, Franklin and his
son went out to the fields.   The kite was raised ; then
Franklin tied an iron key to the lower end of the string.
After waiting some time, he saw the little hair-like
threads of the string begin to stand up like the bristles
of a brush.   He felt certain that the electricity was coming down the string.   He put his knuckle close to the
key and a spark flew out.   Next, he took his Leyden
jar and collected the electricity in that.   He had made
two great discoveries, for he had found out that electricity and lightning are the same thing ; and he had
also found how to fill his bottle directly from the clouds :
that was something that no one had ever done before.

120. Franklin invents the lightning-rod ; *Doctor* Franklin.
— But Franklin did not stop at that.   He said, If I can
draw down electricity from the sky with a kite-string, I
can draw it still better with a tall, sharp-pointed iron rod.
He put up such a rod on his house in Philadelphia ; it
was the first lightning-rod in the world.   Soon other
people began to put them up : so this was another gift
of his to the city which he loved.   Every good lightning-
rod which has since been erected to protect buildings
has been, in some degree, a copy of that invented by
Franklin.

People now began to talk, not only in this country
but in Europe, about his electrical experiments and discoveries.   The oldest college in Scotland[1] gave him a title
of honor and called him Doctor, — a word which means
a learned man.   From this time Franklin the printer was
no longer plain Mr. Franklin, but Dr. Franklin.

[1] The University of St. Andrews.

Dr. Franklin did not think that he had found out all that could be found out about electricity; he believed that he had simply made a beginning, and that other men

would discover still greater things that could be done with it. Do you think he was mistaken about that?

121. Franklin in the Revolutionary War; Franklin and the map of the United States. — When the war of the Revolution broke out, Dr. Franklin did a great work for his country. He did not fight battles like Washington, but he did something just as useful. First, he helped write the Declaration of Independence, by which we declared ourselves free from the rule of the king of England; next, he went to France to get aid for us. We were then too poor to pay our soldiers; he got the king of France to let us have money to give them.

FRANKLIN'S CANE AND WASHINGTON'S REVO-LUTIONARY SWORD

(Preserved in the Patent Office, Washington.)

Franklin lived to see the Revolution ended and America free. When he died, full of years and of honors, he was buried in Philadelphia. Twenty thousand people went to his funeral.

FRANKLIN'S GRAVE IN CHRIST CHURCH BURIAL-GROUND, PHILADELPHIA

If you wish to see what the country thinks of him, you have only to look at a large map of the United States, and count up how many times you find his name on it.   You will find that more than two hundred counties and towns are called FRANKLIN.

122. Summary. — Benjamin Franklin was born in Boston nearly two hundred years ago. He went to Philadelphia when he was seventeen. He started a newspaper there, opened the first public library, and did many other things to help the city. He discovered that lightning and electricity are the same thing, and he invented the lightning-rod to protect buildings. In the Revolution, he got large sums of money from the king of France to pay our soldiers and to help Washington fight the battles which ended in making America free.

What had Philadelphia grown to be by 1733? Who did a great deal for Philadelphia? Tell what you can about Franklin's newspaper. What else did he publish? What sayings did he print in his almanac? What saying of Solomon's did Franklin's father use to repeat to him? Did he ever stand in the presence of any kings? Tell what you can about Franklin as a boy. Where did he live? What did he do? How did he save money to buy books? Why did he run away? Where did he go? Tell what you can about Franklin's landing in Philadelphia. How did Franklin look to Miss Read? Where did Franklin find work? What happened to him when he went back to Boston on a visit? Why did Franklin go to London? What did he do there? What did they nickname him in the printing office? What did Franklin do after he returned to Philadelphia? Tell the story of the "sawdust pudding." Tell about Franklin's plan of life. What did he do for Philadelphia? What experiments did Franklin make? What about the picture of the king? Tell the story of the kite. What two things did he find out by means of this kite? What did he invent? What title did a college in Scotland now give him? Did Franklin think that anything more would be discovered about electricity? What two things did Franklin do in the Revolution? What is said of his funeral? How many counties and towns in the United States are now called by his name?

"Yankee Doodle" or The Spirit of '76

XIV. GEORGE WASHINGTON

(1732-1799)

123. A Virginia boy; what he became; what he learned at school; his writing-books. — In 1732, when Franklin was at work on his newspaper, a boy was born on a plantation[1] in Virginia who was one day to stand higher even than the Philadelphia printer.

That boy when he grew up was to be chosen leader of the armies of the Revolution; he was to be elected the first president of the United States; and before he died he was to be known and honored all over the world. The name of that boy was George Washington.

Washington's father died when George was only eleven years old, leaving him, with his brothers and sisters,

WASHINGTON'S SIGNATURE AT THE AGE OF TWELVE [2]

to the care of a most excellent and sensible mother. It was that mother's influence, more than anything else, which made George the man he became.

---

[1] George Washington was born on a plantation (or farm cultivated by slaves) on Bridges Creek, a small stream emptying into the Potomac. See map, page 106. Not long after George's birth (February 22, 1732), his father moved to an estate on the Rappahannock River, opposite Fredericksburg. See map, page 106, for this place and Mount Vernon.   [2] See Note on page 279.

George went to a little country school, where he learned to read, write, and cipher. By the time he was twelve, he could write a clear, bold hand. In one of his writing-books he copied many good rules or sayings. Here is one:

124. Washington's sports and games; playing at war; "Captain George." — But young Washington was not always copying good sayings; for he was a tall, strong boy, fond of all outdoor sports and games. He was a well-meaning boy; but he had a hot temper, and at times his blue eyes flashed fire. In all trials of strength and in all deeds of daring, George took the lead; he could run faster, jump further, and throw a stone higher than any one else in the school.

Labor to keep alive in your breast that little spark of celestial fire called conscience.[1]

When the boys played "soldier," they liked to have "Captain George" as commander. When he drew his wooden sword, and shouted Come on! they would all rush into battle with a wild hurrah. Years afterward, when the real war came, and George Washington drew his sword in earnest, some of his school companions may have fought under their old leader.

125. The great battle with the colt, and what came of it. — Once, however, Washington had a battle of a different kind. It was with a high-spirited colt which belonged to his mother. Nobody had ever been able to do anything with that colt, and most people were afraid of him. Early one morning, George and some of his brothers were out in the pasture. George looked at the colt prancing about and kicking up his heels. Then he said,

[1] Celestial: heavenly, divine.

"Boys, if you'll help me put a bridle on him, I'll ride him." The boys managed to get the colt into a corner and to slip on the bridle. With a leap, George seated

himself firmly on his back. Then the fun began. The colt, wild with rage, ran, jumped, plunged, and reared straight up on his hind legs, hoping to throw his rider off. It was all useless; he might as well have tried to throw off his own skin, for the boy stuck to his back as though he had grown there. Then, making a last desperate bound into the air, the animal burst a blood vessel and fell dead. The battle was over, George was victor, but it had cost the life of Mrs. Washington's favorite colt.

When the boys went in to breakfast, their mother, knowing that they had just come from the pasture, asked how the colt was getting on. "He is dead, madam," said George; "I killed him." "Dead!" exclaimed his mother. "Yes, madam, dead,"

THE STONE MARKING WASH-
INGTON'S BIRTHPLACE

(The house is no longer standing.)

replied her son. Then he told her just how it happened. When Mrs. Washington heard the story, her face flushed with anger. Then, waiting a moment, she looked steadily at George, and said quietly, "While I regret the loss of my favorite, I rejoice in my son, who always speaks the truth."

126. Washington goes on a visit to Mount Vernon ; he makes the acquaintance of Lord Fairfax. — George's eldest brother, Lawrence Washington, had married the daughter of a gentleman named Fairfax,[1] who lived on the banks of the Potomac. Lawrence had a fine estate a few miles above, on the same river ; he called his place Mount Vernon. When he was fourteen, George went to Mount Vernon to visit his brother.

Lawrence Washington took George down the river to call on the Fairfaxes. There the lad made the acquaintance of Lord Fairfax, an English nobleman who had come over from London. He owned an immense piece of land in Virginia. Lord Fairfax and George soon became great friends. He was a gray-haired man nearly sixty, but he enjoyed having this boy of fourteen as a companion. They spent weeks together on horseback in the fields and woods, hunting deer and foxes.

127. Lord Fairfax hires Washington to survey[2] his land ; how Washington lived in the woods ; the Indian war-dance. — Lord Fairfax's land extended westward more than a hundred miles. It had never been very carefully surveyed ; and he was told that settlers were moving in beyond the Blue Ridge Mountains,[3] and were building log cabins on his property without asking leave. By the time Washington was sixteen, he had learned surveying ; and so Lord Fairfax hired him to measure his land for him.

---

[1] Fairfax: this was the Hon. William Fairfax; he was cousin to Lord Fairfax, and he had the care of Lord Fairfax's land.

[2] Survey: to find out the form, size, and position of a piece of land by measuring it in certain ways.   [3] See map on opposite page.

It has been thought best to number the French Forts instead of giving their names. No. 4, Ft. Duquesne (Du-Kane'), was the most important: it stood where Pittsburg now stands.

LAKE ONTARIO

Oneida L.

Genese River

NEW YORK

Cayuga L.

LAKE ERIE

Erie

French Fort No. 1.

French Fort No. 2.

French Fort No. 3.

O H I O

PENNSYLVANIA

MOUNTAINS

Susquehanna River

Delaware River

Logstown

French Fort No. 4.

Braddock's Defeat

Monongahela Riv.

Allegheny River

Fort Necessity

Fort Cumberland

BLUE RIDGE

Philadelphia

Ohio River

Line

Braddock's March

South Branch

DELAWARE

Frederick

Baltimore

MARYLAND

Potomac Riv.

Winchester

Mt. Vernon

The Fairfax Estate

Washington's Home in Boyhood

Land Surveyed by Washington

VALLEY OF VIRGINIA

Shenandoah River

ALLEGHANY

BLUE RIDGE

VIRGINIA

Fredericksburg

Birthplace of Washington

Rappahannock R.

James

Staunton R.

Richmond

River

Williamsburg

Yorktown

ATLANTIC OCEAN

Dan

Roanoke River

N O R T H   C A R O L I N A

MAP ILLUSTRATING WASHINGTON'S EARLY LIFE

Washington was glad to undertake the work; for he needed the money, and he could earn in this way from five to ten dollars a day.

Early in the spring, Washington, in company with another young man, started off, on foot, to do this business. They crossed the Blue Ridge Mountains, and entered the Valley of Virginia, one of the most beautiful valleys in America.

The two young men would work all day in the woods, with a long chain, measuring the land. When evening came, Washington would make a map of what they had measured. Then they would wrap themselves

WASHINGTON SEES AN INDIAN WAR-DANCE

up in their blankets, stretch themselves on the ground at the foot of a tree, and go to sleep under the stars.

Every day they shot some game, — squirrels or wild turkeys, or perhaps a deer. They kindled a fire with flint and steel,[1] and roasted the meat on sticks held over the coals. For plates they had clean chips; and as clean chips could always be got by a few blows with an axe,

1 Flint and steel · see picture on page 62.

they never washed any dishes, but just threw them away, and had a new set for each meal.

While in the valley they met a band of Indians, who stopped and danced a war-dance for them. The music was not remarkable, — for most of it was made by drumming on a deerskin stretched across the top of an old iron pot, — but the dancing could not be beat. The savages leaped into the air, swung their hatchets, gashed the trees, and yelled till the woods rang.

When Washington returned from his surveying trip, Lord Fairfax was greatly pleased with his work; and the governor of Virginia made him one of the public surveyors. By this means he was able to get work which paid him handsomely.

128. Washington at the age of twenty-one; the French in the west; the governor of Virginia sends Washington to see the French commander. — By the time Washington was twenty-one he had grown to be over six feet in height. He was as straight as an arrow and as tough as a whiplash. He had keen blue eyes that seemed to look into the very heart of things, and his fist was like a blacksmith's sledge-hammer. He knew all about the woods, all about Indians, and he could take care of himself anywhere.

At this time the English settlers held the country along the seashore as far back as the Alleghany Mountains.[1] West of those mountains the French from Canada were trying to get possession of the land. They had made friends with many of the Indians; and, with their help, they hoped to be able to drive out the English and get the whole country for themselves.

[1] Alleghany (Al-le-ga'ni): see map, page 106.   (It is also spelled Allegheny.)

In order to hold this land in the west, the French had built several forts [1] south of Lake Erie; and they were getting ready to build some on the Ohio River. The governor of Virginia was determined to put a stop to this. He had given young Washington the military title of major [2]; he now sent Major Washington to see the French commander at one of the forts near Lake Erie. Washington was to tell the Frenchman that he had built his forts on land belonging to the English, and that he and his men must either leave or fight.

Major Washington dressed himself like an Indian, and attended by several friendly Indians and by a white man named Gist,[3] who knew the country well, he set out on his journey through what was called the Great Woods.

The entire distance to the farthest fort and back was about a thousand miles. Washington could go on horseback part of the way, but there were no regular roads, and he had to climb mountains and swim rivers. After several weeks' travel, he reached the fort; but the French commander refused to give up the land. He said that he and his men had come to stay, and that if the English did not like it they must fight.

129. The journey back; the Indian guide; how Washington found his way through the woods; the adventure with the raft. — On the way back, Washington had to leave his horses and come on foot with Gist and an Indian guide sent from the fort. This Indian guide was in the pay of the French, and he intended to murder Washington in the woods. One day he shot at him from behind a tree, but,

[1] Forts: see map, page 106.
[2] Major (mā′jer): an officer in the army next above a captain, but below a colonel. [3] Gist (Jist).

luckily, did not hit him. Then Washington and Gist
managed to get away from him, and set out to go back
to Virginia by themselves.   There were no paths through
the thick forest ; but Washington had his compass[1] with
him, and with that he could find his way just as the captain of a ship finds his at sea.   When they reached the
Alleghany River, they found it full of floating ice.   They
worked all day and made a raft of logs.   As they were
pushing their way across with poles, Washington's pole
was struck by a big piece of ice which he says jerked
him out into water ten feet deep.   At length the two
men managed to get to a little island, but as there was
no wood on it, they could not make a fire.   The weather
was bitterly cold, and Washington, who was soaked to
the skin, had to take his choice between walking about
all night, or trying to sleep on the frozen ground in his
wet clothes.

130. Major Washington becomes Colonel Washington ; Fort
Necessity ; Braddock's defeat. — When Major Washington
got back to Virginia, the governor made him a colonel.[2]
With a hundred and fifty men, Colonel Washington was
ordered to set out for the west.   He was to "make
prisoners, kill or destroy," all Frenchmen who should
try to get possession of land on the Ohio River.   He
built a small log fort, which he named Fort Necessity.[3]
Here the French attacked him.   They had five men to
his one.   Colonel Washington fought like a man who
liked to hear the bullets whistle past his ears, — as he
said he did, — but in the end he had to give up the
fort.

[1] Compass: see page 30.   [2] Colonel: see note on page 70.
[3] Fort Necessity : see map, page 106.

Then General Braddock, a noted English soldier, was sent over to Virginia, by the king, to drive the French out of the country. He started with a fine army, and Washington went with him.[1] He told General Braddock that the French and the Indians would hide in the

BRADDOCK'S DEFEAT

woods and fire at his men from behind trees. But Braddock paid no attention to the warning. On his way through the forest, the brave English general was suddenly struck down by the enemy; half of his army were killed or wounded, and the rest put to flight.

[1] See map of Braddock's march, page 106.

Washington had two horses shot under him, and four bullets went through his coat. It was a narrow escape for the young man. One of those who fought in the battle said, " I expected every moment to see him fall," — but he was to live for greater work.

131. End of the war with the French; what the king of England wanted to do; how the people here felt toward him. — The war with the French lasted a number of years. It ended by the English getting possession of the whole of America from the Atlantic Ocean to the Mississippi River. All this part of America was ruled by George the Third, king of England. The king now determined to send over more soldiers, and to keep them here to prevent the French in Canada from trying to get back the country they had lost. He wanted the people here in the thirteen colonies[1] to pay the cost of keeping these soldiers. But this the people were not willing to do, because they felt that they were able to protect themselves without help of any kind. Then the king said, If the Americans will not give the money, I will take it from them by force, — for pay it they must and shall. This was more than the king would have dared say about England; for there, if he wanted money to spend on his army, he had to ask the people for it, and they could give it or not, as they thought best. The Americans said, We have the same rights as our brothers in England, and the king cannot force us to give a single copper against our will. If he tries to take it from us, we will fight. Some of the greatest men in England agreed with us, and said that they would fight, too, if they were in our place.

[1] Thirteen colonies: see note on page 84.

132. The king determines to have the money; the tea-ships, and the " Boston tea-party." — But George the Third thought that the Americans did not mean what they said. He tried to make them pay the money, but they would not. From Maine to Georgia all the people were of one mind. Then the king tried a different way. Quantities of tea

THE BOSTON "TEA-PARTY"

were sent over to New York, Boston, Philadelphia, Charleston, and Annapolis. If the tea should be landed and sold, then every man who bought a pound of it would have to pay six cents more than the regular price. That six cents was a tax, and it went into the king's pocket. The people said, We won't pay that six cents. When the tea reached New York the citizens sent it back again to

England. They did the same thing at Philadelphia. At Charleston the tea was landed, but it was stored in damp cellars. People would not buy any of it any more than they would buy so much poison, so it all rotted and spoiled. At Annapolis the citizens forced the owner of the tea-ship *Peggy Stewart* to burn his vessel, tea and all. At Boston they had a grand "tea-party." A number of men dressed themselves up like Indians, went on board the tea-ships at night, broke open the chests, and emptied the tea into the harbor.

133. The king closes the port of Boston; Congress meets at Philadelphia; the names American and British; what General Gage tried to do. — This act of the Bostonians made the king terribly angry, and orders were given to close the port of Boston so that no ships, except the king's war-ships, should come in or go out. Nearly all trade stopped in the city. Many of the inhabitants began to suffer for want of food, but throughout the colonies the people tried their best to help them. The New England towns sent droves of sheep and cattle, New York sent wheat, South Carolina gave two hundred barrels of rice; the other colonies gave liberally in money and provisions. Even in England much sympathy was felt for the distressed people of Boston, and in London a large sum of money was raised to help those whom the king was determined to starve into submission.[1]

The colonies now sent some of their best men to Philadelphia to consider what should be done. As this meeting was made up of those who had come from all

---

[1] When the news reached Virginia that the king of England had determined to close the port of Boston, many people began to talk of taking up arms to defend the rights of the colonists. Washington said little; but he went to church, and fasted all day.

PAUL REVERE'S RIDE

parts of the country, it took the name of the General or Continental Congress.[1]

About this time, too, a great change took place; for the people throughout the country began to call themselves Americans, and to speak of the English troops that the king sent over here, as British soldiers.

In Boston, General Gage had command of these soldiers. He knew that the Americans were getting ready to fight, and that they had stored up powder and ball at Concord,[2] about twenty miles from Boston. One night he secretly sent out a lot of soldiers to march to Concord and destroy what they found there.

134. Paul Revere[3]; the fight at Lexington and Concord; Bunker Hill. — But Paul Revere, a Boston man, was on the watch; and as soon as he found out which way the British were going, he set off at a gallop for Lexington, on the road to Concord. All the way out, he roused people from their sleep, with the cry, "The British are coming!"

When the king's soldiers reached Lexington, they found the Americans, under Captain Parker, ready for them. Captain Parker said to his men, "Don't fire unless you are fired on; but if they want a war, *let it begin here.*" The fighting did begin there, April 19, 1775; and when the British left the town on their way to Concord, seven Americans lay dead on the grass in

---

[1] Congress: this word means a meeting or assembly of persons. The General or Continental Congress was an assembly of certain persons sent usually by all of the thirteen American colonies to meet at Philadelphia or Baltimore, to decide what should be done by the whole country. The first Congress met in 1774, or shortly before the Revolution began, and after that from time to time until near the close of the Revolution.

[2] Concord (Con'kurd).   [3] Revere (Re-veer').

front of the village church.   At Concord, that same day, there was still harder fighting ; and on the way back to Boston, a large number of the British were killed.

Not quite two months later, June 17, 1775, a battle was fought on Bunker Hill in Charlestown, just outside of Boston.   General Gage thought the Yankees wouldn't

WASHINGTON AT MOUNT VERNON

fight ; but they did fight, in a way that General Gage never forgot ; and though they had at last to retreat because their powder gave out, yet the British lost more than a thousand men.   The contest at Bunker Hill was the first great battle of the Revolution ; that is, of that war which overturned the British power in America, and made us a free people.   Many Englishmen thought the king was wrong.   They would not fight against us,

THE NORTHERN STATES IN THE REVOLUTION

and he was obliged to hire a large number of German soldiers to send to America. These Germans had to fight us, whether they wanted to or not, for their king forced them to come.

135. Colonel Washington at Mount Vernon; Congress makes him General Washington, and sends him to take command of the American army. — At the time the battle of Bunker Hill

WASHINGTON TAKING COMMAND OF THE AMERICAN ARMY AT CAMBRIDGE

was fought, Colonel George Washington was living very quietly at Mount Vernon. His brother Lawrence had died, and Mount Vernon was now his home. Washington was very well off; he had a fine estate and plenty of slaves to do the work on it; but when he died, many years later, he took good care to leave orders that all of his slaves should be set free as soon as it could be done.

Congress now made Colonel Washington general-in-chief of all the forces and sent him to Cambridge, a town just outside of Boston, to take command of the American army. It was called the Continental Army because it was raised, not to fight for the people of Massachusetts, but for all the Americans on the continent, north and south. Washington took command of the army under a great elm on what was then the Common.[1] Six months later he raised the first American flag over the camp at Cambridge.[2]

136. American sharpshooters [3]; Washington's need of cannon and powder; the attack on Canada; the British driven out of Boston. — Men now came from all parts of the country to join the Continental Army. Many of them were sharpshooters. In one case an officer set up a board with the figure of a man's nose chalked on it, for a mark. A hundred men fired at it at long distance, and sixty hit the nose. The newspapers gave them great praise for their skill and said, "Now, General Gage, look out for *your* nose."

Washington wanted to drive General Gage and the British soldiers out of Boston; but for months he could not get either cannon or powder. Benjamin Franklin

---

[1] A stone slab marks what is generally believed to be the "Washington Elm." The elm stands not far from the Memorial Hall of Harvard University. On the slab is this inscription: "Under this tree Washington first took command of the American Army, July 3, 1775."

[2] See a picture of this and the other flags of the Revolution on page 126.

[3] Sharpshooters: men who can fire and hit a small mark with a bullet at a long distance.

said that we should have to fight as the Indians used to, with bows and arrows.

While Washington was waiting, a number of Americans marched against the British in Canada; but the cold weather came on, and they nearly starved to death: our men would sometimes take off their moccasins[1] and

" Now, General Gage, look out for *your* Nose "

gnaw them, while they danced in the snow to keep their bare feet from freezing.

At last Washington got both cannon and powder. He dragged the cannon up to the top of some high land overlooking Boston harbor.[2] He then sent word to General Howe (for Gage had gone), that if he did not leave Boston he would knock his ships to pieces. The British saw that they could not help themselves,

[1] Moccasins (mok′ka-sins): Indian shoes made of deerskin.
[2] Dorchester Heights, in what is now South Boston.

so they made haste to get on board their vessels and sail away. They never came back to Boston again, but went to New York.

137. The Declaration of Independence; "Down with the king!" Washington is driven from New York and across the Delaware River. —

"DOWN WITH THE KING!"

Washington got to New York first. While he was there, Congress,[1] on the 4th of July, 1776, declared the United States *independent*, — that is, entirely free from the rule of the king of England. In New York there was a gilded lead statue of King George the Third on horseback. When the news of what Congress had done reached that city, the cry rose: "Down with the king!" That night some of our men pulled down the statue, melted it up, and cast it into bullets.

The next month there was a battle on Long Island,[2] just across from New York City; the British gained the

1 Congress; see note on page 115.
2 See map, page 116.

victory. Washington had to leave New York, and Lord Cornwallis,[1] one of the British generals, chased him and his little army clear across the state of New Jersey. It looked at one time as though our men would all be taken prisoners; but Washington managed to seize a lot of small boats on the Delaware River[2] and get across into Pennsylvania: as the British had no boats, they could not follow.

138. Washington's victory at Trenton, New Jersey. — Lord Cornwallis left fifteen hundred German soldiers[3] at Trenton on the Delaware. He intended, as soon as the river froze over, to cross on the ice and attack Washington's army. But Washington did not wait for him. On Christmas night (1776) he took a large number of boats, filled them with soldiers, and secretly crossed over to New Jersey.[4] The weather was intensely cold, the river was full of floating ice, and a furious snowstorm set in. Many of our men were ragged and had only old, broken shoes. They suffered terribly, and two of them were frozen to death.

The Germans at Trenton had been having a jolly Christmas, and had gone to bed, suspecting no danger. Suddenly Washington, with his men, rushed into the little town and captured a thousand German soldiers. It was all done so quickly that the men found themselves prisoners almost before they knew what had happened. The rest of the Germans escaped to tell Lord Cornwallis how the Americans had beaten them. When Washington was driven out of New York, many Americans thought he would be captured. Now they

---

[1] Cornwallis (Corn-wall'is).
[2] See map, page 116.

[3] German soldiers; see page 117.
[4] See map, page 116.

were filled with joy. The battle of Trenton was the first battle won by the Continental Army.

139. Our victory at Princeton, New Jersey ; the British take Philadelphia ; winter at Valley Forge ; Burgoyne beaten ; the king of France agrees to help us. — Washington took his thousand prisoners over into Pennsylvania. A few days later he again crossed the Delaware into New Jersey. While Cornwallis was fast asleep in his tent, Washington slipped around him, got to Princeton,[1] and there beat a part of the British army. Cornwallis woke up and heard Washington's cannon. "That's thunder," he said. He was right ; it was the thunder of another American victory.

But before the next winter set in, the British had taken the city of Philadelphia, then the capital of the United States. Washington's army was freezing and starving on the hillsides of Valley Forge,[2] about twenty miles northwest of Philadelphia.

But good news was coming. The Americans had won a great victory at Saratoga, New York,[3] over the British general, Burgoyne.[4] Dr. Franklin was then in Paris. When he heard that Burgoyne was beaten, he hurried off to the palace of the French king to tell him about it. The king of France hated the British, and he agreed to send money, ships, and soldiers to help us. When our men, at Valley Forge, heard the news, they leaped and hurrahed for joy. Not long after that the British left Philadelphia, and we entered it in triumph.

140. The war at the south ; Jasper ; Cowpens ; Greene and Cornwallis. — While these things were happening at the

---

[1] Princeton ; see map, page 116.
[2] Valley Forge ; see map, page 116.
[3] Saratoga (Sar-a-toe′gah) ; see map, page 116.
[4] Burgoyne (Bur-goin′).

north, the British sent a fleet of vessels to take Charleston, South Carolina.   They hammered away with their
big guns at a little log fort under command of Colonel
Moultrie.[1]   In the battle, a cannon-ball struck the flag-
pole on the fort, and cut it in two.   The South Carolina
flag fell to the ground outside the fort.   Sergeant[2]
William Jasper leaped down, and, while the British shot

VALLEY FORGE

were striking all around him, seized the flag, climbed
back, fastened it to a short staff, and raised it to its
place, to show that the Americans would never give up
the fort.   The British, after fighting all day, saw that they
could do nothing against palmetto logs[3] when defended

[1] Moultrie (Mole´tree).

[2] Sergeant (sar´jent): a military officer of low rank.

[3] Palmetto (pal-met´toe) logs: the wood of the palmetto tree is very soft and
spongy; the cannon-balls, when they struck, would bury themselves in the logs,
but would neither break them to pieces nor go through them.

by such men as Moultrie and Jasper; so they sailed away with such of their ships as had not been destroyed.

Several years later, Charleston was taken. Lord Corn-

SERGEANT JASPER AND THE FLAG

wallis then took command of the British army in South Carolina. General Greene, of Rhode Island, had command of the Americans. He sent Daniel Morgan with his sharpshooters to meet part of the British army at Cowpens[1]; they did meet them, and sent them flying. Then Cornwallis determined to whip General Greene or drive him out of the state. But General Greene worried Cornwallis so that at last he was glad enough to get into Virginia. He had found North and South Carolina like

[1] Cowpens (Cow′pens); see map on opposite page.

THE SOUTHERN STATES IN THE REVOLUTION

two hornets' nests, and the further he got away from those hornets, the better he was pleased.

141. Cornwallis and Benedict Arnold; Lafayette; Cornwallis shuts himself up in Yorktown. — When Lord Cornwallis got into Virginia, he found Benedict Arnold waiting to help him. Arnold had been a general in the American army; Washington gave him the command of the fort at West Point, on the Hudson River,[1] and trusted him as though he was his brother. Arnold deceived him, and secretly offered to give up the fort to the British. We call a man who is false to his friends and to his country a traitor; it is the most shameful name we can fasten on him. Arnold was a traitor; and if we could have caught him, we should have hanged him; but he was cunning enough to run away and escape to the British. Now he was burning houses and towns in Virginia, and doing all that he could — as a traitor always will — to destroy those who had once been his best friends. He wanted to stay in Virginia and assist Cornwallis; but that general was a brave and honorable man: he despised Arnold, and did not want to have anything to do with him.

LAFAYETTE

A young nobleman named Lafayette[2] had come over from France, on purpose to help us against the British. Cornwallis laughed at him and called him a "boy"; but he found that General

---

[1] West Point; see map. page 116. [2] Lafayette (Lah-fay-et′).

Lafayette was a "boy" who knew how to fight. The British commander moved toward the seacoast; Lafayette followed him; at length Cornwallis shut himself up with his army in Yorktown.[1]

142. Washington marches against Yorktown, and takes it and the army of Cornwallis. — Washington, with his army, was then near New York City, watching the British

THE FLAGS OF THE REVOLUTION[2]

[1] Yorktown; see map, page 124.

[2] The flag with the large crosses on it, on the left, is the English flag at the time of the American Revolution. The flag on the right is that which Washington raised at Cambridge, Massachusetts, January 1, 1776. He simply took the English flag, and added thirteen stripes to represent the union of the thirteen English colonies. The flag in the centre, with its thirteen stars and thirteen stripes representing the thirteen states, is the first American *national* flag. It was adopted by Congress June 14, 1777, not quite a year after we had declared ourselves independent of Great Britain. Beneath this flag is Washington's coat of arms with a Latin motto, meaning "The event justifies the

there. The French king had done as he agreed, and had sent over war-ships and soldiers to help us; but so far they had never been able to do much. Now was the chance. Before the British knew what Washington was about, he had sent the French war-ships down to Yorktown to prevent Cornwallis from getting away by sea. Then, with his own army and a large number of French soldiers besides, Washington quickly marched south to attack Yorktown by land.

When he got there he placed his cannon round the town, and began battering it to pieces. For more than a week he kept firing night and day. One house had over a thousand balls go through it. Its walls looked like a sieve. At last, Cornwallis could not hold out any longer, and on October 19, 1781, his army came out and gave themselves up as prisoners.

The Americans formed a line more than a mile long on one side of the road, and the French stood facing them on the other side. The French had on gay clothes, and looked very handsome; the clothes of Washington's men were patched and faded, but their eyes shone with a wonderful light — the light of victory. The British marched out slowly, between the two lines: somehow they found it pleasanter to look

deed." It is possible that the stars and stripes on our national flag came from the stars and stripes (or bars) on this ancient coat of arms, which may be seen on the tombstone of one of the Washington family, buried in 1583, in the parish church at Sulgrave, Northamptonshire, England.

In 1794, in consequence of the admission of Vermont and Kentucky to the Union, Congress passed an act increasing the number of stars and stripes on the American flag from thirteen to fifteen. Later, it was found that if a *stripe* as well as a star should be added for each new state the flag would in time become too broad and unwieldy. For this reason Congress passed a law in 1818 reducing the number of stripes to thirteen, but ordering that on the admission of each new state a star should be added. That law still remains in force.

at the bright uniforms of the French than to look at the eyes of the Americans.

143. How the news of the taking of Yorktown was carried to Philadelphia ; Lord Fairfax.

"CORNWALLIS IS TAKEN!"

People at a distance noticed that the cannon had suddenly stopped firing. They looked at each other, and asked, "What does it mean?" All at once a man appears on horseback. He is riding with all his might toward Philadelphia, where Congress is. As he dashes past, he rises in his stirrups, swings his cap, and shouts with all his might, "Cornwallis is taken! Cornwallis is taken!" Then the people made the hills ring with "Hurrah! Hurrah!" Later on, Philadelphia night watchmen shouted "Cornwallis is taken!"

Poor Lord Fairfax,[1] Washington's old friend, had always stood by the king. He was now over ninety. When he heard the cry, "Cornwallis is taken!" it was too much

[1] See page 106.

for the old man. He said to his negro servant, "Come, Joe; carry me to bed, for I'm sure it's high time for me to die."

144. Tearing down the British flag at New York ; Washington goes back to Mount Vernon ; he is elected President ; his death ; Lafayette visits his tomb.

— The Revolutionary War had lasted seven years, — terrible years they were, years of sorrow, suffering, and death, — but now the end had come, and America was free. When the British left New York City, they nailed the British flag to a high pole on the wharf; but a Yankee sailor soon climbed the pole, tore down the flag of England, and hoisted the stars and stripes in its place. That was more than a hundred years ago. Now the English and the Americans have become good friends, and the

HOISTING THE STARS AND STRIPES AT NEW YORK

English people see clearly that the Revolution ended in the way that was best for both of us.

When it was certain that there would be no **more** fighting, Washington went back to Mount Vernon. **He** hoped to spend the rest of his life there. But the country needed him, and a few years later it chose him the first President of the United States.

Washington was made President in New York City, which was the capital of the United States at that time. A French gentleman, who was there, tells us how Washington, standing in the presence of thousands of people, placed his hand on the Bible, and solemnly swore that

with the help of God he would protect and defend the United States of America.

Washington was elected President twice. When he died, .many of the people in England and France joined America in mourning for him; for all men honored his memory.

LAFAYETTE AT WASHINGTON'S TOMB

Lafayette,[1] the brave young Frenchman who fought for us in the Revolution, came over to visit us many years afterward. He went to Mount Vernon, where Washington was buried. There he went down into the vault,[2] and, kneeling by the side of the coffin, covered his face with his hands, and shed tears of gratitude to think that he had known such a man as Washington, and that Washington had been his friend.

145. Summary. — George Washington, the son of a Virginia planter, became the leader of the armies of the

[1] Lafayette, see page 125.

[2] This was the old family tomb or vault at Mount Vernon. It is quite near the house. Later, Washington's remains were carried to a new tomb which stands farther away from the house.

United States in the war of the Revolution. At the close of the war, after he had made America free, he was elected our first President. His name stands to-day among those of the greatest men in the history of the world.

When and where was George Washington born? What did he learn at school? What did he write in one of his writing-books? Tell about his sports and games at school. What is said of "Captain George"? Tell the story about the colt. What did George's mother say? Tell about George's visit to his brother and to the Fairfaxes. What is said of Lord Fairfax? What did he hire Washington to do? Tell about his surveying and his life in the woods. Tell about the Indian war-dance. What did the governor of Virginia do when Washington returned? What is said of Washington at the age of twenty-one? Tell about his journey to the French forts and his return. What is said about the Indian guide? What is said about the raft? What did the governor of Virginia do when Washington returned? What did the governor order him to do? What is said about Fort Necessity? Tell about General Braddock, and about what happened to Washington. What is said about the end of the war? What did King George the Third determine to do? What did the king want the Americans to do? How did they feel? What did the king say? What did the Americans say to that? What did some of the greatest men in England say? What did the king then try to do? Tell about the tea-ships. What happened in Boston? What was done to Boston? What help did the people of Boston get? What did the colonies now do? What did the people now begin to call themselves? What did they call the English troops?

Who commanded the British soldiers in Boston? What did he do? What about Paul Revere? What did Captain Parker, of Lexington, say to his men? What happened at Lexington and at Concord? Tell about the battle of Bunker Hill. What did many Englishmen refuse to do? Where was Colonel Washington living? What did Congress do? Where did Washington take command of the army? Tell about the sharpshooters. Tell about the march to Canada. How did Washington take Boston? Where did the British go? Where did Washington go? What did Congress do on July 4, 1776? What happened in New York? What is said about the battle of Long Island? What did Cornwallis do? Tell about the victory at Trenton. What happened at Princeton? What city did the British take? Where was Washington's army? What happened at Saratoga? What did the king of France do? What happened at the south? Tell about Sergeant Jasper. What is said about General Greene? What did Cornwallis do? Where did he go? What is said about Benedict Arnold? What is said about Lafayette? Where did Cornwallis shut himself up with his army? What did Washington do? Tell about the surrender of Cornwallis. How was the news carried to Philadelphia? What is said of Lord Fairfax? How long had the war lasted? What was done at New York? What is said of General Washington after the war? Tell how he was made President. What happened when he died? What is said of Lafayette?

XV. DANIEL BOONE

(1734–1820)

146. Daniel Boone; what the hunters of the west did; Boone's life in North Carolina. — Before Washington began to fight the battles of the Revolution in the east, Daniel

BOONE POUNDING CORN

Boone and other famous hunters were fighting bears and Indians in what was then called the west.[1] By that war in the woods, these brave and hardy men helped us to get possession of that part of the country.

Daniel Boone was born in Pennsylvania.[2] His father moved to North Carolina,[3] and Daniel helped him cut down the trees round their log cabin in the forest. He

[1] That is, the country west of the Alleghany Mountains and between those mountains and the Mississippi River.

[2] He was born in either Bucks or Berks County, Pennsylvania; authorities do not agree on this point.

[3] He settled near Wilkesboro, on the banks of the Yadkin River; see map on page 136.

ploughed the land, which was thick with stumps, hoed the corn that grew up among those stumps, and then, — as there was no mill near, — he pounded it into meal for johnny-cake. He learned how to handle a gun quite as soon as he did a hoe. The unfortunate deer or coon that saw young Boone coming toward him, if he had only been bright enough, might have known that he had seen his best days, and that he would soon have the whole Boone family sitting round him at the dinner-table.

147. Boone's wanderings in the western forests; his bear tree. — When Daniel had grown to manhood, he wandered off with his gun on his shoulder, and, crossing the mountains, entered what is now the state of Tennessee. That whole country was then

BOONE'S BEAR TREE

a wilderness, full of savage beasts and still more savage Indians; and Boone had many a sharp fight with both.

More than a hundred and forty years ago, he cut these words on a beech tree still standing in Eastern Tennessee,[1] — "D. Boon killed a bar on this tree in

[1] The tree is said to be still standing on the banks of Boone's Creek, near Jonesboro, Washington County, Tennessee.

the year 1760." You will see if you examine the tree, on which the words can still be read, that Boone could not spell very well; but he could do what the bear minded a good deal more, — he could shoot to kill.

148. Boone goes hunting in Kentucky; what kind of game he found there; the Indians; the "Dark and Bloody Ground." — Nine years after he cut his name on that tree, Boone, with a few companions, went to a new part of the country. The Indians called it Kentucky. There he saw buffalo, deer, bears, and wolves enough to satisfy the best hunter in America.

This region was a kind of No Man's Land, because, though many tribes of Indians roamed over it, none of them pretended to own it. These bands of Indians were always fighting and trying to drive each other out, so Kentucky was often called the "Dark and Bloody Ground." But, much as the savages hated each other, they hated the white men, or the "pale-faces," as they called them, still more.

149. Indian tricks; the owls. — The hunters were on the lookout for these Indians, but the savages practised all kinds of tricks to get the hunters near enough to shoot them. Sometimes Boone would hear the gobble of a wild turkey. He would listen a moment, then he would say, That is not a wild turkey, but an Indian, imitating that bird; but he won't fool me and get me to come near enough to put a bullet through my head.

One evening an old hunter, on his way to his cabin, heard what seemed to be two young owls calling to each other. But his quick ear noticed that there was something not quite natural in their calls, and, what was stranger still, that the owls seemed to be on the ground instead of being perched on trees, as all well-behaved owls would be. He crept cautiously along through the bushes till he saw something ahead which looked like a stump. He did n't altogether like the looks of the stump. He aimed his rifle at it, and fired. The stump, or what seemed to be one, fell over backward with a groan. He had killed an Indian, who had been waiting to kill him.

150. Boone makes the "Wilderness Road," and builds the fort at Boonesboro'. — In 1775 Boone, with a party of thirty men, chopped a path through the forest from the mountains of Eastern Tennessee to the Kentucky River,[1] a distance of about two hundred

BOONE IN THE WOODS

miles. This was the first path in that part of the country leading to the great west. It was called the "Wilderness Road." Over that road, which thousands of emigrants travelled afterward, Boone took his family,

[1] See map on page 136.

with other settlers, to the Kentucky River. There they built a fort called Boonesboro'. That fort was a great protection to all the first settlers in Kentucky. In fact, it is hard to see how the state could have grown up

Map showing Boone's "Wilderness Road."

without it. So, in one way, we can say with truth that Daniel Boone, the hunter, fighter, and road-maker, was a state-builder besides.

151. Boone's daughter is stolen by the Indians; how he found her. — One day Boone's young daughter was out, with two other girls, in a canoe on the river. Suddenly some Indians pounced on them and carried them off.

One of the girls, as she went along, broke off twigs from the bushes, so that her friends might be able to follow her track through the woods. An Indian caught her doing it, and told her that he would kill her if she did not instantly stop. Then she slyly tore off small bits of her dress, and dropped a piece from time to time.

Boone and his men followed the Indians like bloodhounds. They picked up the bits of dress, and so easily found which way the savages had gone. They came up with the Indians just as they were sitting down round a fire to eat their supper. Creeping toward them behind the trees as softly as a cat creeps up behind a mouse, Boone and his men aimed their rifles and fired. Two of the Indians fell dead, the rest ran for their lives, and the girls were carried back in safety to the fort.

152. Boone is captured by Indians; they adopt him as a son. — Later, Boone himself was caught and carried off by the Indians. They respected his courage so much that

BOONE TRAILING INDIANS

they would not kill him, but decided to adopt him; that is, take him into the tribe as one of their own people, or make an Indian of him.

They pulled out all his hair except one long lock, called the "scalp-lock," which they left to grow in Indian fashion. The squaws [1] and girls braided bright feathers in this lock, so that Boone looked quite gay. Then the Indians took him down to a river. There they stripped him, and scrubbed him with all their

[1] Squaws: Indian women.

might, to get his white blood out, as they said. Next, they painted his face in stripes with red and yellow clay, so that he looked, as they thought, handsomer than he had ever looked before. When all had been done, and they were satisfied with the appearance of their new Indian, they sat down to a great feast, and made merry.

153. Boone escapes, but the Indians find him again; what a handful of tobacco dust did. — After a time Boone managed to escape; but the Indians were so fond of him that they could not rest till they found him again. One day he was at work in a kind of shed, drying some tobacco leaves. He heard a slight noise, and, turning round, saw four Indians with their guns pointed at him. " Now, Boone," said they, "we got you. You no get away this time." " How are you? " said Boone pleasantly; " glad to see you; just wait a minute till I get you some of my tobacco." He gathered two large handfuls of the leaves; they were as dry as powder and crumbled to dust in his hands. Coming forward, as if to give the welcome present to the Indians, he suddenly sprang on them and filled their eyes, mouths, and noses with the stinging tobacco dust. The savages were half choked and nearly blinded. While they were dancing about, coughing, sneezing, and rubbing their eyes, Boone slipped out of the shed and got to a place of safety. The Indians were as mad as they could be, yet they could hardly help laughing at Boone's trick; for cunning as the red men were, he was more cunning still.

154. Boone's old age; he moves to Missouri; he begs for a piece of land; his grave. — Boone lived to be a very old man. He had owned a good deal of land in the west, but he had lost possession of it. When Kentucky began to fill up with people and the game was killed off, Boone moved across the Mississippi into Missouri. He said that he went because he wanted " more elbow room " and a chance to hunt buffalo again.

He now begged the state of Kentucky to give him a small piece of land, where, as he said, he could " lay his bones." The people of that state generously helped him to get nearly a thousand acres; but he appears to have soon lost possession of it. If he actually did lose it, then this brave old hunter, who had opened up the way for such a multitude of emigrants to get farms at the west, died without owning a piece of ground big enough for a grave. He is buried in Frankfort, Kentucky, within sight of the river on which he built his fort at Boonesboro'.

155. Summary. — Daniel Boone, a famous hunter from North Carolina, opened up a road through the forest, from the mountains of Eastern Tennessee to the Kentucky River. It was called the "Wilderness Road," and over it thousands of emigrants went into Kentucky to settle. Boone, with others, built the fort at Boonesboro', Kentucky, and went there to live. That fort protected the settlers against the Indians, and so helped that part of the country to grow until it became the state of Kentucky.

Tell about Daniel Boone. How did he help his father? Where did he go when he became a man? What did he cut on a beech tree? Where did he go after that? What is said of the Indians in Kentucky? Tell about Indian tricks. Tell about the two owls. Tell about the Wilderness Road. What is said of the fort at Boonesboro'? Tell how Boone's daughter and the other girls were stolen by the Indians. What happened next? Tell how Boone was captured by the Indians and how they adopted him. Tell the story of the tobacco dust. What did Boone do when he became old? What did Kentucky get for him? Where is he buried?

XVI. GENERAL JAMES ROBERTSON AND GOVERNOR JOHN SEVIER[1]

(1742-1814 ; 1745-1815)

156. Who James Robertson was ; Governor Tryon ; the battle of Alamance.[2] — When Daniel Boone first went to Kentucky (1769), he had a friend named James Robertson, in North Carolina,[3] who was, like himself, a mighty hunter. The British governor of North Carolina at that time was William Tryon.[4] He lived in a palace built with money which he had forced the people to give him. They hated him so for his greed and cruelty that they nicknamed him the "Great Wolf of North Carolina."

At last many of the settlers vowed that they would not give the governor another penny. When he sent tax-collectors to get money, they drove them back, and they flogged one of the governor's friends with a rawhide till he had to run for his life.

The governor then collected some soldiers and marched against the people in the west. A battle was fought near the Alamance River. The governor had the most men, and had cannon besides ; so he gained the day. He took seven of the people prisoners and hanged them. They all died bravely, as men do who die for liberty.

---

[1] Sevier (Se-veer') : he was born in Rockingham County, Virginia.

[2] Alamance River (Al' a-mance) ; see map on page 136.

[3] Robertson was born in Brunswick County, Virginia ; he emigrated to North Carolina and settled in the neighborhood of Raleigh. See map on page 136.

[4] Tryon (Try'on).

157. James Robertson leaves North Carolina and goes west. — After the battle of Alamance James Robertson and his family made up their minds that they would not live any longer where Governor Tryon ruled. They resolved to go across the mountains into the western wilderness. Sixteen other families joined Robertson's and went with them. It was a long, hard journey; for they had to climb rocks and find their way through deep, tangled woods. The men went ahead with their axes and their guns; then the older children followed, driving the cows; last of all came the women with the little children, with beds, pots, and kettles packed on the backs of horses.

ROBERTSON AND HIS PARTY CROSSING THE MOUNTAINS ON THEIR WAY TO TENNESSEE

158. The emigrants settle on the Watauga River[1] in Tennessee. — When the little party had crossed the mountains into what is now the state of Tennessee, they found a delightful valley. Through this valley there ran a stream of clear, sparkling water called the Watauga

[1] Watauga River (Wa-taw′ga); see map on page 136.

River; the air of the valley was sweet with the smell of wild crab-apples.

On the banks of that stream the emigrants built their new homes. Their houses were simply rough log huts; but they were clean and comfortable. When the settlers put up these cabins, they chopped down every tree near them which was big enough for an Indian to hide behind. They knew that they might have to fight the savages; but they had rather do that than be robbed by tax-collectors. In the wilderness, Governor Tryon could not reach them — they were free; free as the deer and the squirrels were: that one thought made them contented and happy.

159. John Sevier goes to settle at Watauga; what he and Robertson did. — The year after this little settlement was made, John Sevier went from Virginia to Watauga, as it was called. He and Robertson soon became fast friends, — for one brave man can always see something to respect and like in another brave man. Robertson and Sevier hunted together and worked together.

After a while, they called a meeting of the settlers and agreed on some excellent laws, so that everything in the log village might be done decently and in order; for, although these people lived in the woods, they had no notion of living like savages or wild beasts. In course of time President Washington made James Robertson General Robertson, in honor of what he had done for his country.

Out of this settlement on the Watauga River grew the state of Tennessee. Many years ago a small monument was erected to Sevier in the cemetery at Nashville, a city founded by his friend Robertson. Recently a noble monument to Sevier's memory has been erected in Knoxville, formerly the capital of the state of which he became the first Governor.

160. Summary. — James Robertson, of North Carolina, and John Sevier, of Virginia, emigrated across the mountains to the western wilderness. They settled on the Watauga River, and that settlement, with others made later, grew into the state of Tennessee, of which John Sevier became the first governor.

What friend did Boone have in North Carolina? Tell about Governor Tryon. What happened on the Alamance River? Where did Robertson and others go? Where did they settle? Why did they like to be there? Tell about John Sevier. What did he and Robertson do? What did Washington do for Robertson? What state grew out of the Watauga settlement? What did Sevier become? Where are his two monuments?

XVII. GENERAL GEORGE ROGERS CLARK

(1752–1818)

161. The British in the west; their forts; hiring Indians to fight the settlers. — While Washington was fighting the battles of the Revolution in the east, the British in the west were not sitting still. They had a number of forts in the Wilderness,[1] as the country west of the Alleghany Mountains was then called. One of these forts was at Detroit,[2] in what is now Michigan; another was at Vincennes,[3] in what is now Indiana; a third fort was at Kaskaskia,[4] in what is now Illinois.

Colonel Hamilton, the British commander at Detroit, was determined to drive the American settlers out of the

[1] See map on page 168.
[2] Detroit (De-troit′); for these forts see map on page 144.
[3] Vincennes (Vin-senz′).   [4] Kaskaskia ′Kas-kas′ki-a).

west. In the beginning of the Revolution the Americans resolved to hire the Indians to fight for them; but the British found that they could hire them better than we could, and so they got their help. The savages did their work in a terribly cruel way. Generally they did not come out and do battle openly; but they crept up secretly, by night, and attacked the farmers' homes. They killed and scalped the settlers in the west, burned

their log cabins, and carried off the women and children prisoners. The greater part of the people in England hated this sort of war. They begged the king not to hire the Indians to do these horrible deeds of murder and de-

Map showing the forts at Detroit, Kaskaskia, and Vincennes, with the line of Clark's march.

struction. George the Third was not a bad-hearted man; but he was very set in his way, and he had fully made up his mind to conquer the "American rebels," as he called them, even if he had to get the savages to help him do it.

162. George Rogers Clark gets help from Virginia and starts to attack Fort Kaskaskia. — Daniel Boone had a friend in Virginia named George Rogers Clark,[1] who believed that he could take the British forts in the west and drive out the British from all that part of the country. Virginia then owned most of the Wilderness. For

[1] George Rogers Clark was born near Monticello, Virginia. See map, page 124.

this reason Clark went to Patrick Henry, governor of Virginia, and asked for help. The governor liked the plan, and let Clark have money to hire men to go with him and try to take Fort Kaskaskia to begin with.

Clark started in the spring of 1778 with about a hundred and fifty men. They built boats on the banks of the Allegheny[1] River just above Pittsburg,[2] and floated down the Ohio River, a distance of over nine hundred miles. Then they landed in what is now Illinois, and set out for Fort Kaskaskia.[3]

163. The march to Fort Kaskaskia ; how a dance ended. — It was a hundred miles to the fort, and half of the way the men had to find their way through thick woods, full of underbrush, briers, and vines. The British, thinking the fort perfectly safe from attack, had left it in the care of a French officer. Clark and his band reached Kaskaskia at night. They found no one to stop them. The soldiers in the fort were having a dance, and the Americans could hear the merry music of a violin and the laughing voices of girls.

Clark left his men just outside the fort, and, finding a door open, he walked in. He reached the room where the fun was going on, and, stopping there, he stood leaning against the doorpost, looking on. The room was lighted with torches; the light of one of the torches happened to fall full on Clark's face; an Indian sitting on the floor caught sight of him; he sprang to his feet and gave a terrific war-whoop. The dancers stopped

[1] Allegheny (Al-le-gĕn′y): the Allegheny and the Monongahela (Mon-on-ga-he′la) rivers unite at Pittsburg and form the Ohio River.
[2] Pittsburg; see map, page 124.   [3] Fort Kaskaskia; see map on page 144.

as though they had been shot; the women screamed; the men ran to the door to get their guns. Clark did not move, but said quietly, "Go on; only remember you are dancing now under Virginia, and not under Great Britain." The next moment the Americans rushed in, and Clark and his "Long Knives," as the Indians called his men, had full possession of the fort.

CLARK LOOKING ON AT THE DANCE

164. How Fort Vincennes was taken; how the British got it back again; what Francis Vigo[1] did. — Clark wanted next to march against Fort Vincennes, but he had not men enough. There was a French Catholic priest[2] at Kaskaskia, and Clark's kindness to him had made him our friend. He said, I will go to Vincennes for you, and I will tell the French, who hold the fort for the British, that the Americans are their real friends, and that, in this war, they are in the right. He went; the French listened to him; then hauled down the British flag and ran up the American flag in its place.

[1] Vigo (Vee-go).   [2] The priest was Father Gibault (Zhe-bo').

The next year the British, led by Colonel Hamilton, of Detroit, got the fort back again. When Clark heard of it he said, "Either I must take Hamilton, or Hamilton will take me." Just then Francis Vigo, a trader at St. Louis, came to see Clark at Kaskaskia. Hamilton had held Vigo as a prisoner, so he knew all about Fort Vincennes. Vigo said to Clark, "Hamilton has only about eighty soldiers; you can take the fort, and I will lend you all the money you need to pay your men what you owe them."

165. Clark's march to Fort Vincennes; the "Drowned Lands." — Clark, with about two hundred men, started for Vincennes. The distance was nearly a hundred and fifty miles. The first week everything went on pretty well. It was in the month of February; the weather was cold, and it rained a good deal; but the men did not mind that. They would get wet through during the day; but at night they built roaring log fires, gathered round them, roasted their buffalo meat or venison, smoked their pipes, told jolly stories, and sang jolly songs.

The next week they got to a branch of the Wabash River.[1] Then they found that the constant rains had raised the streams so that they had overflowed their banks; the whole country was under water three or four feet deep. This flooded country was called the "Drowned Lands": before Clark and his men had crossed these lands, they were nearly drowned themselves.

166. Wading on to victory. — For about a week the Americans had to wade in ice-cold water, sometimes

[1] See map on page 144.

waist deep, sometimes nearly up to their chins. While wading, the men were obliged to hold their guns and powder horns above their heads to keep them dry. Now and then a man would stub his toe against a root or a stone and would go sprawling headfirst into the water. When he came up, puffing and blowing from such a dive, he was lucky if he still had his gun. For

two days no one could get anything to eat; but hungry, wet, and cold, they k e p t   m o v i n g slowly on.

The last part of the march was the worst of all. They were now near the fort, but they still h a d   t o   w a d e through a sheet of water four miles a c r o s s.   Clark took the lead and

WADING THROUGH FLOOD

plunged in. The rest, shivering, followed. A few looked as though their strength and courage had given out. Clark saw this, and calling to Captain Bowman, — one of the bravest of his officers, — he ordered him to kill the first man who refused to go forward.

At last, with numbed hands and chattering teeth, all got across, but some of them were so weak and blue with cold that they could not take another step, but fell flat on their faces in the mud. These men were so nearly dead that no fire seemed to warm them. Clark ordered two strong men to lift each of these poor fellows up, hold him between them by the arms, and run him up and down until he began to get warm. By doing this he saved every one.

167. Clark takes the fort; what we got by his victory; his grave. — After a long and desperate fight, Clark took Fort Vincennes and hoisted the Stars and Stripes over it in triumph. The British never got it back again. Most of the Indians were now glad to make peace, and to promise to behave themselves.

By Clark's victory the Americans got possession of the whole western wilderness up to Detroit. When the Revolutionary War came to an end, the British did not want to give us any part of America beyond the thirteen states on the Atlantic coast. But we said, The whole west, clear to the Mississippi, is ours; we fought for it; we took it; we hoisted our flag over its forts, and *we mean to keep it*. We did keep it.

CLARK'S GRAVE

There is a grass-grown grave in a burial ground in Louisville, Kentucky, which has a small headstone marked with the letters G. R. C., and nothing more; that is the grave of General George Rogers Clark, the man who did more than any one else to get the west for us — or what was called the west a hundred years ago.

Clark died neglected and in great poverty. In 1895 a fine monument was erected to his memory, in the city of Indianapolis.[1]

---

[1] Indianapolis (In-dian-ap´o-lis).

168. Summary. — During the Revolutionary War George Rogers Clark, of Virginia, with a small number of men, captured Fort Kaskaskia in Illinois, and Fort Vincennes in Indiana. Clark drove out the British from that part of the country; and when peace was made, we kept the west — that is, the country beyond the Alleghany Mountains as far as the Mississippi River — as a part of the United States. Had it not been for Clark and his brave men, we might not have got it.

What did the British have in the west? Where were three of those forts? Who hired the Indians to fight? How did they fight? What did most of the people in England think about this? What is said of George the Third? What friend did Daniel Boone have in Virginia? What did Clark undertake to do? Tell how he went down the Ohio. Tell how he marched on Fort Kaskaskia. What happened when he got there? What did Clark say to the people in the fort? How was Fort Vincennes taken? What did the British do the next year? Tell about Francis Vigo. What did Clark and his men start to do? How far off was Fort Vincennes? Tell about the first part of the march. What lands did they come to? Tell how the men waded. How did Clark save the lives of some of the men? Did Clark take the fort? What did the Americans get possession of by this victory? What happened at the end of the Revolutionary War? What did we say? What is said of the grave at Louisville, Kentucky, and of the monument at Indianapolis? What did Clark get for us?

XVIII. GENERAL RUFUS PUTNAM

(1738-1824)

169. What General Putnam did for Washington, and what the British said of Putnam's work. — When the British had possession of Boston in the time of the Revolution, Washington asked Rufus Putnam,[1] who was a great builder of forts, to help him drive them out. Putnam

---

[1] Rufus Putnam was born in Sutton, Massachusetts.

set to work, one dark, stormy night, and built a fort
on some high land [1] overlooking Boston harbor.

When the British commander woke up the next morning, he saw the American cannon pointed at his ships.
He was so astonished that he could scarcely believe his

"Down the Ohio"

eyes. "Why," said he, "the rebels have done more
in one night than my whole army could have done in
a week." Another officer, who had command of the
British vessels, said, "If the Americans hold that fort, I
cannot keep a ship in the harbor."

[1] Dorchester Heights : now South Boston.

Well, we know what happened. Our men did hold that fort, and the British had to leave Boston. Next to General Washington, General Rufus Putnam was the man who made them go; for not many officers in the American army could build such a fort as he could.

170. General Putnam builds the *Mayflower*; goes down the Ohio River and makes the first settlement in Ohio. — After the war was over, General Putnam started, with a company of people from New England,[1] to make a settlement on the Ohio River. In the spring of 1788 he and his emigrants built a boat at a place on a branch of the Ohio River just above Pittsburg.[2] They named this boat the *Mayflower*,[3] because they were Pilgrims going west to make their home there.

At that time there was not a white settler in what is now the state of Ohio. Most of that country was covered with thick woods. There were no roads through those woods; and there was not a steamboat or a railroad in America or, in fact, in the whole world. If you look on the map[4] and follow down the Ohio River from Pittsburg, you will come to a place where the Muskingum[5] River flows into it. At that place the *Mayflower* stopped, and the emigrants landed and began to build their settlement.

171. What the settlers named their town; the first Fourth of July celebration; what Washington said of the settlers. — During the Revolutionary War the beautiful Queen Mary, of France, was our firm friend, and she was very

---

[1] General Putnam was then living in Rutland, Worcester County, Massachusetts. His house is still standing. From it the emigrants for the Ohio country took their departure in wagons drawn by ox teams. See a very interesting article on "Historic Rutland" in the *New England Magazine* for August, 1893.

[2] Pittsburg; see map, page 124.   [4] See map, page 124.

[3] *Mayflower*; see page 45.   [5] Muskingum (Mus-kin'gum).

kind and helpful to Dr. Franklin when he went to France for us. A number of the emigrants to Ohio had fought in the Revolution; and so the company of settlers decided to name the town Marietta,[1] in honor of the queen.

When the Marietta settlers celebrated the Fourth of July, Major Denny, who commanded a fort just across the river, came to visit them. He said, "These people appear to be the happiest folks in the world." President Washington said that he knew many of them and that he believed they were just the kind of men to succeed. He was right; for these people, with those who came later to build the city of Cincinnati, were the ones who laid the

ON THE LOOKOUT

foundation of the great and rich state of Ohio.

172. Fights with the Indians; how the settlers held their town; Indian Rock; the "Miami[2] Slaughter House." — But the people of Marietta had hardly begun to feel at home in their little settlement before a terrible Indian war

---

[1] The queen's full name in French was Marie Antoinette; the name Marietta is made up from the first and the last parts of her name.   [2] Miami (Mi-am′ĭ).

broke out. The village of Marietta had a high, close fence or palisade[1] built round it, and if a man ventured outside that palisade, he went at the risk of his life; for the Indians were always hiding in the woods, ready to kill any white man they saw. When the settlers worked in the cornfield, they had to carry their guns as well as their hoes; and one man always stood on top of a high stump in the middle of the field, to keep a bright lookout.

On the Ohio River, below Marietta, there is a lofty rock which is still called Indian Rock. It got its name because the Indians used to climb to the top and watch for emigrants coming down the

INDIAN ROCK

river in boats. When they saw a boat, they would fire a shower of bullets at it, and perhaps leave it full of dead and wounded men to drift down the stream. In the western part of Ohio, on the Miami River, the Indians killed so many people that the settlers called that part of the country by the terrible name of the "Miami Slaughter House."

[1] See picture of a palisade (păl-i-sade′) on page 51.

173. What General Wayne[1] did. — But President Washington sent a man to Ohio who made the Indians beg for peace. This man was General Wayne; he had fought in the Revolution, and fought so furiously that he was called " Mad Anthony Wayne." The Indians said that he never slept; and they named him " Black Snake," because that is the quickest and boldest snake there is in the woods, and in a fight with any other creature of his kind he is pretty sure to win the day. General Wayne won; and the Indians agreed to move off and give up a very large part of Ohio to the white settlers. After that, there was not much trouble, and emigrants poured in by thousands.

174. Summary. — In 1788 General Rufus Putnam, with a company of emigrants, settled Marietta, Ohio. The town was named in honor of Queen Mary of France, who had helped us during the Revolution. It was the first town built in what is now the state of Ohio. After General Wayne had conquered the Indians, that part of the country rapidly increased in population.

What did General Rufus Putnam do for Washington? Where did General Putnam go in 1788? What is said of Ohio at that time? Where did the *Mayflower* stop? What is said of Queen Mary of France? What did the settlers name their town? What did Washington say about the settlers? What did these people do? What is said about the Indians? What about Indian Rock? What was the country on the Miami River called? What is said about General Wayne? What did the Indians call him? Why did they give him that name? What did the Indians agree to do? What happened after that?

[1] Wayne (Wāne).

XIX. ELI WHITNEY

(1765-1825)

175. The name cut on a door. — Near Westboro, Massachusetts,[1] there was an old farm-house which was built before the war of the Revolution. Close to the house was a small wooden building ; on the door you could

read a boy's name, just as he cut it with his pocket-knife more than a hundred years ago.[2] Here is the door with the name. If the boy had added the date of his birth, he would have cut the figures 1765 ; but perhaps, just as he got to that point, his father appeared, and said rather sharply : Eli, don't be cutting that door. No, sir, said Eli, with a start ; and shutting his knife up with a snap, he hurried off to get the cows or to do his chores.[3]

176. What Eli Whitney used to do in his father's little workshop ; the fiddle. — Eli Whitney's father used that little wooden building as a kind of workshop, where he mended chairs and did many other small jobs. Eli liked to go to that workshop and make little things for himself, such as water-wheels and windmills ; for it was as natural for him to use tools as it was to whistle.

---

[1] See map, page 116.   [3] Chores : getting in wood, feeding cattle, etc.
[2] The house and the small wooden building (with the famous door) were pulled down a number of years ago.

Once, when Eli's father was gone from home for several days, the boy was very busy all the while in the little shop. When Mr. Whitney came back, he asked his housekeeper, "What has Eli been doing?" "Oh," she replied, "he has been making a fiddle." His father shook his head, and said that he was afraid Eli would never get on much in the world. But Eli's fiddle, though it was rough looking, was well made. It had music in it, and the neighbors liked to hear it: somehow it seemed to say, through all the tunes played on it, *"Whatever is worth doing, is worth doing well."*

177. Eli Whitney begins making nails; he goes to college. — When Eli was fifteen, he began making nails. We have machines to-day which will make more than a hundred nails a minute; but Eli made his, one by one, by pounding them out of a long, slender bar of red-hot iron. Whitney's hand-made nails were not handsome, but they were strong and tough; and, as the Revolutionary War was then going on, he could sell all he could make.

After the war was over, the demand for nails was not so good. Then Whitney threw down his hammer, and said, "I am going to college." He had no money; but he worked his way through Yale College, partly by teaching and partly by doing little jobs with his tools. A carpenter who saw him at work one day noticed how neatly and skilfully he used his tools, and said, "There was one good mechanic spoiled when you went to college."

178. Whitney goes to Georgia; he stays with Mrs. Greene; the embroidery frame. — When the young man had completed his course of study, he went to Georgia to teach in a gentleman's family. On the way to Savannah he became acquainted with Mrs. Greene, the widow of the famous General Greene[1] of Rhode Island. General Greene had done such excellent fighting in the south during the Revolution that, after the war was over, the state of Georgia gave him a large piece of land near Savannah.

NEGROES GATHERING COTTON IN THE FIELD

Mrs. Greene invited young Whitney to her house; as he had been disappointed in getting the place to teach, he was very glad to accept her kind invitation. While he was there, he made her an embroidery frame. It was much better than the old one that she had been using, and she thought the maker of it was wonderfully skilful.

<hr />

[1] General Greene; see page 124.

179. A talk about raising cotton, and about cotton seeds. — Not long after this, a number of cotton-planters were at Mrs. Greene's house. In speaking about raising cotton, they said that the man who could invent a machine for stripping off the cotton seeds from the plant would make his fortune.

For what is called raw cotton or cotton wool, as it grows in the field, has a great number of little green seeds clinging to it. Before the cotton wool can be spun into thread and woven into cloth, those seeds must be pulled off.

At that time the planters set the negroes to do this. When they had finished their day's labor of gathering the cotton in the cotton field, the men, women, and children would sit down and pick off the seeds, which stick so tight that getting them off is no easy task.

After the planters had talked awhile about this work, Mrs. Greene said, "If you want a machine to do

WHITNEY'S FIRST CONTRIVANCE FOR PULLING OFF THE COTTON SEEDS

it, you should apply to my young friend, Mr. Whitney; he can make anything." "But," said Mr. Whitney, "I have never seen a cotton plant or a cotton seed in my life"; for it was not the time of year then to see it growing in the fields.

180. Whitney gets some cotton wool; he invents the cotton-gin; what that machine did. — After the planters had gone, Eli Whitney went to Savannah and hunted about until he found, in some store or warehouse, a little cotton wool with the seeds left on it. He took this back with him and set to work to make a machine which would strip off the seeds.

He said to himself, If I fasten some upright pieces of wire in a board, and set the wires very close together, like the teeth of a comb, and then pull the cotton wool through the wires with my fingers, the seeds, being too large to come through, will be torn off and left behind.

A Cotton-Gin

He tried it, and found that the cotton wool came through without any seeds on it. Now, said he, If I should make a wheel, and cover it with short steel teeth, shaped like hooks, these teeth would pull the cotton wool through the wires better than my fingers do, and very much faster.

He made such a wheel; it was turned by a crank; it did the work perfectly; so, in the year 1793, he had invented the machine the planters wanted.

Before that time it used to take a negro all day to clean a single pound of cotton of its seeds, by picking them off one by one; now, Eli Whitney's cotton-gin,[1] as he called his machine, would clean a thousand pounds in a day.

181. Price of common cotton cloth; what made it cheap; "King Cotton." — In time that machine made cotton cloth

[1] Gin: a shortened form of the word *engine*, meaning any kind of machine.

so cheap that you could buy it for ten or twelve cents a yard;[1] but before Whitney invented his cotton-gin it sold for a dollar and a half a yard. A hundred years ago the planters at the south raised very little cotton, for few people could afford to wear it; but after this wonderful machine was made, the planters kept making their fields bigger and bigger. At last they raised so much more of this plant than of anything else, that they said, "Cotton is king." It was Eli Whitney who built the throne for that king; and although he did not make a fortune by his machine, yet he received a good deal of money for the use of it in some of the southern states.

THE "STAR-SPANGLED BANNER"

Later, Mr. Whitney built a gun-factory near New Haven, Connecticut, at a place now called Whitneyville; in that factory he made thousands of the muskets which we used in our second war with England[2] in 1812, — that famous war which gave us the stirring song of the *Star-Spangled Banner*, and which secured our independence on the sea as the war of the Revolution did on the land.

[1] But when the Great War came (see page 263) cotton jumped in price.

[2] In the war of 1812 the British war-ships attacked Fort McHenry, one of the defences of Baltimore. Francis Scott Key, a native of Maryland, who was then detained on board a British man-of-war, anxiously watched the battle during the night; before dawn the firing ceased. Key had no means of telling whether the British had taken the fort until the sun rose; then, to his joy, he saw the American flag still floating triumphantly above the fort — that meant that the British had failed in their attack; and Key, in his delight, hastily wrote the song of the *Star-Spangled Banner* on the back of a letter which he had in his pocket. In a few weeks his song was heard from one end of the United States to the other.

182. Summary. — About a hundred years ago (1793), Eli Whitney of Westboro, Massachusetts, invented the cotton-gin, a machine for pulling off the green seeds from cotton wool, so that it may be easily woven into cloth. That machine made thousands of cotton-planters and cotton manufacturers rich, and by it cotton cloth became so cheap that everybody could afford to use it.

What name did a boy cut on a door? What did Eli make in that workshop? What did he make while his father was away? What did his father say? What did Eli's fiddle seem to say? What did Eli make next? How did he make his nails? Where did he go after he gave up making nails? When he left college where did he go? What lady did he become acquainted with? What did he make for her? What did the cotton-planters say? What must be done to raw cotton before it can be made into cloth? Who did this work? What did Mrs. Greene say to the planters? What did Mr. Whitney say? What did he do? Tell how he made his machine. What did he call it? How many pounds of cotton would his cotton-gin clean in a day? How much could one negro clean? What is said about the price of cotton cloth? What did the planters say about cotton? Who built the throne for King Cotton? What did Mr. Whitney build at Whitneyville? What did he make there?

XX. THOMAS JEFFERSON

(1743-1826)

183. How much cotton New Orleans sends to Europe; Eli Whitney's work; who it was that bought New Orleans[1] and Louisiana for us. — To-day the city of New Orleans, near the mouth of the Mississippi River, sends more cotton to England and Europe than any other city in America.

If you should visit that city and go down to the river-side, you would see thousands of cotton bales[2] piled up,

[1] New Orleans (Or'le-anz).

[2] A bale or bundle of cotton is usually somewhat more than five feet long, and it generally weighs from 400 to 550 pounds. The cotton crop of this country in 1900 amounted to nearly 9,500,000 bales. The fact is America can now supply cotton enough to clothe the earth.

and hundreds of negroes loading them on ocean steamers. It would be a sight you would never forget.

Before Eli Whitney [1] invented his machine, we sent hardly a bale of cotton abroad. Now we send so much in one year that the bales can be counted by millions. If they were laid end to end, in a straight line, they would reach clear across the American continent from San Francisco to New York, and then clear across the ocean from New York to Liverpool, England, and about three thousand miles further. Eli

THOMAS JEFFERSON

Whitney did more than any other man to build up this great trade. But at the time when he invented his cotton-gin, we did not own New Orleans, or, for that matter, any part of Louisiana [2] or of the country west of

1 See page 156.   2 Louisiana (Lōō′ē-zē-ah′nạ).

the Mississippi River. The man who bought New Orleans and Louisiana for us was Thomas Jefferson.

184. Who Thomas Jefferson was ; Monticello[1]; how Jefferson's slaves met him when he came home from Europe. — Thomas Jefferson was the son of a rich planter who

JEFFERSON'S HOME AT MONTICELLO

lived near Charlottesville in Virginia.[2] When his father died, he came into possession of a plantation of nearly two thousand acres of land, with forty or fifty negro slaves on it.

There was a high hill on the plantation, to which Jefferson gave the Italian[3] name of Monticello, or the little mountain. Here he built a fine house. From it he could see the mountains and valleys of the Blue Ridge for an immense distance. No man in America had a more beautiful home, or enjoyed it more, than Thomas Jefferson.

---

[1] Monticello (Mon-te-sel'lo).   [2] See map, page 124.
[3] Italian (It-ăl'yan).

Jefferson's slaves thought that no one could be better than their master. He was always kind to them, and they were ready to do anything for him.

Once when he came back from France, where he had been staying for a long time, the negroes went to meet

SLAVES MEETING JEFFERSON

his carriage. They walked several miles down the road ; when they caught sight of the carriage, they shouted and sang with delight. They would gladly have taken out the horses and drawn it up the steep hill. When Jefferson reached Monticello and got out, the negroes took him in their arms, and, laughing and crying for joy, they carried him into the house. Perhaps no king ever got such a welcome as that ; for that welcome was not bought with money : it came from the heart. Yet Jefferson hoped and prayed that the time would come when every slave in the country might be set free.

185. Thomas Jefferson hears Patrick Henry speak at Richmond. — Jefferson was educated to be a lawyer; he was not a good public speaker himself, but he liked to hear men who were good speakers. Just before the beginning of the Revolutionary War (1775), the people of Virginia sent men to the city of Richmond to hold a meeting in old St. John's Church. They met to see what should be done about defending those rights which the king of England had refused to grant the Americans.

"We must *Fight!*"

One of the speakers at that meeting was a famous Virginian, named Patrick Henry. When he got up to speak he looked very pale, but his eyes shone like coals of fire. He made a great speech. He said, "We must fight ! I repeat it, sir, — we must *fight !*" The other Virginians agreed with Patrick Henry, and George Washington and Thomas Jefferson, with other noted men who were present at the meeting, began at once to make ready to fight.

186. Thomas Jefferson writes the Declaration of Independence; how it was sent through the country. — Shortly after this the great war began. In a little over a year from the time when the first battle was fought, Congress asked Thomas Jefferson, Benjamin Franklin, and some others to write the Declaration of Independence. Jefferson really wrote almost every word of it. He was called the "Pen of the Revolution"; for he could write quite as well as Patrick Henry could speak.

The Declaration was printed, and was then carried, by men mounted on fast horses, all over the United States. When men heard it, they rang the church bells and sent up cheer after cheer. General Washington had the Declaration read to all the soldiers in his army; and, if powder had not been so scarce, they would have fired off every gun for joy.

187. Jefferson is chosen President of the United States; what he said about New Orleans. — A number of years after the war was over, Jefferson was chosen President of the United States; while he was President (1801–1809) he did something for the country which will never be forgotten.

Louisiana and the city of New Orleans, with the lower part of the Mississippi River, then belonged to the French; for, at that time, the United States only reached west as far as the Mississippi River. Now, as New Orleans stands near the mouth of that river, the French could say, if they chose, what vessels should go out to sea, and what should come in. So far, then, as

Map showing the extent of the United States at the close of the Revolution, and also when Jefferson became President (1801).

that part of America was concerned, we were like a man who owns a house while another man owns one of the principal doors to it. The man who has the door could say to the owner of the house, I shall stand here on the steps, and you must pay me so many dollars every time you go out and every time you come in this way.

Jefferson saw that so long as the French held the door of New Orleans, we should not be free to send our cotton down the river and across the ocean to Europe. He said we must have that door, no matter how much it cost.

188. Jefferson buys New Orleans and Louisiana for the United States. — Mr. Robert R. Livingston, one of the signers of the Declaration of Independence, was in France

Map showing how much larger President Jefferson made the United States by buying Louisiana in 1803. (The Oregon Country is marked in bars to show that the ownership of it was disputed; England and the United States both claimed it.)

at that time, and Jefferson sent over to him to see if he could buy New Orleans for the United States. Napoleon Bonaparte[1] then ruled France. He said, I want money to purchase war-ships with, so that I can fight England; I will sell not only New Orleans, but all Louisiana besides, for fifteen millions of dollars. That was cheap enough, and so in 1803 President Jefferson bought it.

If you look on the map[2] you will see that Louisiana then was not simply a good-sized state, as it is now, but an immense country reaching clear back to the Rocky Mountains. It was really larger than the whole United States east of the Mississippi River. So, through

[1] Napoleon Bonaparte (Na-po'le-on Bo'na-part).
[2] Compare map on this page with that on page 168.

President Jefferson's purchase, we added so much land that we now had more than twice as much as we had before ; and we had got the whole Mississippi River, the city of New Orleans, and what is now the great city of St. Louis besides.

189. Death of Jefferson; the words cut on his gravestone. — Jefferson lived to be an old man.   He died at Monticello on the Fourth of July, 1826, just fifty years, to a day, after he had signed the Declaration of Independence. John Adams, who had been President next before Jefferson, died a few hours later.   So America lost two of her great men on the same day.

Jefferson was buried at Monticello.   He asked to have these words, with some others, cut on his gravestone [1]: —

Here Was Buried

THOMAS JEFFERSON,

Author of the Declaration of American Independence.

190. Summary. — Thomas Jefferson of Virginia wrote the Declaration of Independence.   After he became President of the United States, he bought Louisiana for us.   The purchase of Louisiana, with New Orleans, gave us the right to send our ships to sea by way of the Mississippi River, which now belonged to us. Louisiana added so much land that it more than doubled the size of the United States.

---

[1] The gravestone stands by the side of the road at no great distance from the house at Monticello.   This is the entire inscription cut on the monument: "Here was buried Thomas Jefferson, author of the Declaration of American Independence, of the Statute of Virginia for Religious Freedom, and Father of the University of Virginia."

Before Whitney invented his cotton-gin how much cotton did we send abroad? How much do we send from New Orleans now? Did we own New Orleans or Louisiana when Whitney invented his cotton-gin? Who bought them for us? Who was Thomas Jefferson? What is said about Monticello? Tell how Jefferson's slaves welcomed him home. For what profession was Jefferson educated? Tell about Patrick Henry. What did he say? What did Washington and Jefferson do? What did Jefferson write? What was he called? How was the Declaration sent to all parts of the country? What was Jefferson chosen to be? To whom did New Orleans and Louisiana then belong? How far did the United States then extend towards the west? What could the French say? What were we like? What did Jefferson say? Did we buy it? How much did we pay? How large was Louisiana then? How much land did we get? What else did we get? When did Jefferson die? What other great man died on the same day? What words did Jefferson have cut on his gravestone at Monticello?

XXI. ROBERT FULTON

(1765-1815)

191. The Louisiana country; a small family in a big house; settlements in the west; the country beyond the Mississippi River. — Even before we bought the great Louisiana country,[1] we had more land than we then knew what to do with; after we had purchased it, it seemed to some people as though we should not want to use what we had bought for more than a hundred years. Such people thought that we were like a man with a small family who lives in a house much too large for him; but who, not contented with that, buys his neighbor's house, which is bigger still, and adds it to his own.

If a traveller in those days went across the Alleghany Mountains[2] to the west, he found some small settlements in Ohio, Kentucky, and Tennessee, but hardly any outside of those. The region which is now covered by

See page 169.   [2] See map, page 124.

the great states of Indiana, Illinois, Michigan, and Wisconsin was then a wilderness; and this was true also of what are now the states of Alabama and Mississippi.

If the same traveller, pushing forward, on foot or on horseback, — for there were no steam cars, — crossed the Mississippi River, he could hardly find a white man outside what was then the little town of St. Louis. The country stretched away west for more than a thousand miles, with nothing in it but wild beasts and Indians. In much of it there were no trees, no houses, no human beings. If you shouted as hard as you could in that solitary land, the only reply you would hear would be the echo of your own voice; it was like shouting in an empty room — it made it seem lonelier than ever.

192. Emigration to the west, and the man who helped that emigration. — But, during the last hundred years, that great empty land of the far west has been filling up with people. Thousands upon thousands of emigrants have gone there. They have built towns and cities and railroads and telegraph lines. Thousands more are going and will go. What has made such a wonderful change? Well, one man helped to do a great deal toward it. His name was Robert Fulton. He saw how difficult it was for people to get west; for if emigrants wanted to go with their families in wagons, they had to chop roads through the forests. That was slow, hard work. Fulton found a way that was quick, easy, and cheap. Let us see who he was, and how he found that way.

193. Robert Fulton's boyhood; the old scow; what Robert did for his mother. — Robert Fulton was the son of a poor

Irish farmer in Pennsylvania.[1] He did not care much for books, but liked to draw pictures with pencils which he hammered out of pieces of lead.

Like most boys, he was fond of fishing. He used to go out in an old scow, or flat-bottomed boat, on a river near his home. He and another boy would push the scow along with poles. But Robert said, There is an easier way to make this boat go. I can put a pair of paddle-wheels on her, and then we can sit comfortably on the seat and turn the wheels by a crank. He tried it, and

ROBERT FULTON'S PADDLE-WHEEL SCOW

found that he was right. The boys now had a boat which suited them exactly.

When Robert was seventeen, he went to Philadelphia. His father was dead, and he earned his living and helped his mother and sisters by painting pictures. He stayed in Philadelphia until he was twenty-one. By that time he had saved up money enough to buy a small farm for his mother, so that she might have a home of her own.

194. Fulton goes to England and to France ; his iron bridges ; his diving-boat, and what he did with it in France. — Soon after buying the farm for his mother, young Fulton went to England and then to France. He stayed in those countries twenty years. In England Fulton built some famous iron bridges, but he was more interested in boats than in anything else.

[1] Fulton was born in Little Britain (now called Fulton) in Lancaster County, Pennsylvania. See map, page 116.

While he was in France he made what he called a diving-boat. It would go under water nearly as well as it would on top, so that, wherever a big fish could go, Fulton could follow him. His object in building such a boat was to make war in a new way. When a swordfish [1] attacks a whale, he slips round under him and stabs the monster with his sword. Fulton said, ' If an enemy's war-ship should come into the harbor to do mischief, I can get into my diving-boat, slip under the ship, fasten a torpedo [2] to it, and blow the ship " sky high." '

Napoleon Bonaparte liked nothing so much as war ; and he let Fulton have an old vessel to see if he could blow it up. He tried it, and everything happened as he expected : nothing was left of the vessel but the pieces.

195. What Fulton did in England with his diving-boat ; what he said about America. — Then Fulton went back to England and tried the same thing there. He went out in his diving-boat and fastened a torpedo under a vessel ; when the torpedo exploded, the vessel, as he said, went up like a " bag of feathers," flying in all directions.

The English people paid Fulton seventy-five thousand dollars for showing them what he could do in this way. Then they offered to give him a great deal more — in fact, to make him a very rich man — if he would promise never to let any other country know just how he blew vessels up. But Fulton said, ' I am an American ; and if America should ever want to use my diving-boat in war, she shall have it first of all.' (See also page 284.)

---

[1] Swordfish : the name given to a large fish which has a sword-like weapon, several feet in length, projecting from its upper jaw.

[2] Torpedo : here a can filled with powder, and so constructed that it could be fastened to the bottom of a vessel.

196. Fulton makes his first steamboat. — But while Fulton was doing these things with his diving-boat, he was always thinking of the paddle-wheel scow he used to fish in when a boy. I turned those paddle-wheels by a crank, said he, but what is to hinder my putting a steam engine into such a boat, and making it turn the crank for me? that would be a steamboat. Such boats had already been tried, but, for one reason or another, they had not got on very well. Robert R. Livingston was still in France, and he helped Fulton build his first steamboat. It was put on a river there; it moved, and that was about all.

197. Robert Fulton and Mr. Livingston go to New York and build a steamboat; the trip up the Hudson River. — But Robert Fulton and Mr. Livingston both believed that a steamboat could be built that would go, and that would keep going. So they went to New York and built one there.

In the summer of 1807 a great crowd gathered to see the boat start on her voyage up the Hudson River. They

FULTON'S STEAMER ON ITS WAY TO ALBANY

joked and laughed as crowds will at anything new. They called Fulton a fool and Livingston another. But when Fulton, standing on the deck of his steamboat, waved his hand, and the wheels began to turn, and the vessel began to move up the river, then the crowd became silent with astonishment. Now it was Fulton's turn to laugh, and in such a case the man who laughs last has a right to laugh loudest.

Up the river Fulton kept going. He passed the Palisades[1]; he passed the Highlands[2]; still he kept on, and at last he reached Albany, a hundred and fifty miles above New York.

Nobody before had ever seen such a sight as that boat moving up the river without the help of oars or sails; but from that time people saw it every day. When Fulton got back to New York in his steamboat, everybody wanted to shake hands with him. The crowd, instead of shouting fool, now whispered among themselves, He's a great man — a very great man, indeed.

198. The first steamboat in the west; the Great Shake. — Four years later Fulton built a steamboat for the west. In the autumn of 1811 it started from Pittsburg[3] to go down the Ohio River, and then down the Mississippi to New Orleans. The people of the west had never seen a steamboat before, and when the Indians saw the smoke puffing out, they called it the "Big Fire Canoe."

On the way down the river, there was a terrible earthquake. In some places it changed the course of the Ohio, so that where there had been dry land there was now deep water, and where there had been deep water there was now dry land. One evening the captain of the "Big Fire Canoe" fastened his vessel to a large tree

---

[1] See map on page 38.　　　　[2] See map on page 38.
[3] Pittsburg; see map, page 124.

on the end of an island.   In the morning the people on the
steamboat looked out, but could not tell where they were;
the island had gone: the earthquake had carried it away.
The Indians called the earthquake the "Big Shake":
it was a good name, for it kept on shaking that part of
the country, and doing all sorts of damage for weeks.

THE "BIG FIRE CANOE" ON THE MISSISSIPPI

**199.   The "Big Fire Canoe" on the Mississippi; the fight
between steam and the Great River; what steamboats did;
Robert Fulton's grave.** — When the steamboat reached the
Mississippi, the settlers on that river said that the boat
would never be able to go back, because the current was
so strong.   At one place a crowd had gathered to see
her as she turned against the current, in order to come
up to the landing-place.   An old negro stood watching
the boat.   It looked as if, in spite of all the captain could
do, she would be carried down stream, but at last steam

conquered, and the boat came up to the shore. Then the old negro could hold in no longer : he threw up his ragged straw hat and shouted, 'Hoo-ray ! hoo-ray ! the old Mississippi's just got her master this time, *sure !*'

Soon steamboats began to run regularly on the Mississippi ; and in the course of a few years they began to move up and down the Great Lakes and the Missouri River. Emigrants could now go to the west and the far west, quickly and easily : they had to thank Robert Fulton for that.

Robert Fulton lies buried in New York, in the shadow of the tower of Trinity Church. There is no monument or mark over his grave ; but every steamboat on every great river and lake in America is really a monument to his memory.

200. Summary. — In 1807 Robert Fulton of Pennsylvania built the first steamboat which ran on the Hudson River, and four years later he built the first one which navigated the rivers of the west. His boats helped to fill the whole western country with settlers.

What is said about the Louisiana country? What did some people think we were like? What would a traveller going west then find? What is said of the country west of the Mississippi? Who helped emigration to the west? What did he find? Tell about Robert Fulton as a boy. Tell about his paddle-wheel scow. What did Robert do for his mother? Where did he go? How long did he stay abroad? Tell about his diving-boat. What did he do with it in France? What in England? What did the English people offer him? What did Fulton say? Where did Fulton make and try his first steamboat? Tell about the steamboat he made in New York. How far up the Hudson did it go? Tell about the first steamboat at the west. What did the Indians call it? What happened on the way down the Ohio River? Tell about the steamboat on the Mississippi River. What is said of steamboats at the west? What about emigrants? Where is Fulton buried? Where is his monument?

XXII. GENERAL WILLIAM HENRY HARRISON

(1773-1841)

201. War with the Indians; how the Indians felt about being forced to leave their homes; the story of the log. — The year 1811, in which the first steamboat went west, a great battle was fought with the Indians.   The battle-ground was on the Tippecanoe [1] River, in what is now the state of Indiana.

The Indians fought because they wanted to keep the west for themselves.   They felt as an old chief did, who had been forced by the white men to move many times.

One day a military officer came to his wigwam to tell him that he and his tribe must go still further west. The chief said, General, let's sit down on this log and talk it over. So they both sat down.   After they had talked a short time, the chief said, Please move a little further that way; I have n't room enough. The officer moved along.   In a few minutes the chief asked him to move again, and he did so.   Presently the chief gave him a push and said, Do move further on, won't you?   I can't, said the general.   Why not? asked the chief.   Because I 've got to the end of the log, replied the officer.   Well, said the Indian, now you see how it is with us.   You white men have kept pushing us

---

[1] Tippecanoe (Tip-pe-ka-noo').

on until you have pushed us clear to the end of our country, and yet you come now and say, Move on, move on.

202. What Tecumseh[1] and his brother, the "Prophet,"[2] tried to do. — A famous Indian warrior named Tecumseh determined to band the different Indian tribes together, and drive out the white men from the west.

"MOVE ON"

Tecumseh had a brother called the "Prophet," who pretended he could tell what would happen in the future. He said, The white traders come here, give the Indians whiskey, get them drunk, and then cheat them out of their lands. Once we owned this whole country; now, if an Indian strips a little bark from a tree to shelter him when it rains, a white man steps up, with a gun in his hand, and says, That's my tree; let it alone, or I'll shoot you.

Then the "Prophet" said to the red men, Stop drinking "fire-water,"[3] and you will have strength to kill off

---

[1] Tecumseh (Te-kum′seh).   [3] Fire-water: the Indian name for whiskey.
[2] Prophet (prof′et): one who tells what will happen in the future.

the "pale-faces" and get your land back again. When you have killed them off, I will bless the earth. I will make pumpkins [1] grow to be as big as wigwams, and the corn shall be so large that one ear will be enough for a dinner for a dozen hungry Indians. The Indians liked to hear these things; they wanted to taste those pumpkins and that corn, and so they got ready to fight.

203. Who William Henry Harrison was; the march to Tippecanoe; the "Prophet's" sacred beans; the battle of Tippecanoe. — At this time William Henry Harrison [2] was governor of Indiana territory. He had fought under General Wayne [3] in his war with the Indians in Ohio. Everybody knew Governor Harrison's courage, and the Indians all respected him; but he tried in vain to prevent the Indians from going to war. The "Prophet" urged them on at the north, and Tecumseh had gone south to persuade the Indians there to join the northern tribes.

Governor Harrison saw that a battle must soon be fought; so he started with his soldiers to meet the Indians. He marched to the Tippecanoe River, and there he stopped.

While Harrison's men were asleep in the woods, the "Prophet" told the Indians not to wait, but to attack the soldiers at once. In his hand he held up a string of beans. These beans, said he to the Indians, are sacred. [4] Come and touch them, and you are safe; no white man's bullet can hit you. The Indians hurried up in crowds to touch the wonderful beans.

[1] Pumpkins (pump'kins).   [3] See page 155.

[2] William Henry Harrison was born in Berkeley, Charles City County, Virginia, about twenty-five miles below Richmond. His father, Governor Harrison of Virginia, was one of the signers of the Declaration of Independence. The late President Benjamin Harrison was grandson of General William Henry Harrison.

[4] Sacred: something holy, or set apart for religious uses.

Now, said the "Prophet," let each one take his hatchet in one hand and his gun in the other, and creep through the tall grass till he gets to the edge of the woods. The soldiers lie there fast asleep; when you get close to them, spring up and go for them, like a wild-cat for a rabbit.

THE BATTLE OF TIPPECANOE

The Indians started to do this, but a soldier on guard saw the tall grass moving as though a great snake was gliding through it. He fired his gun at the moving grass; up sprang the whole band of Indians, and, with a terrible yell, they rushed forward : in a moment the battle began.

Harrison won the victory. He not only killed many of the Indians, but he marched against their village, set fire to it, and burned it to ashes.

After that the Indians in that part of the country would not listen to the "Prophet." They said, he is a liar; his beans didn't save us.

The battle of Tippecanoe did much good, because it prevented the Indian tribes from uniting and beginning a great war all through the west. Governor Harrison received high praise for what he had done, and was made a general in the United States army.

204. Tecumseh takes the "Prophet" by the hair; the War of 1812; General Harrison's battle in Canada; President Harrison. — When Tecumseh came back from the south, he was terribly angry with his brother for fighting before he was ready to have him begin. He seized the "Prophet" by his long hair, and shook him as a terrier[1] shakes a rat. Tecumseh then left the United States and went to Canada to help the British, who were getting ready to fight us.

The next year (1812) we began our second war with England. It is called the War of 1812. One of the chief reasons why we fought was that the British would not let our merchant ships alone; they stopped them at sea, took thousands of our sailors out of them, and forced the men to serve in their war-ships in their battles against the French.

In the course of the War of 1812 the British burned the Capitol at Washington; but a grander building rose from its ashes. General Harrison fought a battle in Canada in which he defeated the British and killed Tecumseh, who was fighting on the side of the English.

Many years after this battle, the people of the west said, We must have the "Hero of Tippecanoe" for

---

[1] Terrier (ter'ri-er): a kind of small hunting-dog.

President of the United States. They went to vote for him, with songs[1] and shouts ; and he was elected. A month after he had gone to Washington, President Harrison died (1841), and the whole country was filled with sorrow.

205. Summary. — In 1811 General Harrison gained a great victory over the Indians at Tippecanoe, in Indiana. By that victory he saved the west from a terrible Indian war. In the War of 1812, with England, General Harrison beat the British in a battle in Canada, and killed Tecumseh, the Indian chief who had made us so much trouble. Many years later General Harrison was elected President of the United States.

Where was a great battle fought with the Indians in 1811 ? How did the Indians feel about the west ? Tell the story of the log. What did Tecumseh determine to do ? Tell about the " Prophet." Who was William Henry Harrison ? Tell about the battle of Tippecanoe. Tell about the sacred beans. What did the Indians say about the " Prophet" after the battle ? What good did the battle of Tippecanoe do ? What did Tecumseh do when he got back ? Where did he then go ? What happened in 1812 ? Why did we fight the British ? What did General Harrison do in Canada ? What did the people of the west say ? How long did General Harrison live after he became President ?

XXIII. GENERAL ANDREW JACKSON

(1767-1845)

206. Andrew Jackson and the War of 1812 ; his birthplace ; his school ; wrestling-matches[2] ; firing off the gun. — The greatest battle, on land, of our second war with England — the War of 1812 — was fought by General Andrew Jackson.

---

[1] The chorus of one of the most famous of these songs ended with the words: " Tippecanoe ! and Tyler too ! " (Tyler was the name of the candidate for Vice President.)   [2] Wrestling (res′ling).

He was the son of a poor emigrant who came from the North of Ireland and settled in North Carolina.[1] When Thomas Jefferson wrote the Declaration of Independence in 1776, Andrew was nine years old, and his father had long been dead. He was a tall, slender, freckled-faced, barefooted boy, with eyes full of fun; the neighbors called him "Mischievous little Andy."

He went to school in a log hut in the pine woods; but he learned more things from what he saw in the woods than from the books he studied in school.

He was not a very strong boy, and in wrestling some of his companions could throw him three times out of four; but though they could get him down without much trouble, it was quite another thing to keep him down. No sooner was he laid flat on his back, than he bounded up like a steel spring, and stood ready to try again.

He had a violent [2] temper, and when, as the boys said, "Andy got mad all over," not many cared to face him. Once some of his playmates secretly loaded an old gun almost up to the muzzle, and then dared him to fire it. They wanted to see what he would say when it kicked him over. Andrew fired the gun. It knocked him sprawling; he jumped up with eyes blazing with anger, and shaking his fist, cried out, "If one of you boys laughs, I'll kill him." He looked as though he meant exactly what he said, and the boys thought that perhaps it would be just as well to wait and laugh some other day.

207. Tarleton's [3] attack on the Americans; how Andrew helped his mother. — When Andrew was thirteen, he learned

[1] He settled in Union County, North Carolina, very near the South Carolina line. See map, page 124. Mecklenburg Court House is in the next county west of Union County. Jackson himself insisted that he was born in South Carolina.   [2] Violent: fierce, furious.   [3] Tarleton (Tarl'ton).

what war means. The country was then fighting the battles of the Revolution. A British officer named Tarleton came suddenly upon some American soldiers near the place where young Jackson lived. Tarleton had so many men that the Americans saw that it was useless to try to fight, and they made no attempt to do so. The British should have taken them all prisoners; but, instead of that, they attacked them furiously, and hacked and hewed them with their swords. More than a hundred of our men were left dead, and a still larger number were so horribly wounded that they could not be moved any distance. Such an attack was not war, for war means a fair, stand-up fight; it was murder: and when the people in England heard what Tarleton had done, many cried Shame!

There was a little log meeting-house near Andrew's home, and it was turned into a hospital for the wounded men. Mrs. Jackson, with other kind-hearted women, did all she could for the poor fellows who lay there groaning and helpless. Andrew carried food and water to them. He had forgotten many of the lessons he had learned at school; but here was something he would never forget.

208. Andrew's hatred of the " red-coats " [1]**; Tarleton's soldiers meet their match.** — From that time, when young Jackson went to the blacksmith's shop to get a hoe or a spade mended, he was sure to come back with a rude spear, or with some other weapon, which he had hammered out to fight the "red-coats" with.

Tarleton said that no people in America hated the British so much as those who lived in that part of the

[1] Red-coats: this nickname was given by the Americans to the British soldiers because they wore bright red coats.

country where Andrew Jackson had his home. The reason was that no other British officer was so cruel as "Butcher Tarleton," as he was called. Once, however, his men met their match. They were robbing a farm of its pigs and chickens and corn and hay. When they got through carrying things off, they were going to burn down the farm-house; but one of the "red-coats," in his haste, ran against a big hive of bees and upset it. The bees were mad enough. They swarmed down on the soldiers, got into their ears and eyes, and stung them so terribly that at last the robbers were glad to drop everything and run. If Andrew could have seen that battle, he would have laughed till he cried.

209. Dangerous state of the country; the roving bands. — Andrew knew that he and his mother lived in constant danger. Part of the people in the state of North Carolina were in favor of the king, and part were for liberty. Bands of armed men, belonging sometimes to one side, and sometimes to the other, went roving about the country. When they met a farmer, they would stop him and ask, 'Which side are you for?' If he did not answer to suit them, the leader of the party would cry out, Hang him up! In an instant one of the band would cut down a long piece of wild grape-vine, twist it into a noose, and throw it over the man's head; the next moment he would be dangling from the limb of a tree. Sometimes the band would let him down again, while he was still alive; sometimes they would ride on and leave him hanging there.

210. Playing at battle; what Tarleton heard about himself. — Even the children saw and heard so much of the war that was going on that they played at war, and fought battles with red and white corn, — red for the British and white for the Americans.

At the battle of Cowpens [1] Colonel William Washington [2] fought on the American side, and Tarleton got badly whipped and had to run. Not long afterward he happened to see some boys squatting on the ground, with a lot of corn instead of marbles. They were playing the battle of Cowpens. A red kernel stood for Tarleton, and a white one for Colonel Washington. The boys shoved the corn this way and that ; sometimes the red would win, sometimes the white. At last the white kernel gained the victory, and the boys shouted, " Hurrah for Washington — Tarleton runs ! "

Tarleton had been quietly looking on without their knowing it. When he saw how the game ended, he turned angrily away. He had seen enough of " the little rebels," [3] as he called them.

211. Andrew is taken prisoner by the British ; " Here, boy, clean those boots " ; the two scars. — Not long after our victory at Cowpens, Andrew Jackson was taken prisoner by the British. The officer in command of the soldiers had just taken off his boots, splashed with mud. Pointing to them, he said to Andrew, Here, boy, clean those boots. Andrew replied, Sir, I am a prisoner of war, and it is not my place to clean boots. The officer, in a great passion,

---

[1] Cowpens ; see map, page 124.

[2] Colonel William Washington was a relative of General George Washington.

[3] Rebels : this was the name which the British gave to the Americans because we had been forced to take up arms to overthrow the authority of the English king, who was still lawfully, but not justly, the ruler of this country. Had he been a just and upright ruler, there would probably have been no rebellion against his authority at that time.

whipped out his sword and struck a blow at the boy. It cut a gash on his head and another on his hand. Andrew Jackson lived to be an old man, but the marks of that blow never disappeared: he carried the scars to his grave.

212. The prisoners in the yard of Camden jail; seeing a battle through a knot-hole. —Andrew was sent, with other prisoners, to Camden,[1] South Carolina, and shut up in the jail-yard. There many fell sick and died of small-pox.

One day some of the prisoners heard that General Greene — the greatest American general in the

JACKSON AND THE OFFICER'S BOOTS

Revolution, next to Washington — was coming to fight the British at Camden. Andrew's heart leaped for joy, for he knew that if General Greene should win he would set all the prisoners at liberty.

General Greene with his little army was on a hill in sight of the jail; but there was a high, tight board fence round the jail-yard, and the prisoners could not see them. With the help of an old razor Andrew managed to dig

[1] Camden; see map, page 124.

out a knot from one of the boards.   Through that knot-hole he watched the battle of Hobkirk's Hill.[1]

Our men were beaten in the fight, and Andrew saw their horses, with empty saddles, running wildly about. Then the boy turned away, sick at heart.   Soon after that he was seized with the small-pox, and would have died of it if his mother had not succeeded in getting him set free.

213. Mrs. Jackson goes to visit the American prisoners at Charleston; Andrew loses his best friend; what he said of her. — In the summer Mrs. Jackson made a journey on horse-back to Charleston, a hundred and sixty miles away. She went to carry some little comforts to the poor American prisoners, who were starving and dying of disease in the crowded and filthy British prison-ships in the harbor. While visiting these unfortunate men, she caught the fever which raged among them.   Two weeks later she was in her grave, and Andrew, then a lad of fourteen, stood alone in the world.

Years afterward, when he had risen to be a noted man, people would sometimes praise him because he was never afraid to say and do what he believed to be right ; then Jackson would answer, "*That* I learned from my good old mother."

214. Andrew begins to learn a trade; he studies law and goes west; Judge Jackson; General Jackson. — Andrew set to work to learn the saddler's trade, but gave it up and began to study law.   After he became a lawyer he went across the mountains to Nashville, Tennessee.   There he was made a judge.   There were plenty of rough men in that part of the country who meant to have their own

1 Also called the second battle of Camden.

way in all things; but they soon found that they must respect and obey Judge Jackson. They could frighten other judges, but it was no use to try to frighten him. Seeing what sort of stuff Jackson was made of, they thought that they should like to have such a man to lead them in battle. And so Judge Andrew Jackson became General Andrew Jackson. When trouble came with the Indians, Jackson proved to be the very man they needed.

215. Tecumseh and the Indians of Alabama; Tecumseh threatens to stamp his foot on the ground; the earthquake; war begins. — We have already seen how the Indian chief Tecumseh[1] went south to stir up the red men to make war on the white settlers in the west. In Alabama he told the Indians, that if they fought, they would gain a great victory. I see, said Tecumseh to them, that you don't believe what I say, and that you don't mean to fight. Well, I am now going north to Detroit. When I get there I shall stamp my foot on the ground, and shake down every wigwam you have. It so happened that, shortly after Tecumseh had gone north, a sharp shock of earthquake was felt in Alabama, and the wigwams were actually shaken down by it. When the terrified Indians felt their houses falling to pieces, they ran out of them shouting, "Tecumseh has got to Detroit!"

These Indians now believed all that Tecumseh had said; they began to attack the white people, and they killed a great number of them.

216. Jackson conquers the Indians; the "Holy Ground"; Weathersford and Jackson; feeding the starving. — General Jackson marched against the Indians and beat them in

---

[1] Tecumseh; see page 180.

battle. The Indians that escaped fled to a place they called the "Holy Ground." They believed that if a white man dared to set his foot on that ground he would be struck dead, as if by a flash of lightning. General Jackson and his men marched on to the "Holy Ground," and the Indians soon found that, unless they made peace, they would be the ones who would be struck dead by his bullets.

GENERAL JACKSON AND THE INDIAN CHIEF

Not long after this, a noted leader of the Indians, named Weathersford, rode boldly up to Jackson's tent. "Kill him! kill him!" cried Jackson's men; but the general asked Weathersford into his tent. "You can kill me if you want to," said he to Jackson, "but I came to tell you that the Indian women and children are starving in the woods, and to ask you to help them, for they never did you any harm." General Jackson sent away Weathersford in safety, and ordered that corn should be given to feed the starving women and children. That act showed that he was as merciful as he was brave.

217. The British send war-ships to take New Orleans ; the great battle and the great victory. — These things happened during our second war with England, or the War of 1812. About a year after Jackson's victory over the Indians, the British sent an army in ships to take New Orleans.

General Jackson now went to New Orleans, to prevent the enemy from getting possession of the city.

About four miles below the city, which stands on the Mississippi River,[1] there was a broad, deep ditch, running from the river into a swamp. Jackson saw that the British would have to cross that ditch when they marched against the city. For that reason he built a high bank on the upper side of the ditch, and placed cannon along the top of the bank.

Early on Sunday morning, January 8, 1815, the British sent a rocket whizzing up into the sky ; a few minutes afterward they sent up a second one. It was the signal that they were about to march to attack us.

Just before the fight began, General Jackson walked along among his men, who were getting ready to defend the ditch. He said to them, " Stand to your guns ; see that every shot tells : give it to them, boys ! " The " boys " did give it to them. The British soldiers were brave men ; they had been in many terrible battles, and they were not afraid to die. They fought desperately; they tried again and again to cross that ditch and climb the bank, but they could not do it. The fire of our guns cut them down just as a mower cuts down the tall grain with his scythe.[2] In less than half an hour the great battle was over ; Jackson had won the victory and saved New Orleans. We lost only eight killed; the enemy lost over

1 See map on page 194.   2 Scythe (sithe).

two thousand.[1] We have never had a battle since with England; it is to be hoped that we never shall have another, for two great nations[2] like England and America, that speak the same language, ought to be firm and true friends.

218. We buy Florida; General Jackson made President of the United States; the first railroad. — After the battle of New Orleans, General Jackson conquered the Indians in

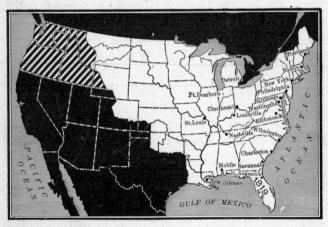

The light parts of this map show the extent of the United States in 1819, after we had bought and added Florida. The black and white bars in the northwest show that the ownership of the Oregon Country was still in dispute between the United States and Great Britain.

Florida; and in 1819 we bought that country of Spain, and so made the United States much larger on the south. This was our second great land purchase.[3]

Ten years after we got Florida, General Jackson became President of the United States. He had fought his way

[1] Killed and wounded.

[2] Nations: a nation is a people born in the same country and living under the same government; as the American nation, the French nation, the English nation.   [3] For our first land purchase, see page 168.

BATTLE OF NEW ORLEANS

(By Act of Congress of 1794 the number of stars and stripes on the national flag was
fixed at fifteen, to correspond with the whole number of states then in the Union;
the flag remained unchanged until 1518, when the present arrangement was
adopted, namely, thirteen stripes, and a star for every state.)

up. Here are the four steps: first the boy, "Andy Jackson"; then "Judge Jackson"; then "General Jackson"; last of all, "President Jackson."

Shortly after he became the chief ruler of the nation, the first steam railroad in the United States was built (1830).

THE GEORGETOWN LOOP
(Near Georgetown, Colorado.)

From that time such roads kept creeping further and further west. The Indians had frightened the white settlers with their terrible war-whoop. Now it was their turn to be frightened, for the locomotive whistle[1] could beat their wildest yell. They saw that the white man was coming

---

[1] The first steam railroad built in the United States extended from Baltimore to Ellicott's Mills, Maryland, a distance of twelve miles. It was opened in 1830. It forms a part of the Baltimore and Ohio Railroad.

as fast as steam could carry him, and that he was determined to get possession of the whole land. The greater part of the Indians moved across the Mississippi; but the white man kept following them, and following the buffalo, further and further across the country, toward the Pacific Ocean; and the railroad followed in the white man's track.

219. Summary.—Andrew Jackson of North Carolina, but later a citizen of Tennessee, gained a great victory over the Indians in Alabama and also in Florida. In 1815, in our second war with England, General Jackson whipped the British at New Orleans, and so prevented their getting possession of that city. A few years later we bought Florida of Spain.

After General Jackson became President of the United States, the first steam railroad was built in this country. Railroads helped to settle the west and build up states beyond the Mississippi.

Who fought the greatest battle on land of the War of 1812? Tell about Andrew Jackson's boyhood. Tell the story of the gun. Tell about Tarleton. What did Mrs. Jackson do? What did Andrew do? What did Andrew use to do at the blacksmith shop?

Tell about Tarleton's men and the bees. What did bands of armed men use to do in the country where Andrew lived? Tell about playing at battle. What did Tarleton say? Tell about Andrew and the boots. Tell how he saw a battle through a knot-hole. Tell how Andrew's mother died. What did he say about her? Tell about Andrew Jackson as a judge. Why was he made a general? Tell about Tecumseh and the Alabama Indians. After General Jackson had beaten the Indians, where did they go? What is said about the "Holy Ground"? What about Jackson and Weathersford? Tell about the great battle of New Orleans. Who gained the victory? When did we buy Florida? What were the four steps in Andrew Jackson's life? What is said about railroads?

XXIV. PROFESSOR MORSE

(1791-1872)

220. How they sent the news of the completion of the Erie Canal to New York City; Franklin and Morse. — The Erie Canal, in the state of New York, connects the Hudson River at Albany with Lake Erie at Buffalo. It is the greatest work of the kind in America, and was completed many years ago. When the water was let into the canal from the lake, the news was flashed from Buffalo to New York City by a row of cannon, about five miles apart,

How they flashed the News of the Completion of the
Erie Canal in 1825

which were fired as rapidly as possible, one after the other. The first cannon was fired at Buffalo at ten o'clock in the morning; the last was fired at New York at half-past eleven. In an hour and a half the sound had travelled over five hundred miles. Everybody said that was wonderfully quick work; but to-day we could send the news in less than a minute. The man who found out how to do this was Samuel F. B. Morse.

We have seen how Benjamin Franklin[1] discovered, by means of his kite, that lightning and electricity are

[1] See page 100.

the same.   Samuel Morse was born in Charlestown,[1] Massachusetts, about a mile from Franklin's birthplace, the year after that great man died.   He began his work where Franklin left off.   He said to himself, Dr. Franklin found out what lightning is ; I will find out how to harness it and make it carry news and deliver messages.[2]

221.   Morse becomes a painter ; what he thought might be done about sending messages. — When Samuel Morse was a little boy, he was fond of drawing pictures, particularly faces ; if he could not get a pencil, he would scratch them with a pin on the furniture at school : the only pay he got for making such pictures was some smart raps from the teacher.   After he became a man he learned to paint. At one time he lived in France with several other American artists.   One day they were talking of how long it took to get letters from America, and they were wishing the time could be shortened.   Somebody spoke of how cannon had been used at the time of the opening of the Erie Canal.   Morse was familiar with all that ; he had been educated at Yale College, and he knew that the sound of a gun will travel a mile while you are counting five; but, quick as that is, he wanted to find something better and quicker still.   He said, Why not try lightning or electricity ?   That will beat sound, for that will go more than a thousand miles while you are counting *one*.

222.   What a telegraph[3] is ; a wire telegraph; Professor Morse invents the electric telegraph. — Some time after that, Mr. Morse set sail for America.   On the way across the Atlantic he was constantly talking about

---

[1] Charlestown is now a part of the city of Boston.

[2] Messages: a message is any word sent by one person to another.

[3] Telegraph (tel′ e-graf) : this name is made up of two Greek words, the first of which means *far off*, and the second *to write*.

electricity and how a telegraph — that is, a machine which would write at a distance — might be invented. He thought about this so much that he could not sleep nights. At last he believed that he saw how he could make such a machine.

Suppose you take a straight and stiff piece of wire as long as your desk and fasten it in the middle so that the ends will swing easily. Next, tie a pencil tight to each end; then put a sheet of paper under the point of each pencil. Now, if you make a mark with the pencil nearest to you, you will find that the pencil at the other end of the wire will make the same kind of mark. Such a wire would

ONE KIND OF TELEGRAPH

be a kind of telegraph, because it would make marks or signs at a distance. Mr. Morse said: I will have a wire a mile long, with a pencil, or something sharp-pointed like a pencil, fastened to the further end; the wire itself shall not move at all, but the pencil shall, for I will make electricity run along the wire and move it. Mr. Morse was then a professor or teacher in the University of the City of New York. He put up such a wire in one of the rooms of the building, sent the electricity through it, and found that it made the pencil make just the marks he wanted it should; that meant that he had invented the *electric telegraph;* for if he could do this over a mile of wire, then what was to hinder his doing it over a hundred or even a thousand miles?

223. How Professor Morse lived while he was making his telegraph. — But all this was not done in a day, for this invention cost years of patient labor. At first, Mr. Morse lived in a little room by himself : there he worked

and ate, when he could get anything to eat ; and slept, if he was n't too tired to sleep. Later, he had a room in the university. While he was there he painted pictures to get money enough to buy food ; there, too (1839), he took the first photograph ever made in America. Yet, with all his hard work, there were times when he had to go hungry ; and once he told a young man that if he did not get some money he should be dead in a week — dead of starvation.

PROFESSOR MORSE AT WORK MAKING
HIS TELEGRAPH

224. Professor Morse gets help about his telegraph ; what Alfred Vail did. — But better times were coming. A young man named Alfred Vail[1] happened to see

---

[1] Alfred Vail: he was the son of Stephen Vail (commonly known as Judge Vail), owner of the Speedwell iron-works, near Morristown, New Jersey. Judge Vail built the engines of the *Savannah*, the first steamship which crossed the Atlantic.

Professor Morse's telegraph. He believed it would be successful. He persuaded his father, Judge Vail, to lend him two thousand dollars, and he became Professor Morse's partner in the work. Mr. Vail was an excellent mechanic, and he made many improvements in the telegraph. He then made a model[1] of it at his own expense, and took it to Washington and got a patent[2] for it in Professor Morse's name. The invention was now safe in one way, for no one else had the right to make a telegraph like his. Yet, though he had this help, Professor Morse did not get on very fast, for a few years later he said, " I have not a cent in the world; I am crushed for want of means."

225. Professor Morse asks Congress to help him build a telegraph line; what Congress thought. — Professor Morse now asked Congress to let him have thirty thousand dollars to construct a telegraph line from Washington to Baltimore. He felt sure that business men would be glad to send messages by telegraph, and to pay him for his work. But many members of Congress laughed at it, and said they might as well give Professor Morse the money to build "a railroad to the moon."

Week after week went by, and the last day that Congress would sit was reached, but still no money had been granted. Then came the last night of the last day

---

[1] Model: a small copy or representation of something. Professor Morse made a small telegraph and exhibited it in Washington, to show what his large telegraph would be like.

[2] Patent : a written or printed right given by the government at Washington to an inventor to make something; as, for instance, a telegraph or a sewing-machine. The patent forbids any one except the inventor, or holder of the patent, from making such a machine, and so he gets whatever money comes from his work. In order to get a patent, a man must send a model of his invention to be placed in the Patent Office at Washington.

(March 3, 1843). Professor Morse stayed in the Senate Chamber[1] of Congress until after ten o'clock; then, tired and disappointed, he went back to his hotel, thinking that he must give up trying to build his telegraph line.

226. Miss Annie Ellsworth brings good news. — The next morning Miss Annie G. Ellsworth met him as he was coming down to breakfast. She was the daughter of his friend who had charge of the Patent Office in Washington. She came forward with a smile, grasped his hand, and said that she had good news for him, that Congress had decided to let him have the money. Surely you must be mistaken, said the professor, for I waited last night until nearly midnight, and came away because nothing had been done. But, said the young lady, my father stayed until it was quite midnight, and a few minutes before the clock struck twelve Congress voted[2] the money; it was the very last thing that was done.

Professor Morse was then a gray-haired man over fifty. He had worked hard for years, and had got nothing for his labor. This was his first great success. He doesn't say whether he laughed or cried — perhaps he felt a little like doing both.

227. The first telegraph line built; the first message sent; the telegraph and the telephone[3] now. — When, at length,

[1] Senate Chamber: Congress (or the body of persons chosen to make the laws of the United States) is divided into two classes, — Representatives and Senators; they meet in different rooms or chambers in the Capitol at Washington. [2] Voted: here this word means given or granted.

[3] Telephone (tel'e-fone): this name is made up of two Greek words, the first of which means *far off*, and the second, *a voice* or *sound*. The telephone was invented by Professor Alexander G. Bell of Boston; he completed it in 1876. Professor Bell now lives in Washington. The late Elisha Gray of Illinois while living in Cleveland, Ohio, invented a telephone the same year that Professor Bell invented his; but the Bell telephone was the first one patented which became practically successful.

Professor Morse did speak, he said to Miss Ellsworth, "Now, Annie, when my line is built from Washington to Baltimore, you shall send the first message over it." In the spring of 1844 the line was completed, and Miss Ellsworth, by Professor Morse, sent these words over it (they are words taken from the Bible): "*What hath God wrought!*" [1]

For nearly a year after that the telegraph was free to all who wished to use it; then a small charge was made, a very short message costing only one cent. On the first of April, 1845, a man came into the office and bought a cent's worth of telegraphing. That was all

CHICAGO   DENVER

HOW A MESSAGE BY TELEGRAPH IS SENT [2]

the money which was taken that day for the use of forty miles of wire. Now there are about two million miles of telegraph wire in the United States, or enough to reach nearly eighty times round the earth, and the messages sent probably bring in a hundred thousand dollars a day. We can telegraph not only across America, but across the Atlantic Ocean, and even to China, by a line laid under the sea.[3] Professor Morse's invention made it possible to write by electricity; but now, by means of the

---

1 See Numbers xxiii. 23.

2 When the button at Chicago is pressed down, the electricity passing over the wire to Denver presses the point there down on the paper, and so makes a dot or dash which stands for a letter on the roll of paper as it passes under it. In this way words and messages are spelled out. The message on the strip of paper above is the question, *How is trade?*   3 See also page 271.

telephone,[1] a man in New York or Boston can talk with any one in Chicago, St. Louis, San Francisco, or in many other large cities, and the man listening at the other end of the wire can hear him and can talk with him in the same way. Professor Morse did not live to see this wonderful invention, which, in some ways, is an improvement even on his telegraph. (See the account of how Professor Alexander G. Bell invented the telephone, on page 289.)

228. Summary. — Professor Morse invented the electric telegraph. He received much help from Mr. Alfred Vail. In 1844, Professor Morse and Mr. Vail built the first line of telegraph in the United States, or in the world. It extended from Washington to Baltimore. The telegraph makes it possible for us to send a written message thousands of miles in a moment; by the telephone, which was invented by Professor Bell after Professor Morse's death, we can talk with people who are hundreds, yes, thousands, of miles away and hear what they say in reply.

Tell how they sent the news of the completion of the Erie Canal. What did Samuel Morse say to himself? Tell about Morse as a painter. What did he want to find? What was he talking about on his voyage back to America? What is a telegraph? How can you make a small wire telegraph? What did Professor Morse make? How did he live? What did he do in 1839? How did he get help about his telegraph? What did he ask Congress to do? What did some men in Congress say? What news did Miss Annie Ellsworth bring him? What was the first message sent by telegraph in 1844? How many miles of telegraph are there now in the United States? Is there a telegraph line under the sea? What is said about the telephone?

[1] There are now more than twenty millions of miles of telephone wire in use in the United States.

XXV. GENERAL SAM HOUSTON

(1793-1863)

229. Sam Houston and the Indians; Houston goes to live with the Indians. — When General Jackson whipped the Indians in Alabama,[1] a young man named Sam Houston [2] fought under Jackson and was terribly wounded. It was thought that the brave fellow would certainly die, but his strong will carried him through, and he lived to make himself a great name in the southwest.

Although Houston fought the Indians, yet, when a boy, he was very fond of them, and spent much of his time with them in the woods of Tennessee.

Long after he became a man, this love of the wild life led by the red men in the forest came back to him. While Houston was governor of Tennessee (1829) he suddenly made up his mind to leave his home and his friends, go across the Mississippi River, and take up his abode with an Indian tribe in that part of the country. The chief, who had known him as a boy, gave him a hearty welcome. " Rest with us," he said ; " my wigwam is yours." Houston stayed with the tribe three years.

230. Houston goes to Texas; what he said he would do; the murders at Alamo [3]; the flag with one star; what Houston did; Texas added to the United States; our war with Mexico. — At the end of that time he said to a friend, " I am going to Texas, and in that new country I will make a man of

[1] See page 191.   [3] Alamo (Al'a-mo).

[2] Sam Houston (Hew'ston): he always wrote his name Sam Houston; he was born near Lexington in Rockbridge County, Virginia.

myself." Texts then belonged to Mexico ; and President
Andrew Jackson had tried in vain to buy it as Jefferson
bought Louisiana.[1]   Houston said, " I will make it part of
the United States."   About twenty thousand Americans
had already moved into Texas, and they felt as he did.

War broke out between Texas and Mexico, and General
Sam Houston led the Texan soldiers in their fight for

" REMEMBER THE ALAMO ! "

independence.   He had many noted American pioneers [2]
and hunters in his little army : one of them was the
brave Colonel Travis [3] of Alabama ; another was Colonel

---

[1] See page 168.   [3] Travis (Tra'vis).
[2] Pioneers: those who go before to prepare the way for others; the first
settlers in a country are its pioneers.

Bowie [1] of Louisiana, the inventor of the "bowie knife"; still another was Colonel David Crockett of Tennessee, whose motto is a good one for every young American — "Be sure you're right, then — *go ahead.*"   Travis, Bowie, and Crockett, with a small force, held Fort Alamo, an old Spanish church in San Antonio.[2]   The Mexicans stormed the fort in overwhelming numbers and killed every man in it.

Not long after that, General Houston fought a great battle near the place where now stands the city called by his name.[3]   The Mexicans had more than two men to every one of Houston's ; but the Americans and Texans went into battle shouting the terrible cry *"Remember the Alamo !"* and the Mexicans fled before them, like frightened sheep.   Texas then became an independent state, and elected General Houston president.   The people of Texas raised a flag having on it a single star. For this reason the state was sometimes called, as it still is, the "Lone Star State."

THE "LONE STAR" FLAG

Texas was not contented to stand alone ; she begged the United States to add her to its great and growing family of states.   This was done [4] in 1845. But, as we shall presently see, a war soon broke out (1846) between the United States and Mexico, and when that war was ended we obtained a great deal more land at the west.

---

[1] Bowie (Bow'e).
[2] San Antonio (Săn An-to'ne-ō).
[3] See map on page 208.
[4] See map on page 208.

231. General Sam Houston in the great war between the North and the South ; what he said. — We have seen the part which General Sam Houston took in getting new country to add to the United States. He lived in Texas for many years after that. When, in 1861, the great war broke out between the North and the South, General Houston was governor of the state. He withdrew

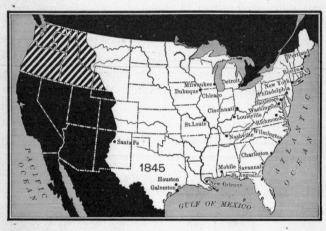

Map showing the extent of the United States after we added Texas in 1845. The black and white bars show that the ownership of the Oregon Country was still in dispute between the United States and Great Britain.

from office, and went home to his log cabin in Huntsville. He refused to take any part in the war, for he loved the Union, — that is, the whole country, North and South together, — and he said to his wife, " My heart is broken." Before the war ended, he was laid in his grave.[1]

[1] General Houston was buried at Huntsville, about eighty miles northwest of the city of Houston, Texas.

232. Summary. — General Sam Houston of Tennessee led the people of Texas in their war against Mexico. The Texans gained the victory, and made their country an independent state with General Houston as its president. After a time Texas was added to the United States. We then had a war with Mexico, and added a great deal more land at the west. General Houston died during the war between the North and the South.

Tell about Sam Houston and the Indians. Where did Houston go after he became governor of Tennessee? Where did Houston go next? What did he say he would do about Texas? What was David Crockett's motto? What is said about Fort Alamo? What about the battle with the Mexicans? What did Texas become? To what office was Houston elected? What is said of the Texas flag? When was Texas added to the United States? What war then broke out? What did we get by that war? What is said of General Houston in the great war between the North and the South?

XXVI. CAPTAIN ROBERT GRAY

(1755-1806)

233. Captain Gray goes to the Pacific coast to buy furs; he first carries the Stars and Stripes round the globe. — Not long after the war of the Revolution had come to an end some merchants of Boston sent out two vessels to Vancouver [1] Island, on the northwest coast of America. The names of the vessels were the *Columbia* and the *Lady Washington*, and they sailed down the long coast of North and South America and then round Cape Horn into the Pacific. Captain Robert Gray went out as commander of one of these vessels.[2] He was born

---

[1] Vancouver (Van-koo'ver): part of it is seen north of Portland, Or., p. 211.
[2] He commanded the *Lady Washington* at first, and afterward the *Columbia*.

in Rhode Island [1] and he had fought in one of our war-ships in the Revolution.

Captain Gray was sent out by the Boston merchants to buy furs from the Indians on the Pacific coast. He had no difficulty in getting all he wanted, for the savages were glad to sell them for very little. In one case a chief let the captain have two hundred sea-otter skins,

MOUNT HOOD

such as are used for ladies' sacks, and which were worth about eight thousand dollars, for an old iron chisel. After getting a valuable cargo of furs, Captain Gray sailed in the *Columbia* for China, where he bought a quantity of tea. He then went down the coast of Asia and of Africa, and round the Cape of Good Hope into the Atlantic; keeping on toward the west, he reached Boston in the summer of 1790. He had been gone

1 Tiverton, Rhode Island.

about three years ; and he was the first man who carried the American flag clear round the globe.

234. **Captain Gray's second voyage to the Pacific coast ; he enters a great river and names it the Columbia ; the United States claims the Oregon Country ; we get Oregon in 1846.** — Captain Gray did not stay long at Boston, for he sailed again that autumn in the *Columbia* for the Pacific coast,

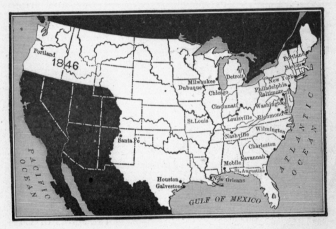

Map showing the extent of the United States after we added the Oregon Country in 1846.

to buy more furs. He stayed on that coast a long time. In the spring of 1792 he entered a great river and sailed up it a distance of nearly thirty miles. He seems to have been the first white man who had ever actually entered it. He named the vast stream the Columbia River, from the name of his vessel. It is the largest American river which empties into the Pacific Ocean south of Alaska.[1]

[1] The Yukon River in Alaska is larger than the Columbia.

Captain Gray returned to Boston and gave an account of his voyage of exploration; this led Congress to claim the country through which the Columbia

EMIGRANTS ON THEIR WAY TO OREGON
FIFTY YEARS AGO

flows [1] as part of the United States.

After Captain Gray had been dead forty years, we came into possession, in 1846, of the immense territory then called the Oregon Country. It was through what he had done that we got our first claim to that country which now forms the states of Oregon, Washington, and Idaho, and parts of Wyoming and Montana.

235. Summary. — A little over a hundred years ago (1790) Captain Robert Gray of Rhode Island first carried the American flag round the world. In 1792 he entered and named the Columbia River. Because he did that the United States claimed the country — called the Oregon Country — through which that river runs.

---

[1] The discovery and exploration of a river usually give the right to a claim to the country watered by that river, on the part of the nation to which the discoverer or explorer belongs.

In 1846 we added the Oregon Country to our possessions; it now forms the three great states of Oregon,
Washington, and Idaho.

Tell about Captain Gray's voyage to the Pacific coast. What did
he buy there? What did he first carry round the globe? Tell about
his second voyage. What did he do in 1792? What happened after
Captain Gray returned to Boston? What happened in 1846? What
states were made out of the Oregon Country?

XXVII. CAPTAIN SUTTER [1]

(1803–1880)

236. Captain Sutter and his fort; how the captain lived.—
At the time when Professor Morse sent his first message by telegraph from Washington to Baltimore (1844),[2]
Captain J. A. Sutter, an emigrant from Switzerland, was
living near the Sacramento [3] River in California. California then belonged to Mexico. The governor of that
part of the country had given Captain Sutter an
immense piece of land; and the captain had built a fort
at a point where a stream which he named the American River joins the Sacramento River.[4] People then
called the place Sutter's Fort, but to-day it is Sacramento City, the capital of the great and rich state of
California.

In his fort Captain Sutter lived like a king. He
owned land enough to make a thousand fair-sized farms;
he had twelve thousand head of cattle, more than ten
thousand sheep, and over two thousand horses and

---

[1] Sutter (Sut'er).   [3] Sacramento (Sac-ra-men'to).
[2] See page 203.   [4] See map on page 214.

mules. Hundreds of laborers worked for him in his wheatfields, and fifty well-armed soldiers guarded his fort. Quite a number of Americans had built houses near the fort. They thought that the time was coming when all that country would become part of the United States.

237. Captain Sutter builds a saw-mill at Coloma[1]; a man finds some sparkling dust. — About forty miles up the American River was a place which the Mexicans called

Coloma, or the beautiful valley. There was a good fall of water there and plenty of big trees to saw into boards, so Captain Sutter sent a man named Marshall to build a saw-mill at that place. The captain needed such a mill very much, for he wanted lumber to build with, and to fence his fields.

Marshall set to work, and before the end of January, 1848, he had built a dam across the river and had got the saw-mill half done. One day as he was walking along the bank of a ditch, which had been dug back of the mill to carry off the water, he saw some bright yellow specks shining in the dirt. He gathered a little of the sparkling dust, washed it clean, and carried it to the house. That evening after the men had come in from their work on the mill, Marshall said to them, "Boys, I believe I 've found a gold mine." They laughed, and one of them said, "I reckon not ; no such luck."

[1] Coloma (Ko-lo′ma).

238. Marshall takes the shining dust to Captain Sutter; what he did with it, and how he felt about the discovery. — A few days after that, Marshall went down to the fort to see Captain Sutter. Are you alone? he asked when he saw the captain. Yes, he answered. Well, won't you oblige me by locking the door; I've something I want to show you. The captain locked the door, and Marshall taking a little parcel out of his pocket opened it and poured some glittering dust on a paper he had spread out. " See here," said he, " I believe this is gold; but the people at the mill laugh at me and call me crazy."

Is it Gold?

Captain Sutter examined it carefully. He weighed it; he pounded it flat; he poured some strong acid on it. There are three very interesting things about gold. In the first place, it is very heavy, heavier even than lead. Next, it is very tough. If you hammer a piece of iron long enough, it will break to pieces; but you can hammer a piece of gold until it is thinner than the thinnest tissue paper, so that, if you hold it up, you can see the light shining through it. Last of all, if you pour strong acids on gold — such acids as will eat into other metals and change their color — they will have no more effect on it than an acid like vinegar has on a piece of glass.

For these and other reasons most people think that gold is a very handsome metal; and the more they see of it, especially if it is their own, the better they are pleased with it.

Well, the shining dust stood all these tests.[1]   It was very heavy, it was very tough, and the sharp acid did not hurt it.   Captain Sutter and Marshall both felt sure that it was *gold*.

But, strange to say, the captain was not pleased.   He wished to build up an American settlement and have

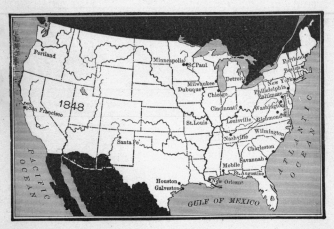

Map showing the extent of the United States in 1848, after Mexico let us have California and New Mexico.

it called by his name.   He did not care for a gold mine — why should he? for he had everything he wanted without it.   He was afraid, too, that if gold should be discovered in any quantity, thousands of people would rush in; they would dig up his land, and quite likely

[1] Tests: here experiments or trials made to find out what a thing is.

take it all away from him. We shall see presently whether he was right or not.

239. War with Mexico; Mexico lets us have California and New Mexico; "gold! gold! gold!" what happened at Coloma; how California was settled; what happened to Captain Sutter and to Marshall. — While these things were happening we had been at war with Mexico for two years (1846–1848), because Texas and Mexico could not agree about the western boundary line[1] of the new state. Texas wanted to push that line as far west as possible, so as to have more land; Mexico wanted to push it as far east as possible, so as to give as little land as she could. This dispute soon brought on a war between the United States and Mexico. Soon after gold was dis-

"GOLD! FROM THE AMERICAN RIVER!"

covered at Coloma, the war ended (1848); and we got not only all the land the people of Texas had asked for, but an immense deal more; for we obtained the great territory of California and New Mexico, out of

---

[1] Western boundary line: the people of Texas held that their state extended west as far as the Rio Grande River, but Mexico insisted that the boundary line was at the Nueces River, which is much further east.

which a number of states and territories have since been made.[1]

In May, 1848, a man came to San Francisco holding up a bottle full of gold-dust in one hand and swinging his hat with the other. As he walked through the streets he shouted with all his might, "Gold! gold! gold! from the American River."

Then the rush for Coloma began. Every man had a spade and a pick-axe. In a little while the beautiful valley was dug so full of holes that it looked like an empty honeycomb. The next year a hundred thousand people poured into California from all parts of the United States; so the discovery of gold filled up that part of the country with emigrants years before they would have gone if no gold had been found there.

Captain Sutter lost all his property. He would have died poor if the people of California had not given him money to live on.

Marshall was still more to be pitied. He got nothing by his discovery. Years after he had found the shining dust, some one wrote to him and asked him for his photograph. He refused to send it. He said, "My likeness . . . is, in fact, all I have that I can call my own; and I feel like any other poor wretch[2]: I want *something* for self."

240. How we bought more land; our growth since the Revolution. — Long before Captain Sutter died, the United States bought from Mexico another great piece of land (**1853**), marked on the map by the name of the Gadsden

---

[1] Namely: California, Nevada, Utah, and part of Wyoming, Colorado, New Mexico, and Arizona.

[2] Wretch: here a very unhappy and miserable person.

Purchase.[1] A number of years later (1867), we bought the territory of Alaska[2] from Russia.

The Revolution ended something over a hundred years ago. If you look on the map on page 168, and compare it with the maps which follow, you will see how we have grown during that time. Then we had

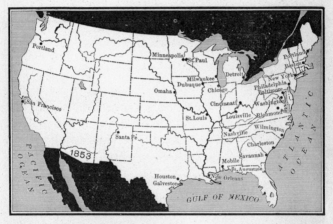

This map shows the extent of the United States in 1853 after we had added the land called the Gadsden Purchase, bought from Mexico; the land is marked on the map, 1853.

only thirteen states.[3] They stretched along the Atlantic, and, with the country west of them, extended as far as the Mississippi River.

Next (1803) we bought the great territory of Louisiana (see map on page 169), which has since been divided

[1] See map, page 220. It was called the Gadsden Purchase because General James Gadsden (Gads'den) of South Carolina bought it from Mexico for the United States, in 1853. It included what is now part of Southern Arizona and New Mexico.

[2] Alaska (A-las'ka); see map, page 220.

[3] Thirteen states; see note on page 84.

into many states; then (1819) we bought Florida (see map on page 194); then (1845) we added Texas (see map on page 208); the next year (1846) we added Oregon territory, since cut up into three great states

SCENE ON AN ALASKAN RIVER

(see map on page 211); then (1848) we obtained California and New Mexico (see map on page 216). Five years after that (1853) we bought the land then known as the Gadsden Purchase (see map on page 219); next (1867) we bought Alaska (see map on opposite page); then we annexed Hawaii [1] (1898), and now (1901) our

---

1 Hawaii (Hah-wy′ee), the Hawaiian or Sandwich Islands.

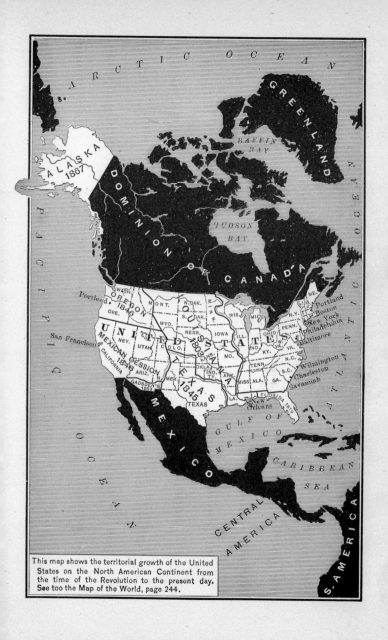

ARCTIC OCEAN

GREENLAND

BAFFIN
BAY

ALASKA
1867

DOMINION

PACIFIC

HUDSON
BAY

OF CANADA

WASH.
OREGON
1846
ORE.

MONT.

N.DAK.

Portland

WIS.

MICH.

ME.
Portland
Boston

N.Y.

New York
Philadelphia

ATLANTIC

San Francisco

UNITED

IDA.

WYO.

S.DAK.

NEBR.

IOWA

ILL.

OHIO

PENN.

Baltimore

LOUISIANA 1803

UTAH

COLO.

MO.

IND.

KY.

W.VA.

VA.

MEXICAN CESSION
1848

NEV.

CALIFORNIA

ARIZ.

STATES

KAN.

OKLA.
IND.
T'Y.

ARK.

TENN.

N.C.

Wilmington

N.MEX.

MISS.

ALA.

GA.

S.C.

Charleston

GADSDEN'S
1853

TEXAS
1845

(TEXAS)

LA.

New
Orleans

FLORIDA 1819

Savannah

OCEAN

MEXICO

GULF OF MEXICO

CARIBBEAN
SEA

OCEAN

CENTRAL

AMERICA

S. AMERICA

This map shows the territorial growth of the United
States on the North American Continent from
the time of the Revolution to the present day.
See too the Map of the World, page 244.

flag floats over a number of other islands in the Atlantic and the Pacific [1] (see map, page 244).

241. "Brother Jonathan's" [2] seven steps. — If you count up the additions we have made on the North American Continent, you will see that, beginning with Louisiana in 1803 and ending with Alaska in 1867, they number seven in all. There is a story of a giant who was so tall that at one long step he could go more than twenty miles ; but "Brother Jonathan" can beat that, for in the seven steps he has taken since the Revolution he has gone over three thousand miles. He stands now with one foot on the coast of the Atlantic, with the other on that of the Pacific, and he holds many islands in his grasp besides.

242. Summary. — In January, 1848, gold was discovered at Captain Sutter's saw-mill at Coloma, California. Soon after that, Mexico let us have California and New Mexico, and they were added to the United States. Thousands of people, from all parts of the country, hurried to California to dig gold ; and so that state grew more rapidly in population than any other new part of the United States ever had grown in the same length of time. Before Captain Sutter died we added the Gadsden Purchase and Alaska.

[1] That is, since our war with Spain, see pages 241, 252, and 253.

[2] "Brother Jonathan": a name given, in fun, to the people of the United States, just as "John Bull" is to the people of England.

One explanation of the origin of the name is this: General Washington had a very high opinion of the good sense and sound judgment of Governor Jonathan Trumbull of Connecticut. At the beginning of the Revolutionary War, when no one seemed to know where to get a supply of powder, General Washington said to his officers, "We must consult Brother Jonathan on this subject." Afterwards, when any serious difficulty arose, it became a common saying in the army that "We must consult Brother Jonathan," and in time the name came to stand for the American people.

Who was Captain Sutter? Where did he live? Tell how he lived. What did he begin to build at Coloma? Tell what Marshall found there, and what was said about it. Tell how Marshall took the shining dust to Captain Sutter, and what the captain did. What made them both certain that the dust was gold? Was the captain pleased with the discovery? What did he think would happen? What is said about our war with Mexico? What did we fight about? What did we get at the end of the war? What happened in May, 1848? Then what happened? How many people went to California? What happened to Captain Sutter? What is said about Marshall? What land did we buy in 1853? What in 1867?

How long ago did the Revolution end? How many states did we have then? [Can any one in the class tell how many we have now?] What land did we buy in 1803? In 1819? What did we add in 1845? In 1846? In 1848? What did we buy in 1853? In 1867? What islands did we annex in 1898? What other islands did we come into possession of the same year? How many additions have we made in all on the North American Continent? What could the giant do? What has "Brother Jonathan" done? Where is one foot? Where is the other?

XXVIII. ABRAHAM LINCOLN

(1809–1865)

243. The tall man from Illinois making his first speech in Congress; how he wrote his name; what the people called him. — Not many days before gold was found at Sutter's saw-mill[1] in California (1848), a tall, awkward-looking man from Illinois was making his first speech in Congress. At that time he generally wrote his name

A. Lincoln

but after he had become President of the United States, he often wrote it out in full, —

Abraham Lincoln

[1] See page 214.

The plain country people of Illinois, who knew all about him, liked best to call him by the title they had first given him, — "*Honest Abe Lincoln*," or, for short, "*Honest Abe.*"   Let us see how he got that name.

244. **The Lincoln family move to Indiana; "Abe" helps his father build a new home; what it was like.** — Abraham

ABRAHAM LINCOLN

Lincoln was born on February 12, 1809, in a log shanty on a lonely little farm in Kentucky.[1]   When "Abe," as he was called, was seven years old, his father, Thomas

[1] Lincoln's old log cabin is now owned by the nation, and a fine granite Memorial Building covers and protects it (see page 279).

Lincoln, moved, with his family, to Indiana[1]; there the boy and his mother worked in the woods and helped him build a new home. That new home was not so good or so comfortable as some of our cow-sheds are. It was simply a hut made of rough logs and limbs of trees. It had no door and no windows. One side of it was left entirely open; and if a roving Indian or a bear wanted to walk in to dinner, there was nothing whatever to stop him. In winter "Abe's" mother used to hang up some buffalo skins before this wide entrance to keep out the cold; but in summer the skins were taken down, so that living in such a cabin was the next thing to living out-of-doors.

245. The new log cabin with four sides to it; how the furniture was made; "Abe's" bed in the loft. — The Lincoln family stayed in that shed for about a year; then they moved into a new log cabin which they had built, and which had four sides to it. They seem to have made a new set of furniture for the new house. "Abe's" father got a large log, split it in two, smoothed off the flat side, bored holes in the under side, and drove in four stout sticks for legs; that made the table. They had no chairs, — it would have been too much trouble to make the backs, — but they had three-legged stools, which Thomas Lincoln made with an axe just as he did the table; perhaps "Abe" helped him drive in the legs.

In one corner of the loft of this cabin, the boy had a big bag of dry leaves for his bed. Whenever he felt like having a new bed, all that he had to do was to go out in the woods and gather more leaves.

[1] Indiana: the Lincoln family moved to a farm on Little Pigeon Creek, near Gentryville, in what is now Spencer County, Indiana.

He worked about the place during the day, helping his father and mother. For his supper he had a piece of cornbread. After he had eaten it, he climbed up to his loft in the dark, by a kind of ladder of wooden pins driven into the logs. Five minutes after that, he was fast asleep on his bed of sweet-smelling leaves, and was dreaming of hunting coons, or of building big bonfires out of brush.[1]

246. Death of " Abe's " mother; the lonely grave in the woods; what Abraham Lincoln said of his mother after he had grown to be a man; what " Abe's " new mother said of him. — " Abe's " mother was not strong; and, before they had been in their new log cabin a year, she fell sick and died. She was buried on the farm. " Abe " used to go out and sit by her lonely grave in the forest and cry. It was the first great sorrow that had ever touched the boy's heart. After he had grown to be a man, he said, with eyes full of tears, to a friend with whom he was talking: " God bless my mother; all that I am or ever hope to be I owe to her."

At the end of a year Thomas Lincoln married again. The new wife that he brought home was a kind-hearted and excellent woman. She did all she could to make the poor, ragged, barefooted boy happy. After he had grown up and become famous, she said: " Abe never gave me a cross word or look, and never refused to do anything I asked him; Abe was the best boy I ever saw."

247. The school in the woods; the new teacher; reading by the open fire; how " Abe " used the fire-shovel. — There was a log schoolhouse in the woods quite a distance off, and

1 Brush: bushes and limbs of trees.

there "Abe" went for a short time.   At the school he learned to read and write a little, but after a while he found a new teacher, that was — himself.   When the rest of the family had gone to bed, he would sit up and read his favorite books by the light of the great blazing

logs heaped up on the open fire.   He had not more than half a dozen books in all.   They were "Robinson Crusoe," "Pilgrim's Progress," Æsop's [1] Fables, the Bible, a Life of Washington, and a small History of the United States.   The boy read these books over and over till he knew a great deal of them by heart and could repeat whole pages from them.

Part of his evenings he spent in writing and

"Abe" and the Fire-Shovel

ciphering.   Thomas Lincoln was so poor that he could

[1] Æsop (E'sop): the name of a noted writer of fables.   Here is one of Æsop's fables: An old frog thought that he could blow himself up to be as big as an ox. So he drew in his breath and puffed himself out prodigiously.   "Am I big enough now?" he asked his son.   "No," said his son; "you don't begin to be as big as an ox yet."   Then he tried again, and swelled himself out still more. "How's that?" he asked.   "Oh, it's no use trying," said his son, "you can't do it."   "But I will," said the old frog.   With that he drew in his breath with all his might and puffed himself up to such an enormous size that he suddenly burst.

Moral: Don't try to be bigger than you can be.

seldom afford to buy paper and pens for his son, so the
boy had to get on without them. He used to take the back
of the broad wooden fire-shovel to write on and a piece of
charcoal for a pencil. When he had covered the shovel
with words or with sums in arithmetic, he would shave
it off clean and begin over again. If "Abe's" father
complained that the shovel was getting thin, the boy
would go out into the woods, cut down a tree, and make
a new one; for as long as the woods lasted, fire-shovels
and furniture were cheap.

**248. What Lincoln could do at seventeen; what he was at
nineteen; his strength.** — By the time the lad was seventeen he could write a good hand, do hard examples in
long division, and spell better than any one else in the
county. Once in a while he wrote a little piece of his
own about something which interested him; when he
read it to the neighbors, they would say, "The world
can't beat it."

At nineteen Abraham Lincoln had reached his full
height. He stood nearly six feet four inches, barefooted. He was a kind of good-natured giant. No one
in the neighborhood could strike an axe as deep into a
tree as he could, and few, if any, were equal to him in
strength. It takes a powerful man to put a barrel of flour
into a wagon without help, and there is not one in a
hundred who can lift a barrel of cider off the ground;
but it is said that young Lincoln could stoop down, lift a
barrel on to his knees, and drink from the bung-hole.

**249. Young Lincoln makes a voyage to New Orleans; how
he handled the robbers.** — At this time a neighbor hired
Abraham Lincoln to go with his son to New Orleans.
The two young men were to take a flatboat, loaded with

corn and other produce, down the Ohio and the Mississippi. It was called a voyage of about eighteen hundred miles, and it would take between three and four weeks.

Young Lincoln was greatly pleased with the thought of making such a trip. He had never been away any distance from home, and, as he told his father, he felt that he wanted to see something more of the world. His father made no objection, but as he bade his son good by he said, Take care that in trying to see the world you don't see the bottom of the Mississippi.

The two young men managed to get the boat through safely. But one night a gang of negroes came on board, intending to rob them of part of their cargo. Lincoln soon showed the robbers he could handle a club as vigorously as he could an axe ; and the rascals, bruised and bleeding, were glad to get off with their lives.

250. The Lincolns move to Illinois ; what Abraham did ; hunting frolics ; how Abraham chopped ; how he bought his clothes. — Not long after young Lincoln's return, his father moved to Illinois.[1] It was a two weeks' journey through the woods with ox-teams. Abraham helped his father build a comfortable log cabin ; then he and a man named John Hanks split walnut rails and fenced in fifteen acres of land for a cornfield.

That part of the country had but few settlers, and it was still full of wild beasts. When the men got tired of work and wanted a frolic, they had a grand wolf-hunt. First, a tall pole was set up in a clearing[2] ; next, the

---

[1] Illinois: he moved to a farm on the North Fork (or branch) of the Sangamon River (Săn′ga-mŏn), Macon County, Illinois. Springfield, the capital of the state, is in the next county west.

[2] Clearing: an open space made in a forest.

hunters in the woods formed a great circle of perhaps ten miles in extent. Then they began to move nearer and nearer together, beating the bushes and yelling with all their might. The frightened deer and other wild creatures inside of the circle of hunters were driven to the pole in the clearing; there they were shot down in heaps.

Young Lincoln was not much of a hunter, but he always tried to do his part. Yet, after all, he liked the axe better than he did the rifle.

He would start off before light in the morning and walk to his work in the woods, five or six miles away. There he would chop steadily all day. The neighbors knew when they hired him that he wouldn't sit down on the first log he came to and fall asleep. Once when he

THE LOG CABIN IN ILLINOIS WHICH LINCOLN HELPED HIS FATHER BUILD

needed a new pair of trousers, he made a bargain for them with a Mrs. Nancy Miller. She agreed to make him a certain number of yards of tow cloth,[1] and dye it brown with walnut bark. For every yard she made, Lincoln bound himself to split four hundred good fence-rails for her. In this way he made his axe pay for all his clothes.

1 Tow cloth: a kind of coarse, cheap, but very strong cloth, made of flax or hemp.

251. Lincoln hires out to tend store ; the gang of ruffians in New Salem ; Jack Armstrong and " Tall Abe." — The year after young Lincoln came of age he hired out to tend a grocery and variety store in New Salem, Illinois.[1] There was a gang of young ruffians in that neighborhood who made it a point to pick a fight with every stranger. Sometimes they mauled him black and blue ; sometimes they amused themselves with nailing him up in a hogshead and rolling him down a hill. The leader of this gang was a fellow named Jack Armstrong. He made up his mind that he would try his hand on "Tall Abe," as Lincoln was called. He attacked Lincoln, and he was so astonished at what happened to him that he never wanted to try it again. From that time Abraham Lincoln had no better friends than young Armstrong and the Armstrong family. Later on, we shall see what he was able to do for them.

252. Lincoln's faithfulness in little things ; the six cents ; " Honest Abe." — In his work in the store Lincoln soon won everybody's respect and confidence. He was faithful in little things, and in that way he made himself able to deal with great ones.

Once a woman made a mistake in paying for something she had bought, and gave the young man six cents too much. He did not notice it at the time, but, after his customer had gone, he saw that she had overpaid him. That night after the store was closed, Lincoln walked to the woman's house, some five or six miles out of the village, and paid her back the six cents. It was such things as this that first made the people give him the name of "Honest Abe."

---

[1] New Salem is on the Sangamon River, in Menard County, about twenty miles northwest of Springfield, the capital of Illinois.

253. The Black Hawk War ; the Indian's handful of dry leaves ; what Lincoln did in the war. — The next year Lincoln went to fight the Indians in what was called the Black Hawk War. The people in that part of the country had been expecting the war ; for, some time before, an Indian had walked up to a settler's cabin and said, " Too much white man." He then threw a handful of dry leaves into the air, to show how he and his warriors were coming to scatter the white men. He never came, but a noted chief named Black Hawk, who had been a friend of Tecumseh's,[1] made an attempt to drive out the settlers and get back the lands which certain Indians had sold them.

Lincoln said that the only battles he fought in this war were with the mosquitoes. He did not kill a single Indian, but he saved the life of one old savage. He seems to have felt just as well satisfied with himself for doing that as though he had shot him through the head.

254. Lincoln becomes postmaster and surveyor ; how he studied law ; what the people thought of him as a lawyer. — After Lincoln returned from the war he was made postmaster of New Salem. He also found time to do some surveying and to begin the study of law. On hot summer mornings he might be seen lying on his back, on the grass, under a big tree, reading a law-book ; as the shade moved round, Lincoln would move with it, so that, by sundown, he had travelled nearly round the tree.

When he began to practise law, everybody who knew him had confidence in him. Other men might be admired because they were smart, but Lincoln was respected because he was honest. When he said a thing, people

[1] Tecumseh ; see page 180.

knew that it was because he believed it; and they knew, too, that he could not be hired to say what he did not believe.   That gave him immense influence.

255. The Armstrong murder trial; how Lincoln saved young Armstrong from being hanged. — But Lincoln was as keen as he was truthful and honest — or perhaps, it would be better to say he was keen because he was truthful and honest.   A man was killed in a fight near where Lincoln had lived, and one of Jack Armstrong's[1] brothers was arrested for the murder.   Everybody thought that he was guilty, and felt sure that he would be hanged. Lincoln made some inquiry about the case, and made up his mind that the prisoner did not kill the man.

Mrs. Armstrong was too poor to hire a lawyer to defend her son; but Lincoln wrote to her that he would gladly defend him for nothing.

When the day of the trial came, the chief witness was sure that he saw young Armstrong strike the man dead. Lincoln questioned him closely.   He asked him when it was that he saw the murder committed.   The witness said that it was in the evening, at a certain hour, and that he saw it all clearly because there was a bright moon.   Are you sure? asked Lincoln.   Yes, replied the witness.   Do you swear to it?   I do, answered the witness.   Then Lincoln took an almanac out of his pocket, turned to the day of the month on which the murder had been committed, and said to the court: The almanac shows that there was no moon shining at the time at which the witness says he saw the murder.[2]   The jury

[1] See Jack Armstrong, on page 230.

[2] The almanac usually gives the time when the moon rises; and so by looking at any particular day of the month, one can tell whether there was a moon on that evening.

was convinced that the witness had not spoken the truth; they declared the prisoner "Not guilty," and he was at once set free.

Lincoln was a man who always paid his debts. Mrs. Armstrong had been very kind to him when he was poor and friendless. Now he had paid that debt.

256. Lincoln and the pig.—Some men have hearts big enough to be kind to their fellow-men when they are in trouble, but not to a dumb animal. Lincoln's heart was big enough for both.

LINCOLN AND THE PIG

One morning just after he had bought a new suit of clothes he started to drive to the court-house, a number of miles distant. On the way, he saw a pig that was making desperate efforts to climb out of a deep mud-hole. The creature would get part way up the slippery bank, and then slide back again over his head in mire and water. Lincoln said to himself: I suppose that I ought to get out and help that pig; for if he's left there, he'll smother in the mud. Then he gave a look at his glossy new clothes. He felt that he really couldn't afford to spoil them for the sake of any pig, so he whipped up his horse and drove on. But the pig was in his mind, and he could think of nothing else. After he had gone about two miles, he said to himself, I've no right to leave that poor creature there to die in the mud, and what is more, I won't leave him. Turning his horse, he drove back to the spot. He got out and carried half a dozen fence-rails to the edge of the hole, and placed them so that he could get to it without falling in himself. Then, kneeling down, he bent over, seized the pig firmly by the fore legs and drew him up on to the solid ground, where he was safe. The pig grunted out his best thanks, and Lincoln, plastered with mud, but with a light heart, drove on to the court-house.

257. Lincoln is elected to the state legislature; he goes to Springfield to live; he is elected to Congress. — Many people in Illinois thought that they would like to see such a man in the state legislature,[1] helping to make their laws. They knew they could trust him. They elected him; and as he was too poor at that time to pay so much horse-hire, he walked from New Salem, a distance of over a hundred miles, to Vandalia,[2] which was then the capital of the state.

Lincoln was elected to the legislature four times; later, he moved to Springfield, Illinois, and made that place his home for the rest of his life.

The next time the people elected him to office, they sent him to Washington to help make laws in Congress, not for his state only, but for the whole country. He had got a long way up since the time when he worked with John Hanks[3] fencing the cornfield round his father's cabin; but he was going higher still, — he was going to the top.

---

[1] Legislature: persons chosen by the people of a state or country to make its laws.   [2] Vandalia (Van-dā'li-a).

[3] John Hanks; see page 228.

258. The meeting for choosing a candidate [1] for President of the United States; the two fence-rails; the Chicago meeting; Abraham Lincoln elected President of the United States.—In the spring of 1860 a great convention, or meeting, was held in one of the towns of Illinois. Lincoln was present at that convention. The object of the people who had gathered there was to choose a candidate that they would like to see elected President of the United States. A number of speeches had been made, when a member of the convention rose and said that a person asked the privilege of making the meeting a present. It was voted to receive it. Then John Hanks and one of his neighbors brought in two old fence-rails and a banner with these words painted on it :—

> ABRAHAM LINCOLN,
> THE RAIL CANDIDATE FOR THE PRESIDENCY
> IN 1860.
> TWO RAILS FROM A LOT OF 3000
> MADE IN 1830
> BY JOHN HANKS AND ABE LINCOLN.

The rails were received with cheer after cheer; and Lincoln was chosen candidate. About a week after that a much greater meeting was held in Chicago, and he was chosen there in the same way. The next November Abraham Lincoln, "the Illinois rail-splitter," was elected

[1] Candidate (can'di-date): a person who seeks some office, such as that of governor or president, or a person who is recommended by a party for such an office. The people in favor of the candidate vote for him; and if he gets a sufficient number of votes, he is elected.

President of the United States. He had reached the top. There he was to die.

259. The great war between the North and the South ; why a large part of the people of the South wished to leave the Union. — In less than six weeks after Lincoln actually became President, in the spring of 1861, a terrible war broke out between the North and the South. The people of South Carolina fired the first gun in that war. They, together with a great part of the people of ten other southern states, resolved to leave the Union.[1] They set up an independent government, called the Confederate States of America, and made Jefferson Davis its president.

The main reason why so many of the people of the South wished to withdraw from the United States was that, little by little, the North and the South had become like two different countries.

At the time of the Revolution, when we broke away from the rule of England, every one of the states held negro slaves ; but in the course of eighty years a great change had taken place. The negroes at the North had become free, but those of the South still remained slaves. In the course of time, all labor at the North had come to be done by free white men, while nearly all the hard work at the South was done by black men who were not free. This difference in the way of doing work made it impossible for the North and the South to agree about many things.

[1] Union: several years after the close of the Revolutionary War, by which we gained our independence of Great Britain, the people of the thirteen states formed a new government. That new government bound all the states together more strongly than before, thus making, as was then said, "a more *perfect union.*"

In 1861 eleven of the southern states endeavored to withdraw from the Union; this attempt brought on the war.

They had come to be like two boys in a boat who want to go in opposite directions. One pulls one way with his oars, the other pulls another way, and so the boat does not get ahead.

At the South most of the people thought that slavery was right and that it helped the whole country; at the North the greater part of the people were convinced that it was wrong, and that it did harm to the whole country.

But this was not all. The people who held slaves at the South wanted to add to the number. They hoped to get more of the new country west of the Mississippi River for slave states, so that there might always be at least as many slave states in the Union as there were free states. But Abraham Lincoln, like most of the people at the North, believed that slavery did no good to any one. He and his party were fully determined that no slaves whatever should be taken into the territories west of the Mississippi River, and that every new state which should be added should be entirely free.

For this reason it happened, that when Lincoln became President, most of the slave states resolved to leave the Union, and, if necessary, to make war rather than be compelled to stay in it.

260. The North and the South in the war; President Lincoln frees the slaves; General Grant and General Lee; peace is made. — The North had the most fighting men and the most money; but the people of the South had the advantage of being able to stay at home and fight on their own ground.

The war lasted four years (1861-1865). Many terrible battles were fought, and thousands of brave men were killed on both sides. During the war President Lincoln gave the slaves their freedom in all the states which were fighting against the Union, and those in the other slave states got their freedom later. After a time, the command of all the armies of the North was given to General Grant, and General Lee became the chief defender of the South.

The last battles between these two great generals were fought around Richmond, Virginia. When the Southern soldiers saw that it was useless to attempt to fight longer, they laid down their arms, and peace was made — a peace honorable to both sides.

261. The success of the North preserves the Union and makes all slaves free ; the North and the South shake hands ; murder of President Lincoln. — The success of the North in the war preserved the Union ; and, as all negro laborers were now free, there was no longer any dispute about slavery. The North and the South could shake hands and be friends, for both were now ready to pull in the same direction.

The saddest thing at the close of the war was the murder of President Lincoln by a madman named Booth. Not only the people of the North, but many of those at the South, shed tears at his death, because they felt that they had an equal place in his great heart. He loved both, as a true American must ever love his whole country.

262. Summary. — Abraham Lincoln, of Illinois, became President of the United States in 1861. He was elected by a party in the North that was determined that slaves should not be taken into free states or territories, and that no more slave states should be made. On this account most of the slave-holding states of the South resolved to withdraw from the Union. A great war followed, and President Lincoln gave the slaves their freedom. The North succeeded in the war, and the Union was made stronger than ever; because the North and the South could no longer have any dispute over slavery. Both sides now shook hands and became friends.

Who was the tall man in Congress from Illinois? What did the people of his state like to call him? When was Abraham Lincoln born? Where was he born? To what state did his father move? Tell about "Abe's" new home. Tell about the new cabin and its furniture. Tell about "Abe's" bed. What is said about the boy's mother? What did "Abe" do? What did he say after he became a man? What did Thomas Lincoln's new wife say about "Abe"? Tell about "Abe's" going to school; about his new teacher; about his books. What did he use to write on? What is said of Abraham Lincoln at seventeen? What about him when he was nineteen? Tell about his voyage to New Orleans.

Tell about his moving to Illinois. What did Abraham Lincoln and John Hanks do? Tell about the hunting frolics. Tell how Lincoln chopped in the woods. What kind of a bargain did he make for a new pair of trousers? What did Abraham Lincoln hire out to do in New Salem? Tell about the gang of ruffians. What is said of Jack Armstrong? Why did Lincoln get the name of "Honest Abe"? Tell about the Black Hawk War. What did Lincoln do in that war?

After he returned from the Black Hawk War, what did Lincoln do? Tell how he used to read law. What did people think of him after he began to practise law? Tell about the Armstrong murder trial. Tell about Lincoln and the pig. To what did the people of Illinois elect Lincoln? Did they ever elect him to the state legislature again? Then where did they send him? Was he going any higher?

Tell about the great meeting in one of the towns of Illinois in 1860. Can any one in the class repeat what was on the banner? What happened at Chicago? What happened the next November? What happened in the spring of 1861? Who fired the first gun in the war? What was done then?

Tell why so many people in the South wished to leave the Union? What is said about negro slaves at the time of the Revolution? What happened in the course of eighty years? What had the North and the South come to be like? How did most of the people at the South feel about slavery? How did most of the people at the North feel about it? What did the people who held slaves at the South want to do? What did most of the people at the North think about this? What is said about Abraham Lincoln and his party? How did most of the people of the slave states feel when Lincoln became President?

What is said about the North and the South in the war? How long did the war last? What is said about it? What did President Lincoln do for the slaves? After a time what general got the command of all the armies of the North? Who became the chief defender of the South? Where were the last battles fought? What did the South do at last? What happened then? What did the success of the North do? What is said about slavery? What could the North and the South do? What was the saddest thing which happened at the close of the war? How did the North and the South feel about President Lincoln?

XXIX. SINCE THE CIVIL WAR — THE GREAT WAR

263. How the North and the South have grown since the war; the great West. — Since the war the united North and South have grown and prospered[1] as never before. At the South many new and flourishing towns and cities have sprung up. Mines of coal and iron have been opened, hundreds of cotton-mills and factories have been built, and long lines of railroads have been constructed.

At the West even greater changes have taken place. Cities have risen up in the wilderness, mines of silver and gold have been opened, and immense farms and cattle ranches[2] produce food enough to feed all America. Many great lines of railroads have been built which connect with railroads at the East, and stretch across the continent from the Atlantic to the Pacific. Into that vast country beyond the Mississippi, hundreds of thousands of industrious people are moving from all parts of the earth, and are building homes for themselves and for their children.

264. Celebration of the discovery of America by Columbus. — More than four hundred years have gone by since the first civilized man crossed the ocean and found this

---

[1] Prospered: to prosper is to succeed, to get on in life, to grow rich.

[2] Ranches (ran´chez): farms at the West for raising horses and cattle, or sheep.

new world which we call America. In 1893 we celebrated that discovery made by Columbus, not only in
the schools throughout the country, but by a great fair
— called the "World's Columbian Exposition" — held
at Chicago. There, on
the low shores of Lake
Michigan, on what
was once a swamp,
the people of the
West had built a
great city. They
had built it, too,
where a United
States govern-
ment engineer
had said that it
was simply impos-
sible to do such a
thing, and in 1893
Chicago had more
than a million of
inhabitants. Mul-
titudes of people

THE MEETING OF THE ENGINES
FROM THE EAST AND THE WEST AFTER THE LAST
SPIKE WAS DRIVEN [1] ON THE COMPLETION OF
THE FIRST RAILROAD TO THE PACIFIC IN 1869

from every state in the Union visited the exposition, and
many came from all parts of the globe to see it.

265. Our Hundred Days' War with Spain.[2] — A little less
than five years after the opening of the Columbian

1 The last spikes (one of gold from California, one of silver from Nevada, and
one made of gold, silver, and iron from Arizona) were driven just as the clock
struck twelve (noon) on May 10th, 1869, at Promontory Point, near Salt Lake,
Utah. Every blow of the hammer was telegraphed throughout the United States.

2 In all, the war lasted from April 21, 1898, to August 12, 1898, but Congress
did not formally declare war until April 25. The fighting covered one hundred
and seven days — namely from May 1 to August 15.

Exposition we declared war against Spain.   It was the first time we had crossed swords with any nation of Europe since General Jackson won the famous battle of New Orleans [1] in the War of 1812 with Great Britain.

When Major McKinley became President (1897) we had no expectation of fighting Spain.   The contest came suddenly, and Cuba was the cause of it.   Spain once

HOW THEY USED TO SHOOT BUFFALO IN THE FAR WEST

owned not only all the large islands in the West Indies, which Columbus had discovered,[2] but held Mexico and Florida, and the greater part of that vast country west of the Mississippi, which has now belonged to the United States for many years.   Piece by piece Spain lost the whole of these enormous possessions, until at last she had nothing left but the two islands of Cuba and Porto Rico.

[1] See page 193.   [2] See page 10.

266. The rebellion in Cuba. — Many of the Cubans hated Spanish rule, and with good reason. They made several attempts to rid themselves of it and fought for ten years (1868–1878), but without success. Finally, in the spring of 1895, they took up arms again, and with the battle cry of "Independence or death!" they set to work in grim earnest to drive out the Spaniards. Spain was determined to crush the rebellion. She sent over thousands of soldiers to accomplish it. The desperate fight continued to go on year after year, until it looked as though the whole island — which Columbus said was

INDIANS ATTACKING A STAGE-COACH IN THE FAR WEST MANY YEARS AGO, BEFORE THE FIRST PACIFIC RAILROAD WAS BUILT

the most beautiful he had ever seen — would be converted into a wilderness covered with graves and ruins. In the course of the war great numbers of peaceful Cuban farmers were driven from their homes and starved to death; and many Americans who had bought sugar and tobacco plantations saw all their property, worth from $30,000,000 to $50,000,000, utterly destroyed.

267. The destruction of the *Maine*. — Cuba is about the size of the State of Pennsylvania. It is our nearest island neighbor on the south, and is almost in sight from Key West, Florida. The people of the United States could not look on the war of devastation unmoved. While we were sending ship-loads of food to feed the starving Cubans, it was both natural and right that we should earnestly hope that the terrible struggle might be speedily brought to an end.

Our Government first urged and then demanded that Spain should try to make peace in the island. Spain did try, tried honestly so far as we can see, but failed. The Cuban Revolutionists had no faith in Spanish promises; they positively refused to accept anything short of separation and independence. Spain was poor and proud; she replied that come what might she would not give up Cuba.

While we were waiting to see what should be done a terrible event happened. We had sent Captain Sigsbee[1] in command of the battle-ship *Maine* to visit Havana. In the night (February 15, 1898), while the *Maine* was lying in that port, she was blown up. Out of three hundred and fifty-three officers and men on board the vessel, two hundred and sixty-six were instantly killed, or were so badly hurt that they died soon after. We appointed a Court of Inquiry, composed of naval officers, to examine the wreck. After a long and careful investigation of all the facts, they reported that the *Maine* had been blown up by a mine[2] planted in the harbor or placed under her

---

[1] Sigsbee (Sigs'bee).

[2] Mine : here this word means a quantity of powder or some other explosive substance placed under water for the purpose of blowing up a vessel. See account of Fulton's torpedo on page 174.

ISLAND POSSESSIONS, AMERICA
UNITED STATES

SHOWN IN BLACK

NOTE.—The total distance from San Francisco
to Manila, via Hawaii and Guam, is 8100
Statute Miles, and to China 8600 Miles.

THE M'N.CO.

hull. Whether the mine was exploded by accident or by design, or who did the fatal work, was more than the Court could say.

268. Declaration of war and the blockade of Cuba. — President McKinley sent a special message to Congress in which he said, "The war in Cuba must stop." Soon afterward Congress resolved that the people of Cuba "are, and of right ought to be, free and independent." [1] They also resolved that if Spain did not proceed at once to withdraw her soldiers from the island, we would take measures to make her do it. Spain refused to withdraw her army, and war was forthwith declared by both nations.

The President then sent Captain Sampson [2] with a fleet of war-ships to blockade Havana and other Cuban ports, so that the Spaniards should not get help from Spain to carry on the contest. He next put Commodore Schley [3] in command of a "flying squadron" of fast war-vessels, so that he might stand ready to act when called upon.

269. Dewey's victory at Manila. — In the Pacific Spain owned the group of islands called the Philippines. [4] Many of the people of those islands had long been discontented with their government, and when the Cubans rose in revolt against Spain it stirred the inhabitants of the Philippines to begin a struggle for liberty. They, too, were fighting for independence.

[1] See page 253 on the vote of the Cuban people in 1901 accepting the guardianship and protection of the United States.

[2] Captain William T. Sampson, who was then "Acting Rear-Admiral," has since been promoted to the full rank of Rear-Admiral, and so, too, has Commodore Winfield Scott Schley.   [3] Schley (Shlī).

[4] Philippine Islands, or the Philippines (Fil'ip-peens); see the Map of the World, page 244.

President McKinley resolved to strike two blows at once, and while we hit Spain in Cuba, to hit her at the same time at Manila,[1] the capital of the Philippines.   It

BATTLE OF MANILA

happened, fortunately for us, that Commodore Dewey[2] had a fleet of six war-ships at Hong Kong, China.

[1] Manila (Man-il′ah).   [2] Commodore George Dewey — now Admiral Dewey.

The President telegraphed to him to start at once for Manila and to "capture or destroy" the Spanish fleet which guarded that important port. The Spaniards at that place were brave men who were determined to hold Manila against all attack; they had forts to help them; they had twice as many vessels as Commodore Dewey had; on the other hand, our vessels were larger and better armed; best of all, our men could fire straight, which was more than the Spaniards knew how to do.

Commodore Dewey carried out his orders to the letter. On the first day of May (1898) he sent a despatch to the President, saying that he had just fought a battle and had knocked every Spanish war-ship to pieces without losing a single man in the fight. The victorious Americans took good care of the wounded Spaniards.

The President at once sent General Merritt from San Francisco with a large number of soldiers to join Commodore Dewey. Congress voted the "Hero of Manila" a sword of honor, and the President, with the consent of the Senate of the United States, made him Rear-Admiral, and later Admiral, thus giving him the highest rank to which he could be promoted in the navy.

270. Cervera " bottled up " ; Hobson's brave deed. — Spain had lost one fleet, but she still had another and a far more powerful one under the command of Admiral Cervera.[1] Where Cervera was we did not know — for anything we could tell he might be coming across the Atlantic to suddenly attack New York or Boston or some other of our cities on the Atlantic coast. The

[1] Cervera: English pronunciation Sur-vee′rah.

President sent Commodore Schley with his "flying squadron" to find the Spanish fleet. After a long search the Commodore discovered that the Spanish war-ships had secretly run into the harbor of Santiago [1] on the southeastern coast of Cuba.

A day or two afterward Captain Sampson with a number of war-vessels went to Santiago and took command of our combined fleet in front of that port. One of Captain Sampson's vessels was the famous battle-ship *Oregon*, which had come from San Francisco round South America, a voyage of about thirteen thousand miles, in order to take a hand in the coming fight.

The entrance to the harbor of Santiago is by a long, narrow, crooked channel guarded by forts. We could not enter it without great risk of losing our ships. It was plain enough that we had "bottled up" Cervera's fleet, and so long as Cervera remained there he could do us no harm. But there was a chance, in spite of our watching the entrance to the harbor as a cat watches a mouse-hole, that the Spanish commander might, after all, slip out of his hiding-place and under cover of darkness or fog escape our guns.

Captain Sampson believed that he saw a way by which he could effectually cork the bottle and make Cervera's escape impossible. By permission of Captain Sampson, Lieutenant [2] Hobson proceeded to carry out his daring scheme. With the help of seven sailors, who were eager to go with him at the risk of almost certain death, Hobson ran the coal ship *Merrimac* into the narrow channel, and by exploding torpedoes sank

---

[1] Santiago (San-te-ah'go).

[2] Lieutenant (Loo-ten'ant), an officer in the navy below the rank of captain.

the vessel part way across it. Then he and his men jumped into the water to save themselves as best they could. It was one of the bravest deeds ever done in war and will never be forgotten. The Spaniards captured Hobson and his men, but they treated them well, and after a time sent all of them back to us in exchange for Spanish prisoners of war.

271. Fighting near Santiago ; the " Rough Riders " ; Cervera caught. — A few weeks later General Shafter landed a large number of American soldiers on the coast of Cuba near Santiago. The force included General Wheeler's cavalry, and among them were the " Rough Riders." A good many of these " Rough Riders " had been Western " cowboys " ; Colonel Roosevelt was one of their leaders, and on horseback or on foot they were a match for anything, whether man or beast.

The Americans at once set out to find the enemy. The Spaniards had hidden in the underbrush, where they could fire on us without being seen. They opened the battle, and as they used smokeless powder, it was difficult for our men to tell where the rifle balls came from or how to reply to them. But in the end, after pretty sharp fighting, we got possession of some high ground from which we could plainly see Santiago, where Cervera's fleet lay concealed behind the hills.

A week later our regular soldiers, with the " Rough Riders " and other volunteers, stormed up the steep heights,[1] drove the Spaniards pellmell into Santiago, and

[1] Of El Caney and San Juan (San Wahn), suburbs of Santiago. The battles of El Caney and San Juan were fought mainly by the " regulars " — that is, by the soldiers of the regular standing army of the United States. Volunteers are men who enlist to fight in a war but do not belong to the regular standing or permanent army of the country.

forced them to take refuge behind the earthworks which protected the town.

Meanwhile Captain Sampson had gone to consult with General Shafter. While he was absent Commodore Schley and the other commanders of the fleet kept up a sharp lookout for Cervera, who was anxious to escape.

On Sunday morning, July 3 (1898), a great shout was sent up from the flagship *Brooklyn*, and another from Captain Evans's ship, the *Iowa:* "The Spaniards are coming out of the harbor!" It was true, for the sunken *Merrimac* had only half corked the bottle after all, and Cervera was making a dash out, hoping to reach the broad Atlantic before we could hit him.

Then all was excitement. "Open fire!" shouted Schley. We did open fire. The Spanish Admiral was a brave man; he did the best he could with his guns to answer us, but it was of no use, and in less than three hours all of the enemy's fleet were helpless, blazing wrecks. Cervera himself barely escaped with his life. He was rescued by the crew of the *Gloucester;* as he came on board that ship, Commander Wainwright said to him, "I congratulate you, sir, on having made a most gallant fight." When not long afterward one of our cruisers[1] reached Portsmouth, New Hampshire, with Cervera and more than seven hundred other prisoners of war taken in the battle, the people sent up cheer after cheer for the Spanish Admiral who had treated Lieutenant Hobson and his men so handsomely.

272. The end of the war; what the "Red Cross Society" did. — Soon after this crushing defeat the Spaniards surrendered Santiago. Next Porto Rico[2] surrendered

---

[1] Cruisers (krew′zers), vessels of war.   [2] Porto Rico (Por′to Rēē′kō).

to General Miles. By that time Spain had given up the struggle and begged for peace. An agreement for making a treaty of peace was signed at Washington (August 12, 1898). Our Government at once sent a despatch to our forces at the Philippines ordering them to

CHARGE UP SAN JUAN HILL

stop fighting. Before the despatch could get there, Rear-Admiral Dewey and General Merritt had taken Manila.

The war was not without its bright side. That was the noble work done by the "American Red Cross Society" under Clara Barton. They labored on battle-fields and in hospitals to help the wounded and the sick of both armies, and to soothe the last moments of the dying.   Many a poor fellow who was called to lay down his life for the American cause, and many another who fell fighting for Spain, blessed the kind hands that did everything that human power could do to relieve their suffering.   For the " Red Cross " helpers and nurses treated all alike.   They did not ask under what flag a

"The Red Cross"

man served or what language he spoke — it was enough for them to know that he needed their aid. So, too, it is pleasant to find that the Spanish prisoners of war were so well treated by our people that when they sailed for Spain they hurrahed for America and the Americans with all their might.

While the war was going on we peacefully annexed the Republic of Hawaii,[1] or the Sandwich Islands (July 7, 1898). Before the end of the contest with Spain our flag waved above those islands, as a sign that they had become part of the territory of the United States.   Later, it floated, as a sign of conquest, over Porto Rico, Manila, the capital of the Philippines, and

[1] Hawaii: pronounced (Hah-wy'ee). See page 220, and the Map of the World, page 244.

Guam,[1] the principal island of the Ladrones, in the Pacific. On New Year's Day, 1899, the Spanish colors were hauled down at Havana, and the stars and stripes took their place, as our sign of guardianship over Cuba.

Less than three years later (1901) the people of Cuba declared themselves independent. At the same time they voted to accept the friendly offer of the United States to continue to watch over life, liberty, and property in that island. In 1902 we withdrew the American flag and acknowledged the independence of the Republic of Cuba.[2]

It will be remembered that Havana is the city in which Columbus was believed to be buried.[3] By order of the Queen of Spain, his remains were sent back after the war (December 12, 1898) to the city of Valladolid,[4] his old home in Spain.[5] To-day the Spaniards have nothing left on this side of the Atlantic which they can call their own — not even the corpse of the great navigator who discovered the New World, unless by chance his body still rests in the old church in San Domingo.[6]

Many of our people wish to keep all of the islands we have conquered from Spain.[7] They believe that by so doing we shall open new markets for our goods in the East, and in China; and that by having possessions in various parts of the globe we shall make the United States a great "world-power," — the greatest, perhaps, that has ever existed in history.

[1] Guam (Gwam).
[2] Provided Cuba fulfilled certain conditions.
[3] See account of the burial of Columbus on page 13.
[4] Valladolid (Väl-yä-dō-leed'). Columbus spent the last years of his life there.
[5] But it is said that the remains of Columbus were not actually carried to Valladolid, but were deposited in the Cathedral at Seville in Spain.
[6] San Domingo : see page 13.
[7] We paid Spain $20,000,000 for the Philippines.

Many other Americans, who are equally patriotic and equally proud of their country, believe that it would be a mistake for us to keep all of these islands. They say that distant possessions would make us weaker instead of stronger, that they would be likely to get us into quarrels with other nations, and that in the end we should have to spend enormous sums of the people's money in building more war-ships and fitting out new armies.

Time tests all things and all men. Time will not fail to show which of these two parties is right. That decision will add another chapter to the history of our country. Let us hope it will be a chapter that both you and I shall be glad to read.

273. The murder of President McKinley. — In the autumn of 1900 Major McKinley[1] was re-elected President of the United States with Colonel Theodore Roosevelt[2] as Vice President.

The next spring (1901) a grand exhibition, called the Pan-American Exposition,[3] was opened at Buffalo, New York. In the autumn President McKinley attended a public reception at the Exposition. On this occasion (September 6) great numbers of people came forward to shake hands with him. Among these was a young man who was the son of emigrants that had come to the United States from Poland.[4] At the moment the President was reaching out his hand to the young man the

[1] See page 242.   [2] See page 249.

[3] Pan-American Exposition, that is, the exhibition of *all* the nations of North, South, and Central America.

[4] The name of the young man was Leon F. Czolgosz (pronounced Chol′gosh). He declared himself an Anarchist, that is, one who wishes to overthrow all government. He was executed at Auburn, New York, October 29, 1901. President McKinley is the third President who has been murdered; President Lincoln, shot by Booth in 1865, and President Garfield, killed by Guiteau (Gē-toe′) in 1881, being the first two.

latter shot him twice with a revolver which he held concealed in a handkerchief. The President fell back fatally wounded and died about a week later (September 14). His last words to his friends were: "Good-bye, all; good-bye. It is God's way. His will be done."

WILLIAM McKINLEY

In accordance with law, Vice-President Roosevelt then became President. Five days later (September 19) the body of the dead President was laid in its last earthly resting-place at his late home in Canton, Ohio. President Roosevelt appointed that day for mourning and prayer. It was solemnly kept, not only by all the people of the United States, but by great numbers of the people of Europe, who joined with us in our sorrow.

In London, in Paris, in Berlin, in Edinburgh, and
other European cities, the American flag was displayed
draped in black, and funeral services were held in
Westminster Abbey and other churches.   Throughout
America a great silence fell upon the people when the

THEODORE ROOSEVELT

body of the murdered President was laid in the grave.
In New York, and in many other of our chief cities,
cars and steamboats ceased to run for a time; the ever-
busy telegraph ceased to click its messages, and thousands of people stood reverently in the streets as if
they felt that they were present at the burial-ground in
Ohio.   It was an occasion that no one who took part in
it will ever forget.

274. Why we hired a strip of land on the Isthmus [1] of Panama. — While Mr. Roosevelt [2] was President, the United States hired a strip of land on the Isthmus of Panama which we can keep as long as we like [3] (see maps facing pages 220 and 244). The strip is ten miles wide and it extends clear across the Isthmus from the Atlantic to the Pacific, a distance of nearly fifty miles. Not far from there Columbus attempted to build a town on the Atlantic coast, but it came to nothing. On the other side Balboa, [4] the Spanish explorer, climbed a mountain from which he discovered the largest ocean on the globe. We paid a number of millions of dollars for the right to use that narrow and crooked piece of land which we have named the Canal Zone, yet in itself it is worth very little. Very few of our farmers would give much of anything for it, because most of it is made up of rocks, hills, and swamps. Then again, very few Americans would care to stay long in a climate which is either terribly hot and dry or terribly hot and wet, so that people there are baked one half of the year and stewed the other half.

Why, then, were we so eager to get possession of such a bit of territory? It was because after our war with Spain, when the battleship *Oregon* had to sail around the whole continent of South America to get from California to Cuba, [5] we made up our minds that we must construct a canal across the Isthmus of Panama. Then our steamships and our warships could pass through both ways, say from

[1] Isthmus (Iss'mus) of Panama (Pan-a-mah').

[2] Roosevelt (Ro'ze-velt); see page 255.

[3] In 1904 we paid the Republic of Panama $10,000,000 for the Panama " Canal Zone " and agreed that from 1913 we would pay $250,000 every year as long as we continued to hold the Zone.

[4] Balboa; see pages 19 and 20.

[5] On the voyage of the *Oregon* see page 248.

New York to San Francisco or from San Francisco to New York, and save thousands of miles in distance and several weeks in time. We had already made some use of the Isthmus, for after gold was discovered in California an American company built a railway across that neck of land, which proved to be a complete success. Then a French company tried to construct a canal alongside of the railway, but they wasted so much money and lost so many men from sickness that they were glad to sell out their rights to us for what we chose to offer. Everybody expected that when we began to build our canal in 1905 we should "make the dirt fly," but it was slow business, and for several years we did not seem to get ahead much. Finally, in 1907, President Roosevelt appointed Colonel George W. Goethals[1] to see what he could do about it. Colonel Goethals was an engineer[2] in the United States army, and he knew just how to push the work to completion.

He saw that the first thing to be done was to make the Canal Zone so clean and healthful that forty or fifty thousand men could labor there all day in the hot sun and still keep well and strong. Perhaps the greatest enemy he had to contend with was mosquitoes — not common mosquitoes, but certain dangerous kinds which abound in that climate and whose bite means sickness and sometimes death. In his fight against these winged pests the new chief engineer was entirely successful.[3] He barred the mosquitoes out of

[1] Goethals (Go'thalz). Colonel Goethals is a descendant of an old Dutch family that settled in Brooklyn, New York, a great many years ago. He was educated at the United States Military Academy at West Point on the Hudson.

[2] Engineer: a military engineer is an officer who makes use of engines and machines of different kinds to construct canals, roads, bridges, dams, forts, and other important works.

[3] One chief reason why he was successful was that the officer who took charge of the cleaning up was Colonel Gorgas (Gor'gas), who is now Surgeon-General

the houses with wire screens, and then killed them off by millions by pouring kerosene in their breeding places. That battle never stopped even for a day, and never can stop.

Next, Colonel Goethals, the "Great Digger," whose motto has been "to dig the most dirt for the least money," set to work to tame the Chagres River.[1] It was a very difficult stream to deal with. At that time it flowed across the line of the canal he had set out to dig, and in the rainy season it became a raging torrent. The Colonel found a cure for this. He took the earth he had dug out and built a dam over a hundred feet high and nearly a mile and a half long.[2] This dam held the troublesome river in check and converted it into a peaceful lake thirty miles long and deep enough for the largest ships to pass through.[3] That lake is many feet above the level of the sea, but Colonel Goethals built some immense locks, or water-stairs, by which vessels entering the canal can ascend to the lake and can go down from it when they pass out at the other end.

But, hard as this job about the river was, there was a harder one to come. The line of the canal was blocked by the Culebra Hills.[4] The highest of these hills are about five hundred feet above the canal. They form part of that great range of mountains which begins in Alaska and extends down through the western part of the United States, then across the Isthmus of Panama, and then down

of the Army of the United States. One of his efficient helpers was Miss Gertrude Beeks, who did excellent work in improving health conditions among the Canal workmen and their families.

[1] Chagres (Chag′res).

[2] This is the Gatun (Gat-oon′) Dam. It is on the Atlantic side, not far from the entrance of the Canal.

[3] This is called Gatun Lake. It is eighty-five feet above the level of the sea

[4] Culebra Hills (Coo-la′brah). A Spanish word meaning "snake."

the western coast of South America to Cape Horn. Get your atlas and you will see that these mountains are the backbone of the American Continent. In order to construct the canal we had to dig a ditch nearly nine miles long, directly through that backbone. At first that seemed an easy thing for our steam shovels to do, for each shovel could scoop up a big cartload of earth and stone at a mouthful. But just here came an unexpected difficulty : as

THE GATUN LOCKS ON THE PANAMA CANAL

fast as we dug the stuff out, the rock above kept crumbling to pieces, sliding down and filling up the ditch. Heaps as big as a whole row of houses would come roaring down and would cover up everything in a moment. Then all the wearisome labor of scooping it out had to be done over again. This happened time after time and month after month. Some of the workmen began to feel discouraged and to think we must give it up. The young officer who had charge of this particular work never lost heart, but he became so worn out with it that all the strength went out of him and he died. Still the battle went on day by day, and after seven years of toil the cut was made so wide that it was believed the sliding rocks could not fall into the ditch. Then Colonel Goethals spoke the word, and President Wilson, sitting in his office at the ·White House in Washington, pressed an electric button ; the water rushed in, and the great American Canal across the Isthmus of Panama was practically finished.[1]

One reason why it was finished was that during all the seven years Colonel Goethals made a practice of setting apart one day of every week to meet his men. He would see them at his office and talk with them in a sensible and friendly way about what they were doing, and would find out what he could do for them. In this way they all worked together like a great family, each one of whom meant to do his "level best."

Now that the Canal is open and boats are going through it, the next thing is to finish several forts at each end of it. These forts will be armed with cannon — not cannon to make war but to keep peace in case any unfriendly battleships should be foolish enough to come to break it. One gun alone can fire a shell as big as a man and weighing more than a ton, and it can send that shell whizzing through the air for more than twenty miles. These huge guns will not be fired unless we are forced to defend the work

---

[1] Since the Canal was opened there have been more rock-slides, which have caused much labor and expense ; but Colonel Goethals expects that in time this difficulty can be entirely overcome. This work will increase the cost of the Canal so that the total bill may be upwards of $400,000,000. But it is thought that so many vessels will want to use our new waterway that the tolls we shall collect from them will help us a great deal in paying for it. At a charge of $1.20 a ton a steamship of ten thousand tons would pay $12,000. Still even at that rate it will take us many years to reduce the debt and also meet the expense of keeping the whole Canal in good working order.

we have completed. Let us hope that the necessity for that will never come and that our great waterway will always be a highway of peace, which the whole world can use and can profit by.

Now to go back a little. When the eminent French engineer began his unsuccessful attempt to cut his canal

WILLIAM H. TAFT

through the Isthmus, many years ago, the company set up a statue of him there. Colonel Goethals has no monument or statue on the Isthmus. He would not want one. He likes best to keep in the background and let you look at what he has done. That speaks for him; it always will speak for him.[1]

275. The discovery of the North Pole; the outbreak of the Great War in Europe. — While the laborers on the Isthmus were digging

the canal and while Mr. Taft was President, a remarkable piece of work was done at the North. For many years explorers had tried to make their way to the North Pole, but had always failed to get there. It was a terrible journey

---

[1] A man went down to Panama
　　Where many a man had died
　To slit the sliding mountains
　　And lift the eternal tide:
　A man stood up in Panama,
　　And the mountains stood aside.
　　　　　　　　　　　PERCY MACKAYE

over ice and snow and not a few who started on it perished miserably of cold and starvation. But in the spring of 1909 Commander Robert E. Peary[1] of the United States navy succeeded in getting to the Pole, and he put up an American flag there. Later Captain Amundsen[2] of Norway discovered the South Pole ; so we can now say we have seen the top and the bottom of the world.

In the summer of 1914, after Mr. Wilson became President, the greatest war ever known began in Europe.[3] The people of the United States resolved not to take any part in it if they could avoid it, but to do everything they could to hasten the coming of peace. To show our good will towards all, we sent a ship to Europe loaded with Christmas presents for thousands of poor children whose fathers had left their homes to go and fight. After a time we resolved to enter the Great War. This happened because the German submarines (see page 285), which had destroyed many English vessels, began to blow up American merchant ships trading with England. President Wilson told Germany the destruction must stop. But it did not stop. When we found that Germany meant to keep on making war on us by destroying our ships, we saw that we must declare war against her, and Congress made that declaration in the spring of 1917.

Later on, the President of the United States, who, in time of war, is commander-in-chief of all the soldiers and sailors in our army and navy, ordered Admiral Sims to begin the fight. He accordingly went, as speedily as possible, with a number of our warships, to help the

---

[1] Peary (pee´ry): afterwards Rear Admiral.   [2] Amundsen (ah´mun-sen).

[3] In the Great War, Germany and Austria fought on one side, and Russia, France, England, and finally America on the other. Italy and several other nations also entered the war ; but meanwhile a revolution made Russia quit fighting.

English fleet hunt down and destroy the terrible German submarines, which were enemies to both of us.

The battle with the submarines was long and hard, for these vessels could quickly sink out of sight, could stay under water for many hours, or could slyly travel miles away without being seen or heard. In the end, however, the American and English sailors managed, by working together, to get the better of these slippery craft so that fewer and fewer escaped.

Copyright by Harris & Ewing.

ADMIRAL SIMS

But we soon discovered that we should need many more warships and that we must also have a great number of transport ships to carry our fighting men across the ocean. Nor was that all, for we should need a whole fleet of other ships to carry over food and clothing and powder and guns for our men. It took us a great while to get ready to build these new vessels. But after we really set our hands to the work, no country in the world ever completed so many ships in the same number of days.

Then we had to meet a still greater difficulty. We found that our money was running short, because it always costs far more to carry on war, even for a single year, than it does to pay the expenses of many years of peace. Well, we did not shrink back frightened and declare that we never could raise all the dollars that the Government at Washington called for. On the contrary we met the case bravely. We declared that we stood ready to give money in taxes and to lend money to the Government to use as it saw fit. We did this because we felt that we must push the war forward — no matter

Copyright by Committee on Public Information.

A UNITED STATES WAR-SHIP

what it might cost — until we should win a victory that would make us safe in every way. We wanted also to make the friendly nations of Europe that were fighting along with us as safe as ourselves, on land and sea.

This feeling explains why so many people took out their pocketbooks and paid their taxes, and also bought Liberty Bonds.[1] So too, later on, thousands of boys used to

[1] **Liberty Bonds.** When a man bought one of these bonds — say for $100 — he received a printed promise from the Government that the money should be paid back to him at the end of a certain number of years, and that in the meantime he should get interest every year on the bond.

go to the Post Offices and buy War Savings Stamps,[1] or, if they had not money enough for that, they would buy Thrift Stamps.[2] Thousands of girls did the same thing. They also set to work at home and knit great piles of woolen sweaters and socks to send abroad to our soldiers. Then, for fear that they had not done enough, they made up little boxes of good things to add to what they had sent.

GENERAL PERSHING

While these preparations were going on, the President dispatched General Pershing with a small American army of regular troops[3] to France. They went there to help the people in their desperate fight against the powerful German armies which had entered their country and vowed that they would conquer it. The enemy was rapidly marching forward to capture the great city of Paris,[4] the capital of the

[1] **War Savings Stamps.** These were little bonds which the Government sold for $4.12 and for which the purchaser received $5.00 at the end of five years. These stamps and those mentioned below are still for sale.

[2] **Thrift Stamps.** These stamps were sold for 25 cents each and when the purchaser had bought sixteen of them and pasted them on a "Thrift Card" he could exchange them, by paying a little more, for a War Savings Stamp which would bring him $5.00. Great numbers of our young people used to spend their quarters for these stamps.

[3] **Regular troops** are those who make up the permanent army of the United States in peace as well as in war.

[4] **Paris.** See your School Geography map of France or of Europe.

French Republic, which means as much to every true Frenchman as the city of Washington does to every one of us.

The people over there swung their hats and cheered with all their might when they saw our men landing from the vessels. They had good reason for giving such a rousing welcome, for these were the first American soldiers that we had ever sent to fight anywhere on the continent of Europe. Our soldiers went there because France, England, and America had joined hands to beat back Germany, whose emperor was determined not to let any free country rest in peace unless it would give in to him and do whatever he ordered. That would have made the American people, and those of England and France as well, no better than slaves.

Before our regular troops had gone abroad, we had begun getting ready to raise a new and much stronger army to follow them. We resolved that this should be the largest army that we had ever collected since we first called ourselves the "United States of America" and since we adopted the Stars and Stripes as our country's flag. That, as you know, was more than a hundred and forty years ago. (See pages 120, 126, and 129.)

It is interesting to see how we started to raise such an army. It was done in this way : The President commanded all the young men in the whole country to write their names and the names of the places where they lived on cards which were to be sent to Washington. These cards were then numbered and put in small drawers so that they could be easily examined when wanted.

When this task had been accomplished, the Government officer who had charge of the cards gave notice that on July 20, 1917, he would proceed to select those young men who would enter the new fighting force. The selection was made in the fairest possible manner so that all might be treated alike, and no one could say that his name had been picked out on purpose. This was the method : Many slips of paper, each of which

SALVATION ARMY LASSIES

had a number printed on it, were deposited in a large glass jar. Then the officer in charge of the draft closed his eyes, bound his handkerchief over them, and, thus blindfolded, drew out one of the slips from the jar. The slip was then opened, and the number on it decided who should first have the privilege of entering the new American Army of Liberty.

All of the young men thus chosen were examined to see if they were strong enough to go to war; if they

were, and were not excused on some other account, they
went to military camps in different states, to be trained
as soldiers. A good many of them had never in their
lives held a gun in their hands, and some had never
seen a gun fired. But they showed themselves quick to
learn, prompt to act, and
eager to do their part in
the Great War.

When our men were
ready they sailed for
France—many thousands
going over at a time. The
Germans, knowing that
they were coming, ordered
the captains of their submarines to be on the
watch and to sink every
Yankee transport ship
with all on board. But
we too were on the watch,
and American or English
war vessels always crossed
the Atlantic along with
"our boys" to guard them
from attack. No Ameri-

RED CROSS NURSE AND RED
CROSS DOG

can transport ship was ever sunk on its way to Europe.

These steamers also carried over to France great numbers of Red Cross nurses and of Salvation Army Lassies,
as the girls called themselves. They went to look after
the comfort and welfare of the "boys." The Salvation
Army Lassies kept near the firing line, and in their huts
they always held themselves ready to serve the tired

fighters with hot coffee and hot doughnuts. The Red
Cross nurses took good care of those who fell sick or who
were wounded in battle. These faithful nurses were as-
sisted by Red Cross dogs that were trained to go out and
search for missing soldiers who had been so badly hurt
that they could neither move nor call for help. When
the dogs found such cases they would trot back and get

A FIGHT IN THE SKY

some one to go with
them and bring the
poor fellows to the
hospital.

Now let us see
how our soldiers lived
and what they did.
You might think that
the first thing they
would do would be to
use their guns. No,
the first thing they
did was to use their
spades. They dug
long lines of deep
trenches or ditches, and they also hollowed out rude
rooms and passages underground. These were for shelter and for defense against attack. So, too, they built
strong fences and entanglements of barbed wire to keep
the enemy at a distance. It is safe to say that no one
likes to stand very long in a ditch, but our soldiers had
to do it, and when it rained they often stood in mud and
water a foot deep or more.

In these trenches and underground "dugouts" the
men did something more than fight, for there many of

them ate and slept. They lived there because oftentimes "dugouts" were the only safe places where they could live. What did they see when they looked out? In front of them, not very far away, they saw long stretches of barbed wire, and back of those cruel-looking entanglements they saw trenches like their own, but which swarmed with

FIRING A BIG SHELL

German soldiers. These soldiers always fired at ours when they had a good chance, just as our men fired at the Germans. That was what they were there for.

Again, both sides used the same kinds of weapons, such as guns and machine-guns, each one of which could shoot hundreds of bullets in a minute.[1] So, too,

---

[1] **Machine-gun.** R. J. Gatling, an American inventor, brought out the first successful gun of this kind in 1861. It was greatly improved in later years, so that it would fire 1200 bullets a minute.

both sides threw many thousands of cast-iron explosive shells,[1] about as big as an orange, at each other. Then those who worked the cannon fired huge shells, sometimes weighing a ton or more, which rushed screaming through the sky, bursting with a terrific crash when they struck, and tearing everything to pieces around them.

WHAT THE BIG SHELL WAS AIMED AT

While this fighting was taking place on the ground desperate battles would often be going on overhead between American and German airplanes. Then there

[1] **Shells** or bombs are made of metal of different forms and sizes. All the larger ones are fired from cannon. They are charged with a kind of powder much more powerful than our common gunpowder. They are made so that they will explode either when they strike or after a certain time, which is often only a few seconds from the moment they leave the gun.

would be days when the soldiers in the trenches, on both sides, would suddenly climb out and engage in fierce hand-to-hand fights in " No Man's Land," as the strip was called which separated the combatants from each other.

But there was still another kind of fighting which proved to be wonderfully effective, and which was entirely different

WHAT THE BIG SHELL DID

from anything we have described. Strange to say, though the English, French, and Americans made use of this new method, the Germans did not learn how to employ it until considerably later, and they never accomplished very much with it.

This new war-machine had in the beginning nothing at all that was warlike about it. It was a big, strong

automobile invented by an American,[1] and was manu-
factured in one of our Western States. It was built to
do certain kinds of farm work, on rough ground where
neither horses nor oxen could be used. Because it had
enormous pulling power it was called a Tractor, and as it
crept along very slowly, it got the name of the "Caterpillar Tractor." It could easily force its way over stones
and through brush and up and down steep places where
an ordinary automobile would have been upset and
knocked to pieces. In doing this the Tractor could drag
gangs of heavy plows which would break up the hardest
soil and prepare it for raising crops of wheat and corn.

An English military officer happened to see this go-ahead
machine. He gazed at it in silence and then exclaimed,
"This is just the sort of thing we want in the war against
the Germans, for *this thing can be made to fight*!" He
bought several of these tractors before the parts were put
together, and had the parts boxed up and shipped to England. There some alterations were made in the strange
machines and they were covered over with plates of steel.
All work on them was done secretly in order that the Germans might not find out what they were. Luckily a report
got abroad that they were water-carriers, though in reality
they were forts on wheels, made to carry men and guns.
When they were finished they were sent off by night to
the battlefields of France. As soon as the English soldiers over there caught sight of them they laughed out-
right at the awkward way in which these new water-carriers
stumbled along. They nicknamed them "Tanks," and
predicted that they would speedily get wrecked. But the
"Tanks" astonished everybody by beating down and

[1] Benjamin Holt of Stockton, California.

breaking through German barbed-wire entanglements and utterly destroying the enemy's nests of machine-guns. Besides, what harm could their showers of bullets do to these slow-moving monsters, protected by walls of steel, which stopped at nothing, but went straight across trenches or down into them and out again without tipping over?

A TANK ON THE BATTLEFIELD

From that time on, it was plain that however queer the "Tanks" might look or act, they would certainly "do their bit." They did do it, and so helped to gain some hard-fought battles that might have been lost without them.

But the war itself was now changing. Our men were no longer standing in muddy trenches week after week, since the armies on both sides had begun to move. Little by little, General Pershing's great American army in the east of France was gaining ground from the enemy. So, too, the Americans who were acting with the French and English armies on the west were gaining. All of them working together were steadily pushing the Germans out of France and out of Belgium and compelling them to

move back toward Germany.

Still the German troops, even while they were retreating, continued their terrible work of destruction. Often when they left a city or a country village which they had captured and held, they left it a mass of smoking ruins. The officers accomplished this by ordering a certain number of men to remain behind long enough to burn down buildings, blow up bridges, destroy roads, fill

WOODROW WILSON

up wells, and saw down fruit trees. So far as practicable they seemed determined to leave nothing that could be of use or value to the French or Belgian people who had made these places their homes.

Notwithstanding this far-reaching destruction, the time had at last arrived when everyone could see that the end of the Great War was near. Our men had not been fighting long, but they had fought bravely and well. Their reward came on November 11, 1918 — "Victory Day." On that memorable day the Germans gave up, and solemnly bound themselves to do what France, England, America,

PERSHING'S VICTORIOUS ARMY IN WASHINGTON

and Italy demanded. Then the last gun was fired, and the fighting stopped. Not very long afterward " Our Boys " began to return, full of joy at the thought of setting foot on American soil again. Later, General Pershing came back and marched at the head of a division of his

victorious soldiers through the streets of Washington. It was a sight never to be forgotten. Since then England, France, and Italy, with other nations, have made a final peace with Germany. We, too, shall publicly declare, in some way that everyone can understand, that the Great War is over and that we believe Peace has come to make her home with us all.

Copyright by Baker Art Gallery

WARREN G. HARDING

In 1921 Warren G. Harding became President. He declares that he is ready to do all that he can to help forward whatever is best for all.

276. The unfinished pyramid ; making history. — On one of the two great seals[1] of the United States a pyramid is represented partly finished. It stands for our country. The American republic now has forty-eight states, and it

[1] Seals: the first great seal, having the eagle and the Latin motto " *E Pluribus Unum*," meaning " *Many in One*," — or one nation made up of many states, — was adopted June 20, 1782. The spread eagle signifies strength ; the thirteen stars above his head and the thirteen stripes on the shield on his breast represent the thirteen original states ; the olive branch, held in the eagle's right

stretches clear across the continent from the Atlantic to the Pacific.[1]   But that is not all, for we now own a number of islands in both oceans.   That pyramid shows how much has been done and how much still remains to be done.   The men whose lives we have read in this little book were all builders.   By patient and determined labor

FIRST GREAT SEAL OF THE
UNITED STATES

SECOND GREAT SEAL OF THE
UNITED STATES

they added stone to stone, and so the good work grew. Now they have gone ; and it is for us to do our part and make sure that the pyramid, as it rises, shall continue to stand square and strong and true.

talon, shows that America seeks peace, while the bundle of arrows in his left talon shows that we are prepared for war.   This seal is used in stamping agreements or treaties made by the United States with other nations, and also for other important papers.

The second great seal, adopted at the same time, was never used.   It was intended for stamping the wax on a ribbon attached to a treaty or other important paper, thus making a hanging seal.   The Latin motto "*Annuit Cœptis*," above the all-seeing eye looking down with favor on the unfinished pyramid, means "*God has favored the work*."   The date MDCCLXXVI, or 1776, marks the Declaration of Independence.   The Latin motto at the bottom, "*Novus Ordo Seclorum*," means "*A New Order of Ages*," — or a new order of things, such as we have in this New World of America.

[1] See map facing page 220.

What is said about the North and the South since the Civil War? Tell about the growth of the South. What is said about the West? What is said about railroads? What is said about people going West?

How long is it since Columbus discovered America? What is said about the celebration of that discovery? What is said about the possessions which Spain once had in North America? What is said of the rebellion in Cuba? What is said about the destruction of the *Maine?* What did the United States do? Give an account of Commodore Dewey's victory. What is said of Cervera's fleet? What did Hobson do? What is said about the fighting near Santiago? Who were the "Rough Riders"? What happened to Cervera's fleet? When did the end of the war come? What is said of the "Red Cross"? What is said of Hawaii? Over what islands does our flag now wave? What is said about the remains of Columbus? What do people think in regard to keeping all the islands now under our control? What terrible event occurred at Buffalo in the autumn of 1901?

What strip of land did we buy while Mr. Roosevelt was President? Why did we buy it? Can you give some account of the great work Colonel Goethals did there?

What great discovery did Commander Peary make in 1909? What terrible thing happened in the summer of 1914? What did the United States resolve to do about it? Can you give some account of the Great War and of what we did in it? How did it end?

What is said about one of the great seals of the United States? What does the unfinished pyramid stand for? What does it show us? What is said of the men whose lives we have read in this book? Is there anything left for us to do?

NOTE on Washington's Signature shown on page 103, and on the Day of his Birth cut on the old stone shown on page 105.

The English year formerly began on March 25, but in 1752 Parliament ordered it to begin on January 1.

In the case given here (page 103), according to the first method, March 12 would occur in 1744, while according to the second method, which was gradually coming into use before the law of 1752 was passed, March 12 would occur in 1745. For the sake of convenience Washington, like many others, used both dates.

Another important change made in 1752 was the adding of eleven days to the year, in order to correct an error through which it fell short. For this reason we now make February 22 the date of Washington's birth, although the date cut on the old stone shown on page 105 is "The 11th of February."

On these changes in reckoning time see Chambers's Encyclopædia, under "Chronology," page 229.

A noble gift to the nation (see page 223). After President Lincoln's death an Association was formed which purchased the farm and log cabin where he was born (1809), near Hodgenville, in Hardin (now La Rue) County, Kentucky. The Association erected a beautiful granite Memorial Hall to shelter and preserve the simple home of his childhood. On September 4, 1916, the Hall, cabin, and farm were presented to the nation, with a fund of $50,000 to maintain them for the future. Above the entrance to the Hall is the following inscription:

Here, over the log cabin where Abraham Lincoln was born, destined to preserve the Nation and to free the slave, a grateful people have dedicated this Memorial to unity, peace, and brotherhood among these States.

In 1920 the American people completed a grand Memorial Building in Washington in honor of Lincoln's life and services to our country. It stands at the farther end of the beautiful park which extends from the National Capitol to the Potomac River.

XXX. A SUPPLEMENTARY CHAPTER ON SOME REMARKABLE AMERICAN INVENTIONS

A World's Fair was held at San Francisco in 1915 to celebrate Balboa's discovery of the Pacific, more than four hundred years ago,[1] and Colonel Goethals's completion of the Panama Canal, uniting the waters of the Atlantic and the Pacific.[2]

Of the multitude of things exhibited at that Fair nothing was more interesting than some of the inventions which have made Americans famous. One of these inventions was a little machine which would add up a long column of figures in less than half the time that you or I could do it. Another interesting thing was a model of one of the big steam shovels used in digging the Panama Canal. Those big shovels did more hard work in an hour than six hundred men could do, with hand shovels, in that time. A third invention was a press which could print more than a thousand newspapers in a minute, fold them, and pile them up. Looking at these things we can understand why American machines are sold and used throughout the world. In this book you have read something about Whitney's Cotton Gin,[3] Fulton's Steamboat,[4] and Morse's Telegraph[5]; the telephone too has been mentioned[6]; but there are several other inventions which should be spoken of here.

[1] See page 20.
[2] See pages 257–262.
[3] See page 159.
[4] See page 175.
[5] See page 198.
[6] See page 202.

277. Robert Fulton's "Diving-Boat." — You have already seen that Fulton spent a great deal of work on this boat.[1] He said he hoped the time would come when it would destroy so many warships that it would put an end to all fighting on the ocean. That was more than a hundred

Captain of a submarine, under water, looking through a peculiar kind of spyglass at a steamer in the distance

years ago. Well, within a short time a large number of these "Diving-Boats" have been built in Europe, in Japan, and in the United States. They are now called Submarines,[2] because they can travel beneath the surface of the sea. Some of them can go many hundreds of miles. When one of these vessels gets sight of an enemy's ship, it sends out a torpedo to destroy it. The torpedo looks like a large fish. It moves swiftly under water toward the ship, and when it strikes, it explodes and tears a great hole in the ship, which soon sinks. We all know that the Submarines did some terrible work in the Great War.[3] But in times of peace these "Diving-Boats" can often be used to explore parts of the ocean, to find the remains of wrecked vessels, and also to take very interesting moving pictures of life under the sea.

278. A machine for cutting grain. — A hundred years ago wheat and other grain were cut by hand. A Virginia

[1] See page 174.   [2] Submarines (sub-ma-reens').   [3] See pages 263–264.

farmer said to himself, "Why can't I make a machine which my horses can draw and which will cut my wheat in less time than a dozen men can do it with sickles or cradles?" He constructed a machine but it did not satisfy him, and he left it to rust to pieces where it stood.

His son, Cyrus H. McCormick, made up his mind that he would find out why his father's Reaper would not work. Cyrus had learned to do one thing at a time, and *to do*

SUBMARINE ATTACKING A STEAMER

the hardest thing first. Now the hardest thing in this case was to discover why the Reaper, when it cut the wheat, would not throw it down straight, so that it could be easily made up into bundles for the thrashing-machine which separated the grain from the straw.[1]

By patient effort young McCormick succeeded in making a Reaper which would do what was wanted. This was in 1831. But he had to wait nine years before any one bought one of his new machines, and even then he found

[1] The Thrashing-Machine was invented in England many years before McCormick invented his Reaper.

that he must make it still better. This he set to work and did ; but not many farmers there could afford to purchase it. Finally a friend said to him, " Cyrus, why don't you go West with your Reaper, where the land is level and where it is difficult for the farmers to hire men enough to cut all the grain that grows ? " " Yes," answered Cyrus, " I will go West." He started at once, and for the first time in his life saw a prairie.[1] It stretched out as far as the eye could see, and seemed as smooth as a barn floor. Then the thought came to him, " What must this country

CUTTING WHEAT WITH SICKLE, CRADLE, AND REAPER

look like when it is covered with golden fields of wheat ? " " Now," said he, " I see what I really made my machine for. I must come out here and build it, for every farmer will be sure to buy it."

He traveled on until he came to Lake Michigan. On the southern shore of the lake he stopped at a town called Chicago. " Here," said Mr. McCormick, " I shall start business, for this town is going to grow, and my business will grow with it." He made no mistake that time. He built Reapers and found no difficulty in selling them. He kept steadily at work, and he kept making improvements

[1] Prairie (pra´ry).

in his work. He got his Reapers so that they would cut the grain rapidly and smoothly and then tie it up in bundles.

Having done all this, he took the last step. He made a new Reaper or Harvester which would do all that the old one did, and would even thrash out the grain besides. This accomplished everything that the Western farmer could ask, for it filled row after row of bags with the precious wheat which gives us " our daily bread." Meanwhile other men had entered the business, so that now no city in the world makes so many Reapers and Harvesters as the great city of Chicago does.

279. What Elias[1] Howe did. — While Cyrus H. McCormick was busy in the West, a young man of the name of Howe was just as busy in the garret of a house in Cambridge, Massachusetts. When some one asked him what he was trying to make, he answered, " I am trying to make a machine that will sew cloth." His answer was met by a loud laugh. Mr. Howe paid no attention to the laugh, but kept quietly at work. By the end of the winter he managed to put together a clumsy contrivance which he called his " Iron Needle-woman." This was in 1845.

He hoped that in time his machine would be able to sew faster than any girl, but in the end people found that the " Iron Needle-woman " could sew faster than ten girls. The young man expected to sell his invention to the tailors, but they were afraid that if they bought the machines, the men they hired to do sewing by hand would refuse to use them for fear of losing their jobs of hand-sewing, so they declined to have anything to do with him.

Then Mr. Howe took ship for London, thinking that perhaps he could dispose of his invention in that city.

---

[1] Elias (E-li′as).

There he was worse off than he was at home, for though the tailors would try his machine, they would not pay him anything for it. He decided that he must leave England and go back to America. He found that the only way he could get money enough to pay his passage across the ocean was to borrow it and leave his " Iron Needle-woman " as security. When he landed in New York he had less than a dollar in his pocket. That was discouraging. Then came a still harder experience. He learned that while he was abroad some one had been making and selling his invention who had no lawful right to do so.

In fact, a man in western New York was traveling about, at that very time, and exhibiting his machine to any one who would pay twelve cents to see it. Here is one of the showman's hand-bills.

A GREAT

CURIOSITY

THE YANKEE SEWING MACHINE

is now

EXHIBITING

AT THIS PLACE

FROM

8 A.M. to 5 P.M.

Many ladies went to see it and bought fancy work done on it — all frills and flourishes. They carried the work home to show their friends what the wonderful " Iron Needle-woman " could do. Still very few believed that the machine would ever prove to be of any real use in a family.

Mr. Howe was too poor to go to law to protect his rights, but he at length found means to prevent others from taking his machine away from him. Then he became prosperous, and this man who once did not have a dollar in his pocket, began to complain that he had n't pockets enough to hold all the dollars that poured in on him.

At the same time several other inventors made various improvements in the Sewing Machine. Finally one of them constructed a machine that would sew leather with a waxed thread. This opened a new field of work. To-day most of our clothing is made by sewing machines, and our boots and shoes are generally stitched together by them. The result is that now both clothing and footwear are far cheaper than they would be if they were made by hand.

280. How the Telephone [1] **was invented.** — Long after the Sewing Machine had come into use, Professor Alexander G. Bell, of Boston, began to make experiments with the human voice.[2] His friends thought that he was wasting his time, but he said, " Professor Morse made an electric wire write,[3] while I hope to do still better, for I believe I can make an electric wire talk."

After many disappointments he succeeded in sending a faint sound over a wire which passed from one room to another. Next he stretched one from the basement of a building in Boston up to the third floor. One day when he was at work he called down through this wire to his assistant, " Mr. Watson, come up here ; I want you." Mr. Watson rushed upstairs greatly excited, crying out,

[1] See page 202.

[2] Professor Bell had been teaching some deaf-and-dumb children in Canada. Then he left there and took up the same work in Boston.

[3] See page 198.

" Mr. Bell, I can hear your words!" Then Mr. Bell knew that he had made the wire speak.

That was in the spring of 1876. In the summer a World's Fair was held at Philadelphia to celebrate the remarkable things which had been done in the United States since the Declaration of Independence a hundred years before.[1] Mr. Bell took his Speaking Wire, or " Talking Telegraph," to exhibit it at the Fair.[2] Nobody seemed to pay much attention to it. But one evening

the Emperor of Brazil came in and said, " Professor Bell, I am delighted to meet you again ; I want to see your new machine."

Mr. Bell went to the end of the long hall and took up the mouthpiece of the wire, while the Emperor, standing where Mr. Bell had left him, picked up the other end and put it to his ear. He listened a moment, and then, suddenly throwing his head back, he exclaimed : " Why, it *talks* ! "

Yes, it did talk, and it has been talking ever since. At first the Telephone, as it was finally named, could only be used for very short distances. But now, after many years of improvement, it will talk clear across the United States from the Atlantic to the Pacific. This was done in January, 1915. To-day a boy, going into a Telephone office in New York, can speak to a boy in San Francisco and

[1] See page 120.
[2] Professor Bell at first called his invention a " Talking Telegraph."

hear what he says in reply. The Telephone makes the two boys just as near together, so far as talking is concerned, as though they lived in the same house. This is done by using an electric wire over three thousand miles long. But people are beginning to telephone to each other without using any wire, just as they can telegraph without one. In both cases they send their messages through the air.

281. Mr. Edison and his work. — Thomas A. Edison began earning his living by selling newspapers on a railroad train in Michigan. He was then a boy of twelve. A few years later he began printing a small weekly paper of his own in the baggage car of the train. After he had grown to manhood he invented (1877), the " Talking-machine," or Phonograph.[1] That machine makes a record of what is said to it and can repeat the words years afterward. It can also repeat music in the same way. Once people would have declared such a thing impossible, but Mr. Edison found a way of doing it. Now his Phonograph has become so common that almost every one has heard it talk or sing. Besides being used for amusement it is used for business.

Next Mr. Edison invented (1879) the Electric Light, which we see in so many houses and stores. The next year (1880) he built an Electric Car, which he used for a while at Menlo Park, New Jersey, where he then lived. That set people thinking how convenient it would be to have electric cars to travel by; now they are rushing in all directions over the United States.

Later on, Mr. Edison took up a small toy which showed a few pictures in motion, the size of postage stamps. He greatly improved that toy, and out of it, in 1895, he produced the Moving-Pictures which we know so well.

[1] Phonograph (fo'no graf).

How often, in the past, people had looked at pictures hanging on a wall, or shown on a screen by a magic lantern, and felt that they lacked only one thing to make them complete. That one thing was motion. A painting representing a vessel bounding over the waves in a stiff breeze, or an express train flying through the country, might be excellent — but then not a wave rolled, not a wheel turned. Suddenly, to everybody's astonishment, all this was changed.

SOME MOVING-PICTURES OF A FOOTBALL GAME

When some Indians in Colorado went to see Edison's pictures of a fast train, the sight was too much for them. They jumped up with a yell and ran wildly out of the hall; for there, directly facing them, they saw the engine coming straight at them at a speed of a mile a minute. The Red Men felt sure that if they had kept their seats a few seconds longer, they would all have been dead Indians. It is this wonderful reality in Moving-Pictures which draws crowds who never tire of looking at them.

So when we go to one of these exhibitions and see a fleet of United States warships sailing into the harbor of New York, with every flag flying, or when we look on some merry scene which rouses a hearty laugh all around, we are glad that Edison's inventive skill made these things possible.

282. The Flying-Machine. — Eight years after Edison began to astonish people with his marvelous pictures, two brothers, Orville Wright and Wilbur Wright, of Dayton, Ohio, did something remarkable that the world had never seen done before. It is true that an old Greek story[1] tells us that a daring boy once made an attempt of the same kind. He took a pair of wings made of birds' feathers and wax, fastened them on his shoulders, and flew up into the sky; but his wings dropped off and he fell into the sea and was drowned. The two Wright brothers also set out to learn to fly, but instead of making wings they made a flying-machine. It was simply a long, light frame of wood covered with cotton cloth which they called a " Glider." They would take it to the top of a hill, and when the wind blew strong and steadily, one of them would mount the " Glider " and slide down hill on the air. It was good fun unless the wind happened to give out and let the rider down with a bump. But after all, this was not flying as a bird flies, so the Wrights decided to do something different.

They made a very light engine, like the engine of an automobile, and fastened it on the " Glider." The engine drove an air-wheel which pushed it forward, somewhat as the paddle-wheels of a steamboat push that forward. They practised awhile with this, and at last, in 1903, their " Flying-Machine " — for it was more than a " Glider " now — actually flew with one of them, against the wind, for fifty-nine seconds! They tried hard to keep up in the air for a whole minute, but could not. After a while they succeeded, one at a time, in keeping up for several minutes; but they nearly always had to fly in a straight

[1] See " A Lost Secret " in *Gods and Heroes*, published by Ginn and Company.

line, for if they tried to turn corners — especially sharp
corners — they were in great danger of tumbling down.

However, they were not the kind of men to give up.
They were determined that their machine should turn and
twist like a letter S ; so they watched the hawks and gulls
to see how they managed.   These big birds seemed to be
laughing at them, for they would spread their wings and

THE SIMPLEST FORM OF AIRSHIP

fly swiftly round and round as if they enjoyed the game.
At length the two brothers found out how the birds did it,
and the next year they made two circular flights of three
miles each.   Then it was their turn to laugh.

In 1909 they went to Fort Myer, near Washington,
to show some officers of the United States Government
what they could do.   The Government offered to give a
prize of twenty-five thousand dollars to any man who
could accomplish these three things :

1. He must fly a whole hour without coming down.
2. He must take a passenger with him in his flight.
3. He must fly at the rate of not less than forty miles an hour.

One of the Wrights did all these things, and better too. He went up in his Airship, or Airplane,[1] as it is now generally called, and flew with a passenger for more than an hour. Next, he flew at the rate of a little more than forty-two miles an hour. Thousands watched him as he glided like a bird through the sky and then lighted on the grass as easily and gracefully as a bird lights.

The great crowd cheered and shouted like mad. The United States Government was entirely satisfied. It not only paid the Wright brothers twenty-five thousand dollars for their Airship, but it gave them five thousand dollars more because they had made greater speed than was demanded. These two men, by years of patient and persistent effort, had won the victory. They had taught the world how to travel through the air. Some of their friends asked them if it was very hard work finding out how to do it. They answered, "Yes; it was." But they said, "After all, it is easier for a man to learn to fly than for a child to learn to walk."

Now Airplanes are an everyday sight in many parts of the world, and Flying-Boats are frequently seen. They can skim over the surface of the sea at a great rate, and can then rise and fly if they like. Airplanes have been employed to cross deserts, and mountains, and regions covered with ice. They are of immense value in war, and no armies to-day would feel like fighting without their

---

[1] At first it was usually called the Aëroplane (a'er-o-plane).

help. They are also coming into use for carrying mail and passengers and express parcels.

In 1919 Commander Read, an officer in our navy, started in one of these winged boats and flew through the air across the Atlantic Ocean from Long Island, New York, to the city of Lisbon in Europe.[1] No such wonderful thing had ever been done before, and some of the papers called him the "American Columbus of the air," because he had discovered a new way of crossing the ocean.

While the Wright brothers were growing up and while they were learning to travel through the air, two more remarkable machines came into use. One of these was the Typewriter, which was exhibited at the World's Fair in Philadelphia in 1876, and which now writes business letters all over the world. The other machine was the "Horseless Carriage," which we call the Automobile,[2] and which began to attract a good deal of attention about 1900. It did not move very rapidly at first, for it was simply a buggy or a wagon moved by a small steam engine, but now it enables people to rush through the country at a rate of speed which sometimes beats even the railway trains.

Neither of these wonderful inventions was made by one man. Like Topsy, in the story of *Uncle Tom's Cabin*, both "grow'd." Both were thought out and built up, little by little, by a number of men, each one adding something until at last Typewriter and Automobile have become very nearly perfect.

[1] He flew first from America to the island of Newfoundland, where he took a rest; then he flew to the Islands of the Azores (A-zorz'), and after another short rest he flew to Lisbon and then on to England. By taking a school atlas you can follow him clear across.

[2] Automobile (aw-to-mo⁴bil).

What two things did the World's Fair at San Francisco celebrate? Can you mention three inventions exhibited at that Fair?

What is said about Fulton's Diving-Boat? How does a Submarine attack a vessel? How can a Submarine be used in times of peace?

Who invented a Reaper for cutting grain? Why did Cyrus McCormick go West? Did he succeed there? What did Elias Howe do? Did he succeed? Can you tell how the Telephone was invented? How far can we telephone now? What is said about Edison's Talking-Machine? Did Mr. Edison make any electrical inventions? What is said about Moving-Pictures? What did the Indians think of Edison's pictures? What do you think about them?

What did the Wright brothers try to invent? Can you give some account of their " Glider "? What did the Wrights do in 1903? What did one of them do at Fort Myer in 1909? What did the Wrights teach the world? What are Airships used for?

What is said about the Typewriter? What about the Automobile? Was either of these inventions made by one man?

APPENDIX

A SHORT LIST OF BOOKS OF REFERENCE

(For the Use of Teachers)

This brief list is arranged alphabetically. It consists, with a few exceptions, of small, one-volume biographies; all of which are believed to be of acknowledged merit.

A much fuller reference list will be found in the appendix to the author's larger work, entitled *The Leading Facts of American History*.

Balboa: Irving's Companions of Columbus, and Winsor's America, Vol. II.

Baltimore, Lord: William H. Browne's Lords Baltimore[3]; G. W. Burnap's Baltimore.[1]

Boone, Daniel: C. B. Hartley's Boone (including Boone's autobiography); J. M. Peck's Boone[1]; and see the excellent sketch of Boone's life in Theodore Roosevelt's The Winning of the West, Vol. I.

Cabot (John and Sebastian): William H. Johnson's The World's Discoverers: The Story of Bold Voyages by Brave Navigators (Little, Brown & Co., Boston); J. F. Nicholls's Cabot; C. Hayward's Cabot.[1]

Clark, George Rogers: see Theodore Roosevelt's The Winning of the West, Vol. II.

Columbus: William H. Johnson's The World's Discoverers: The Story of Bold Voyages by Brave Navigators (Little, Brown & Co., Boston); Irving's Columbus, abridged edition; Charles K. Adams's Columbus[3]; Edward Everett Hale's Columbus.

De Leon: Irving's Companions of Columbus, and Winsor's America, Vol. II.

De Soto: see Winsor's America, Vol. II.

Franklin, Benjamin: D. H. Montgomery's Franklin (autobiography and continuation of life)[2]; John T. Morse's Franklin.[7]

Fulton, Robert: J. Renwick's Fulton[1]; R. H. Thurston's Fulton[3]; Thos. W. Knox's Fulton.[4]

Gray, Robert: see H. H. Bancroft's Pacific States, Vol. XXII.

Harrison, William Henry: H. Montgomery's Harrison; S. J. Burr's Harrison.

Holland, R. S.: Historic Inventions.

Houston, Sam: Henry Bruce's Houston[3]; C. E. Lester's Houston.

Hudson, Henry: H. R. Cleveland's Hudson.[1]

Jackson, Andrew: James Parton's Jackson; W. G. Sumner's Jackson.[7]

Jefferson, Thomas: James Schouler's Jefferson[3]; John T. Morse, Jr.'s Jefferson.[7]

i

Lincoln, Abraham: Carl Schurz's Lincoln; Isaac N. Arnold's Lincoln; Noah Brooks's Lincoln[4]; J. G. Holland's Lincoln; F. B. Carpenter's Six Months at the White House with Lincoln.

Morse, Samuel F. B.: S. I. Prime's Morse; Denslow and Parke's Morse (Cassell).

Oglethorpe, James Edward: Bruce's Oglethorpe[3]; W. B. O. Peabody's Oglethorpe.[1]

Penn, William: G. E. Ellis's Penn[1]; W. H. Dixon's Penn; J. Stoughton's Penn.

Philip, King: H. M. Dexter's edition of Church's King Philip's War (2 vols.); Richard Markham's King Philip's War.

NOTE. — The story of Colonel Goffe's appearance at Hadley during the Indian attack on that town rests on tradition. Some authorities reject it; but Bryant and Gay say (History of the United States, II, 410), "There is no reason for doubting its essential truth."

Putnam, Rufus: see H. B. Carrington's Battles of the Revolution, Rufus King's History of Ohio, and Bancroft's United States.

Raleigh, Walter: L. Creighton's Raleigh; E. Gosse's Raleigh; W. M. Towle's Raleigh.[8]

Robertson, James: see Theodore Roosevelt's The Winning of the West, Vol. I.

Sevier, John: see Theodore Roosevelt's The Winning of the West, Vol. I.

Smith, John: G. S. Hillard's Captain John Smith[1]; C. D. Warner's Smith.[6]

NOTE. — The truth of the story of Pocahontas has been denied by Mr. Charles Deane and some other recent writers; but it appears never to have been questioned until Mr. Deane attacked it in 1866 in his notes to his reprint of Captain John Smith's *True Relation or Newes from Virginia.* Professor Edward Arber discusses the question in his Introduction (pp. cxv–cxviii) to his excellent edition of Smith's writings. He says, "To deny the truth of this Pocahontas incident is to create more difficulties than are involved in its acceptance." See, too, his sketch of the life of Captain Smith in the *Encyclopædia Britannica.*

Standish, Myles: see J. A. Goodwin's Pilgrim Republic, and Alexander Young's Chronicles of the Pilgrims.

Sutter, John A.: see H. H. Bancroft's Pacific States, Vol. XVIII.

Washington, George: John Fiske's Irving's Washington and his Country[2]; E. E. Hale's Washington[4]; Horace E. Scudder's Washington.[6]

Whitney, Eli: Denison Olmsted's Whitney.

Williams, Roger: W. R. Gammell's Williams[1]; H. M. Dexter's Williams.

Winthrop, John: Joseph H. Twichell's Winthrop.[3]

[1] In Sparks's *Library of American Biography:* Little, Brown & Co., Boston.
[2] In *Classics for Children Series:* Ginn & Company, Boston.
[3] In *Makers of America Series:* Dodd, Mead & Co., New York.
[4] In *Boys and Girls' Library of American Biography:* G. P. Putnam's Sons, New York.
[5] In the *Riverside Library for Young People:* Houghton, Mifflin & Co., Boston.
[6] In *Lives of American Worthies:* Henry Holt & Co., New York.
[7] In *The American Statesmen Series:* Houghton, Mifflin & Co., Boston.
[8] In *The Heroes of History Series:* Lee & Shepard, Boston.

INDEX

Admiral (Ad'mi-ral) (note), 6.
Æsop's Fables, The Frog (note), 226.
Airship, the, or Airplane, invented, 293–296.
Alamance (Al'a-mance), battle of, 140.
Alamo (Al'a-mo), battle of, 207.
Alaska purchased, 219.
America, Northmen discover (note), 15.
    Columbus discovers, 8, 9.
    Cabot's voyage to, 14, 15.
    name of, given, 18, 19.
    Spaniards settle in, 20, 21.
    English first settle in, 23, 25, 26.
    independence of, declared, 120, 167.
Americans, name of, 115.
Amerigo (A-ma-ree'go), see Vespucci, 18.
Anarchist (note), 254.
Apprentice (note), 92.
Armstrong, Jack, 230, 232 ; murder trial, 232.
Army, the Continental, 118.
Arnold, Benedict, 125.
Atlantic called the "Sea of Darkness," 6.
    crossed by the Northmen (note), 15.
    crossed by Columbus, 8, 9.
    crossed by a Flying-Boat (1919), 296.
Augustine, St. (Aw'gus-teen'), founded, 20.
Automobile (Aw-to-mo'bil), invented, 296.

Bacon's war in Virginia, 34.
Balboa (Bal-bo'ah) discovers the Pacific, 20.
Baltimore founded, 59.
    in the Revolution, 60.
Baltimore, Lord, in Newfoundland, 55.
    Maryland granted to, 56.
    power of, 57.
    son of, settles Maryland, 57.
    grants religious liberty, 58, 59.
    is persecuted, 59.
    summary of, 60.
Barton, Clara, 251.
Battle, playing at, 188.
Battle of Alamance (Al'a-mance), 140.
    Alamo (Al'a-mo), 207.
    Braddock's defeat, 111, 112.
    Bunker Hill, 88, 116.
    Burgoyne's defeat, 122.

Battle of Camden, 189.
    Concord, 116.
    Cowpens, 124, 188.
    El Caney, 249.
    Fort Moultrie, 123.
    Fort Necessity, 110.
    Hadley, 70, 71.
    Hobkirk's Hill, 190.
    Lexington, 115.
    Long Island, 120.
    Manila, 245–247.
    New Orleans, 193, 194.
    Princeton, 122.
    San Juan (San Wahn), 249.
    Santiago (San-te-ah'go), 249, 250.
    Saratoga, 122.
    Swamp fight, 72.
    Tippecanoe, 181–183.
    Trenton, 121.
    Vincennes (Vin-senz'), 149.
    Yorktown, 126–128.   [War, 263–278.
Battles of Civil War, 236, 237, 238 ; of Great
Beans, the sacred, 181, 183.
Bees, the, and the "Red-Coats," 187.
Bell, Alexander G., inventor, 289.
Berkeley, governor of Virginia, 34.
Black Hawk War, 231.
"Blazing" trees, 87.
Boone, Daniel, birth and boyhood of, 132.
    how he could handle a gun, 133.
    his bear tree, 133.
    goes to Kentucky, 134.
    makes the "Wilderness Road," 135.
    builds a fort, 136.
    his daughter stolen by Indians, 136.
    he is captured and adopted by Indians,
      137.
    his escape, 138.
    how he used tobacco dust, 138.
    his old age, 138, 139.
    goes to Missouri, 139.
    Kentucky helps him, 139.
    grave of, 139.
    summary of, 139.
Boston founded, 53.

Boston, name of, 53.
"Tea Party," 114.
port of, closed, 114.
British driven from, 118-120, 150-152.
Bowie (Bow'e), Colonel, 207.
Braddock's defeat, 111.
Bradford, William, caught in trap, 46.
Bradford, Governor, 46, 50.
and Canonicus, 50.
Brewster, Elder, 48.
British, the name, 115.
Brookfield burnt by Indians, 70.
"Brother Jonathan," 221.
his seven steps, 221.
origin of name (note), 221.
Brush (note), 225.
Burgoyne's defeat, 122.

Cabot (Cab'ot), John and Sebastian, 14, 15.
discover continent of America, 15.
take possession of, for England, 15, 16.
return to Bristol, 17.
what they carried back, 17.
second voyage of, 17.
how much of America they discovered, 18.
summary of, 18.
California, Captain Sutter in, 213.
gold discovered in, 214-216.
effects of discovery of gold, 218.
acquisition of, 217.
emigration to, 218.
Camden, battle of, 189, 190.
Canal, Erie, opened, 197.
Canal, Panama (Pan-a-mah′), 257, 263, 264.
Candidate (note), 235.
Canonchet (Ka-non′chet), death of, 74.
Canonicus (Ka-non′i-kus) sends challenge
to Bradford, 50.
and Roger Williams, 63, 64.
Cape Cod, arrival of Pilgrims at, 46.
explored by Pilgrims, 46.
Capitol, the, at Washington, burned, 183.
rebuilt, 183.
Carolina, North, Governor Tryon in, 140.
battle of Alamance in, 140.
the Revolution in, 124, 125, 186.
South, in the Revolution, 123, 124, 125.
secedes, 236.
begins the Civil War, 236.
Carver chosen governor, 46.
his kindness to the sick, 48.
makes treaty with Massasoit, 49.
Catholics cruelly treated in England, 55.
colony of, in Newfoundland, 55.
colony of, in Maryland, 57.

Catholics give equal religious rights to
Protestants, 58, 59.
persecuted in Maryland, 59.
first English Church of, in America, 58.
help George Rogers Clark, 146.
Cervera (Sur-vee′rah), Admiral, 247, 248, 250.
Charles II and Penn, 76, 77.
Charleston helps Georgia, 86.
in the Revolution, 123, 124.
Chicago, rapid growth of, 241.
Columbian Exposition at, 241.
Church, Captain Benjamin, 72.
Church, the first English Protestant, in
America, 27.
first English Catholic, in America, 58.
Civil War, the, 236.
causes of the, 236, 237.
battles of the, 237, 238.
Grant and Lee in the, 238.
Lincoln in the, 237, 238.
result of the, 238.
Clark, George Rogers, birth of (note), 144.
expedition against Fort Kaskaskia, 144, 145.
march against, 145.
takes the fort, 146.
is helped by a Catholic priest, 146.
his march to Vincennes, 147.
in the "Drowned Lands," 147.
wading to victory, 147, 148.
takes Fort Vincennes, 149.
results of the victory, 149.
grave of, 149.
summary of, 150.
Clearing (note), 228.
Coloma (Ko-lo′ma), gold discovered at, 217.
Colonel (kur′nel) (note), 70.
Colonies, the thirteen (note), 84.
Colony (note), 54.
"Columbus," the "American," 296.
Columbus, birth and boyhood of, 1.
becomes a sailor, 2.
has a sea-fight, 2.
goes to Lisbon, 3.
his maps of the world, 3.
plan for reaching Indies, 4.
goes to Spain for help, 4, 5.
his reception at the convent, 5.
leaves his son at the convent, 5.
gets help for his voyage, 5, 6.
sails from Palos, 6.
voyage of, 6, 8.
discovers land, 8.
names it San Salvador, 9.

Columbus names the "West Indies," 10.
　calls the natives Indians, 10.
　discovers large islands, 10, 11.
　returns to Spain, 11.
　his reception in Spain, 11, 12.
　last voyages of, 12.
　sent back to Spain in chains, 13.
　his sorrowful old age, 13.
　his letter to Ferdinand and Isabella, 13.
　death and burial, 13.
　summary of, 14.
　celebration of his discovery of America, 241.
Compass, Roger Williams's, 63.
　Smith's use of the, 29.
　Washington's use of the, 110.
Concord (Kon'kurd), battle of, 116.
Congress, meeting of the first, 115.
　makes Washington commander-in-chief, 118.
　declares independence, 120.
　meaning of word (note), 115.
　Senate and House of Representatives (note), 202.
　votes money for first telegraph lines, 202.
Continental Army, the, 118.
Convent (note), 4.
　of St. Mary at Palos, 4.
Cornwallis, Lord, in the Revolution, 121, 125, 127.
　his pursuit of Washington, 121.
　and Benedict Arnold, 125.
　shuts himself up in Yorktown, 126.
　surrender of, 127.
　news sent to Philadelphia, 128.
　"Cornwallis is taken!" 128.
Cotton, how it grows, 159.
　seeds of, 159.
　price of, 160, 161.
　effect of cotton-gin on, 160, 161.
　export of, 162, 163.
　size of bales (note), 162.
Cotton-gin, invention of, 159, 160.
　effect of the, 160, 161.
Cowpens, battle of, 124, 188.
Crockett, David, motto of, 207.
Cuba, formerly owned by Spain, 242.
　people of, rebel against Spain, 243.
　destruction of the *Maine* in, 244.
　blockaded by the United States, 245.
　Cervera "bottled up" in Santiago, 248.
　fighting at Santiago, 249.
　Cervera captured at Santiago, 250.
　the Stars and Stripes hoisted at Havana, 253.

Cuba, people of the island accept the guardianship of the United States, 253.

Declaration of Independence made, 120, 167.
　written by Jefferson, 167.
　Franklin has part in, 101.
　sent throughout the country, 167.
De Leon, pronunciation of name (note), 19.
　discovers Florida, 19.
De Soto, pronunciation of name (note), 19.
　discovers the Mississippi, 20.
Detroit, Fort, 143.
Dewey, Admiral, 246, 247.
　his great victory at Manila, 247.
Discovery, right of (note), 212.
"Drowned Lands," the, 147.

Earthquake, great, of 1811, 176, 191.
　Tecumseh predicts an, 191.
Ebenezer (Eb-e-ne'zer), settlement of, 87.
Edison, the inventor, 291.
Electricity, Franklin's experiments in, 98–101.
Eliot, Rev. John, 68.
Elizabeth, Queen, names Virginia, 23.
Ellsworth, Miss Annie, 202, 203.
Elm, the treaty, at Philadelphia, 80.
　the Washington, at Cambridge, 118.
Emigrants (note), 23.
Exhibition, the Columbian, 241.
　the Pan-American, 254.
　the San Francisco, 263.
Experiments (note), 98.
Explorer (note), 2.

Fable of the Frog and the Ox (note), 226.
Fairfax estate, 106.
Fairfax, Lord, and Washington, 106.
　hires Washington to survey land, 106.
　death of, 128.
Father Gibault (Zhe-bo') (note), 146.
　White, 58, 59.
Ferdinand and Isabella, 5, 12.
Flag, first American, 118; (note), 126, 127.
　the English (note), 126, 127.
　torn down at New York, 129.
　United States, origin of (note), 126, 127.
　carried round the world, 211, 212.
　"Star Spangled Banner," 161; (note), 161.
　of Texas, 207.
　Jasper saves the, of Fort Moultrie, 123.

Flag in our island possessions, 252.
   hoisted at Havana, Cuba, 253.
   draped in black for McKinley, 256.
Flint and steel, 63.
Florida, discovery of, 19.
   name of (note), 19.
   settlement of, 20, 21.
   Indian war in, 194.
   purchase of, 21, 194.
Flying-Machine, the, invented, 293.
Fort, Boone's, 136.
   Detroit, 143.
   Dorchester Heights, 151.
   Indian, 72.
   Jamestown, 26.
   Kaskaskia, 145, 146.
   Manhattan, 41.
   McHenry (note), 161.
   Moultrie, 123.
   Necessity, 110.
   Plymouth, 51.
   St. Augustine, 20.
   Sutter's, 213.
   Vincennes, 146-149.
Fortifications on Dorchester Heights, 151
   at New Orleans, 193.
Forts, British, at the west, 143.
   French, at the west, 109.
Founds (note), 53.
Fountain, the magic, 19.
France, the king of, helps us in the Revo-
      lution, 101, 122, 125, 127.
   See French, and Lafayette.
Franklin, Benjamin, boyhood of, 92.
   works for his father, 92.
   is apprenticed to his brother, 92.
   boards himself, 92.
   is badly treated, 92.
   runs away, 93.
   his walk across New Jersey, 93.
   lands in Philadelphia, 93.
   buys some rolls, 93.
   sees Miss Read, 94.
   goes to a Quaker meeting, 94.
   gets work in a printing office, 95.
   goes to Boston on a visit, 95.
   learns to stoop, 95.
   returns to Philadelphia, 96.
   goes to London, 96.
   called the "Water-American," 96.
   returns to Philadelphia, 96, 97.
   sets up a newspaper, 97.
   his "sawdust pudding," 97.
   his almanac, 91.
   his sayings, 91.
   his plan of life, 97.

Franklin, Benjamin, what he did for Phila-
      delphia, 89, 98.
   experiments with electricity, 98.
   his electrical picture, 98.
   his electrical kite, 99.
   his discoveries in electricity, 100, 101.
   invents the lightning-rod, 100.
   receives title of Doctor, 100.
   services in the Revolution, 101.
   thinks we must fight with bows and
      arrows, 118, 119.
   gets help for us from France, 101.
   his funeral, 101.
   counties and towns named for him,
      102.
   summary of, 102.
French, the, in America, 108.
   the war with the, 110-112.
   the, conquered, 112.
   the, at battle of Yorktown, 127.
   the, in the west, 145, 146, 167-169.
   See France, Lafayette.
Friends (or Quakers), religion of, 77.
   persecuted in England, 78.
   go to Pennsylvania, 78.
   friendly relations with the Indians, 79,
      81.
   See William Penn.
Frog, fable of the (note), 226.
Fulton, Robert, birth and boyhood of,
      172, 173.
   his paddle-wheel scow, 173.
   care of his mother, 173.
   goes to England and France, 173.
   builds iron bridges, 173.
   his diving-boat, 174, 284.
   torpedo experiments in France, 174.
   torpedo experiments in England, 174.
   England's offer of money, 174.
   his reply, 174.
   builds his first steamboat, 175.
   returns to America, 175.
   builds steamboat here, 175.
   trip up the Hudson, 175, 176.
   builds steamboat for the west, 176,
      177.
   his "Big Fire Canoe" on the Missis-
      sippi, 177, 178.
   what he did for western emigration,
      178.
   his grave, 178.
   summary of, 178.

Gadsden Purchase, the, 220.
Gage, General, in Boston, 115, 116.
   his nose, 118.

Gage, General, leaves Boston, 119.
Genoa (Jen'o-ah) (note), 1.
George II and Georgia, 84, 85.
George III, resolves to tax Americans, 112, 113.
    sends over taxed tea, 113, 114.
    closes port of Boston, 114.
    hires German soldiers, 117.
    his statue pulled down, 120.
    his character, 144.
Georgia, name of, 84.
    settlement of, 85.
    Savannah, 85.
    Ebenezer, 87.
    silk raised in, 87.
    keeps out Spaniards, 88.
    in the Revolution, 88.
    sends powder to Bunker Hill, 88.
    summary of, 89.
Gibault (Zhe-bo'), Father (note), 146.
Gin, invention of the cotton, 159–161.
Goethals (Go'thalz), Colonel George W., 258.
Goffe, Colonel, at Hadley, 71.
Gold, discovered in California, 214.
    tested by Sutter, 215, 216.
    carried to San Francisco, 218.
    excitement over, 218.
    effect of discovery of, 218.
Grant, General, 238.
Gray, Captain, voyage to the Pacific, 209.
    his fur trade with the Indians, 210.
    carries American flag around the world, 211.
    names the Columbia River, 211.
    helps us to get Oregon, 212.
    summary of, 212.
Greene, General (Revolution), 124, 158, 189.
Greene, Mrs. General, 158, 159.
Guam (Gwam), we acquire, 253.

Hadley, Indian attack on, 70, 71.
    Goffe at, 70, 71.
Hamilton, Colonel, 143, 147.
Hanks, John, and Lincoln, 228, 234, 235.
Harding, President, 278.
Harrison, General (note), 181.
    governor of Indiana territory, 181.
    marches against the Indians, 181.
    gains victory of Tippecanoe, 182, 183.
    beats the British, 183.
    elected President, 184.
    death of, 184.
    summary of, 184.
Hawaii (Hah-wy'ee) annexed, 220, 252.
Henry, Patrick, speech of, 166.

Henry, Patrick, sends Clark to take British forts, 145.
Henry VII, sends Cabot on voyage, 14.
    claims part of North America, 15, 16.
Hobson, Lieutenant, tries to "bottle up" Cervera, 248.
Holland, gives Pilgrims a refuge, 44, 45.
    takes possession of the country on the Hudson, 41.
"Holy Ground," the Indians', 192.
Houston (Hew'ston), Sam, birthplace of (note), 205.
    in war with Indians, 205.
    governor of Tennessee, 205.
    goes to live with the Indians, 205.
    goes to Texas, 205, 206.
    fights for Texas, 206, 207.
    is made president of Texas, 207.
    in the Civil War, 208.
    death of, 208.
    summary of, 209.
Howe, General, driven from Boston, 119.
Hudson, Henry, first voyage of, 36.
    hired by the Dutch, 37.
    sails for America, 37.
    discovers the "Great River," 37.
    what he said about the country, 38.
    voyage up the river, 38, 39.
    is feasted by the Indians, 39.
    what the Indians thought of him, 39.
    has fight with Indians, 40.
    sails for Europe, 40.
    Hudson River is named for him, 40.
    death of, in Hudson Bay, 40.
    what he would think of New York now, 42.
    summary of, 42.
Hudson River, described, 38.
    named, 40.
    Dutch settle on the, 41.

Illinois, Clark's conquest of, 145, 146.
Independence, see Declaration of Independence.
Indians, Columbus names the, 10.
    described, 10, 11, 17, 28, 29.
    welcome the English, 22, 39, 48, 64.
    welcome Sam Houston, 205.
    thought the white men came down from the sky, 39.
    of Virginia, 28.
    how they lived, 28, 29.
    and Captain Smith, 29, 30, 31.
    Pocahontas saves Smith's life, 30.
    feast Henry Hudson, 39.
    make treaty with Pilgrims, 49.

Indians contribute to the Thanksgiving
    of the Pilgrims, 49.
  help the Pilgrims, 49, 50.
  challenge Pilgrims to fight, 50.
  Standish's fight with the, 51, 52 f.
  help the settlers of Maryland, 58.
  Roger Williams defends rights of, to
    land, 61.
  how they helped Williams, 63.
  how they lost their lands, 67, 155, 179,
    180, 195, 196.
  great war with, in New England, 67-76.
  driven off by a woman, 71.
  Penn defends rights of, to land, 79.
  make treaty with Penn, 80, 81.
  Penn's frolic with the, 81.
  their love for him, 82, 83.
  present his widow with rich furs, 82, 83.
  friendly to the Quakers, 81.
  Washington is present at a war-dance
    of, 108.
  act as guides to Washington, 109.
  attempt to murder Washington, 109.
  attack General Braddock, 111.
  and Daniel Boone, 132, 133, 134.
  their tricks and stratagems, 134.
  capture Boone's daughter, 136.
  capture Boone and adopt him, 137,
    138.
  Boone escapes from the, 138.
  in the Revolution, 144.
  war in Ohio, 153-155.
  victory of General Wayne over the,
    155.
  what they called the steamboat, 176.
  forced to move west, 179.
  story of the log, " Move on ! " 179.
  badly treated by the white men, 180.
  the " Prophet's " influence over the,
    180-183.
  his " sacred beans," 181, 183.
  victory of Harrison over, 182.
  what Tecumseh told the, 191.
  the, and the earthquake, 191.
  the " Holy Ground " of the, 192.
  victory of Jackson over, 191, 192.
  Captain Gray buys furs from the, 210.
  Sam Houston goes to live with the,
    205.
  General Jackson and Weathersford,
    192.
  " fire-water " hurts the, 180.
  the, and the locomotive whistle, 195,
    196.
  move west of the Mississippi, 196.
  Abraham Lincoln and the, 231.

Indians. See Black Hawk, Canonchet,
    Canonicus, King Philip, Massasoit,
    Pocahontas, Powhatan, Samoset,
    Squanto, Tecumseh, the " Prophet,"
    Wamsutta, Weathersford.
Indian treaty with Pilgrims, 49.
  with Penn, 80, 81.
Indian wars, Captain Standish's fight, 51, 52.
  King Philip's War, 67.
  in Kentucky, 134, 135, 136.
  at the west, in the Revolution, 144.
  in Ohio, 153-155.
  in Indiana, 179, 182.
  in Alabama, 191, 192.
  in Florida, 194.
  in Illinois, 231.
  Black Hawk War, 231.
Inventions, American, 159, 174, 175, 198,
    263-264, 271, 273-274, 283-297.

Jackson, Andrew, boyhood of, 185.
  and the gun, 185.
  and Tarleton, 186.
  his mother, 186, 190.
  his hatred of the British, 186.
  dangers exposed to, 187.
  playing at battle, 187, 188.
  taken prisoner, 188.
  and the boots, 188.
  sees a battle through a knot-hole,
    189, 190.
  death of his mother, 190.
  what he said of her, 190.
  begins to learn a trade, 190.
  studies law, 190.
  goes to Tennessee, 190.
  becomes judge, 190, 191.
  becomes general, 191.
  fights the Indians, 191, 192.
  interview with Weathersford, 192.
  wins the great battle of New Orleans,
    193, 194.
  conquers Indians in Florida, 194.
  elected President, 194.
  four steps in life of, 195.
  first steam railroad, 195.
  summary of, 196.
James I, Jamestown named for, 26.
  denies religious liberty to his subjects,
    44, 53.
Jamestown settled, 26.
  burned, 34.
Jasper, Sergeant, how he saved the flag,
    123.
Jefferson, Thomas, birth of, 164.
  home at Monticello, 164.

Jefferson, Thomas, beloved by his slaves, 165.
  desires to free his slaves, 166.
  hears Patrick Henry speak, 166.
  writes Declaration of Independence, 167.
  elected President, 167.
  what he said about New Orleans and Louisiana, 167, 168.
  buys Louisiana, 168, 169.
  his death, 170.
  inscription on his tombstone, 170.
  summary of, 170.
" Jonathan, Brother," 221.
  his seven steps, 221.
  origin of name (note), 221.
Jury (note), 27.
Jury trial, first in America, 27.

Kaskaskia (Kas-kas'ki-a), Fort, 143, 145, 146.
King Philip, son of Massasoit, 66.
  becomes chief, 66.
  how he dressed and lived, 66.
  his hatred of the whites, 67.
  determines to make war, 67.
  Indians attack Swansea, 68.
  attack other towns, 69.
  burn Brookfield, 70.
  attack Hadley, 70, 71.
  bravery shown by a woman, 71.
  the great swamp fight, 72.
  Canonchet taken, 74.
  Philip's wife and son taken, 74.
  wife and son sold into slavery, 74.
  Philip shot, 74, 75.
  destruction caused by the war, 75.
  cost of the war, 75.
  Indian power broken, 75.
  summary of, 75.

Lafayette (Lah-fay-et'), helps us in the Revolution, 125.
  pursues Cornwallis, 126.
  at the tomb of Washington, 130.
Land, rights of Indians to, 61, 79.
Land acquired from the Indians, 67, 155, 179, 180, 195, 196.
Land acquired by the United States, see Territory and United States.
Lee, General, in the Civil War, 238.
Legislature (note), 234.
Lexington, battle of, 115.
Leyden (Li'den), Holland, 44.
Leyden jar, 98, 99, 100.
Liberty, religious, in Maryland, 58, 60.

Liberty, religious, in Rhode Island, 64, 65.
  religious, none formerly in England, 44, 55, 78.
Liberty, Sons of, in the Revolution, 41.
Liberty, statue of, 42.
Library, the first public, in America, 98.
Lincoln, Abraham, birth and boyhood of, 223.
  how he lived, 224, 225.
  death of his mother, 225.
  what he said of her, 225.
  what his step-mother said of him, 225.
  at school, 225, 226.
  teaches himself at home, 226, 227.
  what he read, 226.
  how he used the fire-shovel, 227.
  description of, at seventeen, 227.
  his strength, 227.
  goes to New Orleans, 227, 228.
  drives off a gang of robbers, 228.
  moves to Illinois, 228.
  splits rails, 229.
  hunting frolics, 228, 229.
  tends store at New Salem, 230.
  is attacked by Jack Armstrong, 230.
  he teaches Jack a lesson, 230.
  his faithfulness in little things, 230.
  called " Honest Abe," 230.
  in the Black Hawk War, 231.
  becomes postmaster and surveyor, 231.
  studies law, 231.
  begins to practise law, 231.
  respected by all men, 231, 232.
  in Armstrong murder trial, 232.
  how he saved the pig, 233.
  goes to the legislature, 234.
  goes to Congress, 234.
  chosen candidate for President, 235.
  elected President, 235, 236.
  his election brings on the Civil War, 236, 237.
  emancipates the slaves, 238.
  murdered by Booth, 238.
  grief of the nation at his death, 238.
  summary of, 238.
Log, the story of the, 179.
Louisiana, purchase of, 169.
  original extent of, 169, 170, 171, 172.

McKinley, President, 242, 245, 246, 254.
  is murdered, 254.
  his funeral, 255, 256.
Maine, the destruction of the, 244.
Major (note), 109.
Manhattan Island, 37, 41, 42.
Manila, battle of, see Battles.

Manila, capital of the Philippines, 246, 252.
General Merritt takes, 251.
Map of the world before Columbus discovered America, 2, 3.
of voyage of Columbus, 9.
of parts of America discovered by Columbus, 12.
showing where John Cabot lived, 15.
of John Cabot's landing in America, 15.
of the coast of America discovered by the Cabots, 18.
of first English settlement in Virginia, 23.
of Jamestown, Virginia, 27.
of Henry Hudson's plan for reaching Asia, 36.
of the Hudson River, 38.
of homes of the Pilgrims in England and Holland, 44.
of first English settlements in Massachusetts, 46.
of first settlement of Maryland, 58.
of Roger Williams's route to Mount Hope, 62.
of first settlement of Rhode Island, 65.
of King Philip's War, 68.
of first settlement of Pennsylvania, 79.
of first settlement of Georgia, 85.
of Franklin's journey to Philadelphia, 93.
illustrating the early life of Washington, facing 106.
of the northern states in the Revolution, facing 116.
of the southern states in the Revolution, facing 124.
of Boone's " Wilderness Road," 136.
of George Rogers Clark's line of march, 144.
of the battle of Tippecanoe, 179.
of Sutter's Fort California, 214.
Maps showing the territorial growth of the United States :
1. The United States at the close of the Revolution and in 1801, 168.
2. The United States after our purchase of Louisiana in 1803, 169.
3. The United States after our purchase of Florida in 1819, 194.
4. The United States after we added Texas in 1845, 208.
5. The United States after we added the Oregon Country in 1846, 211.

Maps showing the territorial growth of the United States :
6. The United States after we added California and New Mexico in 1848, 216.
7. The United States after the Gadsden Purchase in 1853, 219.
8. The United States after we added Alaska in 1867, facing 220.
9. The United States after we added our island possessions in 1898, facing 244.
Marietta, Ohio, settled, 152, 153.
name of, 153.
what Washington said of, 153.
and the Indians, 153, 154.
summary of, 155.
Marshall finds gold in California, 214-216.
his poverty, 218.
Maryland, name of, 56.
granted to Lord Baltimore, 56.
rent of, 56.
settlement of, 57.
first Catholic church in America in, 58.
home of religious liberty, 58.
trouble with Virginia, 59.
Catholics of, badly treated, 59.
Baltimore city founded, 59.
in the Revolution, 60.
summary of, 60.
Massachusetts, name of, 54.
settlement of, 53, 54.
in the Revolution, 54.
Massasoit (Mas-sa-soit'), makes treaty with the Pilgrims, 49.
and Roger Williams, 61, 62, 63.
death of, 66.
King Philip, his son, 66.
Mayflower, voyage of the, 45, 46, 47, 48, 53.
Ohio boat so named, 152.
Messages (note), 198.
Mexico, war with, 217.
territory obtained from, 217.
Miami (Mi-am'i), Ohio, 154.
Mine, the, in Havana harbor, 244.
(note), 244.
Mississippi, De Soto discovers the, 20.
lower part of, belonged to France, 167.
we get possession of the, 170.
first steamboat on the, 177, 178.
Moccasins (note), 119.
Model (note), 201.
Monticello (Mon-te-sel'lo), described, 164.
Morgan's sharpshooters, 124.
Morse, Samuel F. B., birth and boyhood of, 198.

Morse, Samuel F. B., becomes a painter, 198.
  goes to France, 198.
  thinks of using electricity to send messages, 198.
  returns to America, 198.
  invents electric telegraph, 198, 199.
  his poverty, 200, 201.
  takes the first photograph in America, 200.
  gets assistance from Mr. Vail, 200, 201.
  obtains patent for the telegraph, 201.
  receives help from Congress, 202.
  and Miss Annie Ellsworth, 202, 203.
  builds line of telegraph, 203.
  the first message sent. 203.
  how a message is sent (note), 203.
  the first year of telegraphy, 203.
  the ocean telegraph, 203.
  the telephone (note), 202, 204.
  summary of, 204.
Moultrie (Mole'tree), Colonel, 123.
  Fort, 123.
Mount Vernon, Washington at, 106, 117, 129, 130.
"Move on, won't you?" 179.
Moving-Pictures, Edison's, 291.

Nations (note), 194.
Negroes (see Slaves) made free, 238.
New Amsterdam, 41.
New England, name of, 33, 47.
  first settlements in, 48, 53.
New Netherland, name of, 41.
  seized by the English, 41.
New Orleans (New Or'le-anz), 167, 168.
  cotton exported from, 162.
  purchase of, 169, 170.
  battle of, 193.
New Salem, Illinois, 230, 231.
Newspaper, Franklin's, 97, 103
New York, name of, 41.
New York City, name, 41.
  in the Revolution, 41, 126, 129.
  the greatest city in America, 42.
  became the capital of the United States 130.
  Washington made President in, 130.
North and South in the Civil War, 237.
Northmen discover America (note), 15.
North Pole, discovery of the, 262.
Nurses, the Red Cross, 251, 252.

Oglethorpe (O'gel-thorp), General, who he was, 84.
  and prisoners for debt, 84, 85.

Oglethorpe (O'gel-thorp), General, gets grant of Georgia, 85.
  object of settling Georgia, 85.
  builds Savannah, 85, 86.
  welcomes German settlers, 86, 87.
  attempts to produce silk, 87.
  sends silk as present to the queen of England, 88.
  keeps out the Spaniards, 88.
  in his old age, 88, 89.
  summary of, 89.
Ohio, first settlement in, 152.
  Indian wars in, 153, 154, 155.
Ohio River, first steamboat on, 176.
Oregon, how we got our claim to, 212.
  added to the United States, 212, 220.

Pacific, Balboa discovers the, 20.
Pacific Railroad completed (note), 241.
Pacific railroads, the five, 240.
Palisade, 51.
Palisades of the Hudson (note), 38.
Palmetto logs (note), 123.
Palos (Pä'lōs), convent at, 4.
  Columbus sails from, 6.
Panama (Pan-a-mah') Canal, 257, 263, 264.
Pan-American Exposition, 254.
Parker, Captain, at Lexington, 115.
Patent (note), 201.
Penn, William, receives grant of Pennsylvania, 76.
  belongs to the Society of Friends or Quakers, 77.
  his religion, 77.
  sends emigrants to Pennsylvania, 78.
  his conversation with Charles II, 79.
  founds Philadelphia, 79, 80.
  his treaty with the Indians, 81.
  his treaty elm protected by a British officer, 81.
  visits the Indians, 81.
  beats them at their athletic sports, 81.
  said the people should make their own laws, 82.
  goes back to England, 82.
  the victim of a dishonest agent, 82.
  goes to prison for debt, 82.
  death of, 82.
  the Indians present his widow with rich furs, 82, 83.
  love of the Indians for him, 82, 83.
  his grave, 83.
  summary of, 83.
Pennsylvania, named by Charles II, 77.
  granted to William Penn, 76.
  natural wealth of, 77.

Pennsylvania in the Revolution, 82, 83.
Philadelphia, founded, 79, 80.
    name of, 80.
    prosperity of, 81, 82, 89, 98.
    in the Revolution, 82, 83, 114, 115, 122, 228.
    first Continental Congress meets in, 82, 83, 114, 115.
    Declaration of Independence, made in, 82, 83.
    what Franklin did for, 98.
    Franklin buried in, 101.
Philip, King, see King Philip.
Philippine (Fil'ip-peen) Islands, the, 245, 246, 251, 252; (note), 253.
    we pay Spain for the (note), 253.
Phonograph, the, invented, 271, 272.
Photograph, first, in America, 200.
Pictures, Moving-, 272–273.
Pilgrims, the, in Holland, 44.
    name of, 44.
    persecuted in England, 44, 45.
    why they wished to leave Holland, 45.
    sail for America, 45.
    Captain Myles Standish goes with them, 45.
    number of the, 45.
    make a compact of government, 46.
    elect John Carver first governor, 46.
    land on Cape Cod, 46.
    wash-day, 46.
    explore the cape, 46.
    land on Plymouth Rock, 47.
    settle in Plymouth, 48.
    why they chose that place, 47.
    name of Plymouth, 47.
    sickness and death, 48.
    meet Indians, 48.
    make treaty with Massasoit, 49.
    their first Thanksgiving, 49.
    Canonicus dares them to fight, 50.
    Governor Bradford's reply, 50.
    build a fort, 51.
    build a palisade around the town, 51.
    fight the Indians at Weymouth, 52.
    what Myles Standish did for the Pilgrims, 52, 53.
    summary of, 54.
    See Myles Standish.
Pioneers (note), 206.
Pittsburg, 145, 152, 176; and see map, 124.
Plantation (note), 103.
Planter (note), 34.
Plymouth, the Pilgrims settle, 47, 48.
    natural advantages of, 47.
    name of, 47.

Plymouth. See Pilgrims.
Plymouth Rock, Pilgrims land on, 47.
Pocahontas (Po-ka-hon'tas) saves Smith's life, 30; and see under Smith, in List of Books in Appendix.
    marries John Rolfe, 30.
    her descendants, 30.
Pole, the North, discovered, 262.
Ponce de Leon, see De Leon.
Porto Rico, how we got, 250, 252.
Potato, the, sent to England, 23.
    Raleigh plants it in Ireland, 23.
Powder, lack of, in Revolution, 116.
    sent to Bunker Hill, 88.
Powhatan (Pow-ha-tan') and Captain John Smith, 30.
Prison-ships, British, 190.
"Prophet," the, and Tecumseh, 180–183.
    promises gigantic corn and pumpkins, 181.
    his sacred beans, 181, 183.
    at the battle of Tippecanoe, 182.
    Indians say he is a liar, 183.
    Tecumseh takes him by the hair, 183.
Prophet (note), 180.
Providence, name of, 64.
    settled, 64.
    religious liberty in, 64.
Pudding, Franklin's sawdust, 97.
Puritans (note), 44, 53.
    settle Boston, 53.
Putnam, General Rufus, services in the Revolution, 150–152.
    builds fortifications, 151, 152.
    builds the *Mayflower*, 152.
    settles Marietta, Ohio, 152, 153.
    summary of, 155.
Pyramid, the great American, 278.

Quakers, see Friends.

Railroad, the first, in America, 195 and note.
    growth of railroads, 196.
    the, and the Indians, 195, 196.
    first Pacific (note), 241.
    the five Pacific railroads, 240.
Raleigh (Raw'li), Sir Walter, a favorite of Queen Elizabeth, 22.
    sends exploring expedition to America, 22.
    receives title of honor, 23.
    sends settlers to Virginia, 23.
    receives tobacco and potato plants from Virginia, 23.
    plants them in Ireland, 23.

Raleigh (Raw'li), Sir Walter, spends a great deal of money on his Virginia colony, 23.
  fails to establish a settlement, 24.
  last days of, 24.
  is beheaded, 24.
  power of his example, 24.
  summary of, 24.
Ranches (note), 240.
Randolph, John, of Virginia, 30.
Reaper, the, invented, 284-287.
Rebels (note), 188.
Red-coats (note), 186.
Red-coats, the, and the bees, 187.
Red Cross Society, the, 250, 251, 252, 269.
Religious liberty, formerly none in England, 44, 53, 55, 78.
  liberty in Maryland, 58.
  liberty in Rhode Island, 64.
  persecution in England, 44, 45, 53, 55, 78.
  persecution of Catholics, 55.
  persecution of Pilgrims, 44, 45.
  persecution of Puritans, 53.
  persecution of Quakers, 78.
Revere's (Re-veer'), Paul, ride, 115.
Revolution, the cause of, 112, 113, 166.
  first blood shed in, 115, 116.
  Patrick Henry says, "We must fight," 166.
  "Sons of Liberty" in the, 41.
  progress of, 112-127.
  Declaration of Independence, 120, 167.
  battles of, see Battles.
  British prison-ship of the, 190.
  help given by France and the French in the, 101, 122, 125, 127, 146.
  end of the, 126-129.
  See Greene, Lafayette, Clark, Franklin, Jefferson, Putnam, Washington.
  the, in Delaware, 82.
  Georgia, 88.
  Maryland, 60.
  Massachusetts, 54, 114-116, 118, 119, 150-152.
  New England, 54.
  New Jersey, 82, 121, 122.
  New York, 41, 114, 120, 122, 126, 129.
  North Carolina, 88, 124, 140, 186, 190.
  Pennsylvania, 82, 114, 115, 122, 128.
  Rhode Island, 65.
  South Carolina, 88, 114, 123, 124, 188-190.
  Virginia, 35; (note), 114, 124, 125-128, 145, 146, 166, 167.

Revolution in the west, 143-149.
Rhode Island, settled, 64.
  religious liberty in, 64.
  in the Revolution, 65.
Robertson, James, birthplace of (note), 140.
  his home in North Carolina, 140.
  emigrates to Watauga, Tennessee, 141.
  and Sevier, 142.
  what he did for the new settlement, 142.
  Washington makes him general, 142.
  summary of, 143.
Rolfe, John, marries Pocahontas, 30.
Roosevelt, Colonel, 249.
  President, 255.
"Rough Riders," the, in Cuba, 249.

Sacramento, Sutter's Fort at, 213.
Sacred (note), 181.
St. Louis a hundred years ago, 172.
St. Mary's, settlement of, 58.
Salem, Roger Williams' church at, 60, 61.
Samoset (Sam'o-set) and the Pilgrims, 48.
Sampson, Rear-Admiral, 245, 248, 250.
San Salvador (Sal'va-dor), Columbus names, 9.
Saratoga, battle of, 122.
Savannah settled, 85.
  in the Revolution, 88.
"Sawdust pudding," Franklin's, 97.
Schley, Rear-Admiral, 245, 248, 250.
Seal, great, of United States, 278 and note.
Seekonk, Roger Williams at, 63.
Senate Chamber (note), 202.
Sergeant (Sar'jent) (note), 123.
Sevier (Se-veer'), John, born in Virginia, (note), 140, 142.
  emigrates to Watauga, Tennessee, 142.
  and Robertson, 142.
  what he did for Watauga, 142.
  becomes governor of Tennessee, 143.
  summary of, 143.
Sewing Machine, the, invented, 287-289.
Sharpshooters in the Revolution, 118, 124.
Silk, attempt to produce, in Georgia, 87.
  sent to England, 88.
  the queen has a dress made of it, 88.
Silkworm (note), 87.
Slaves, negro, first brought to Virginia, 33, 34.
  employed in raising tobacco, 34.
  planters grow rich by, 34.
  all the colonies buy, 34.
  at the Revolution all of the states held, 236.

Slaves, Washington's, 117.
  Jefferson beloved by his, 165, 166.
  Jefferson's feeling in regard to, 166.
  how employed on cotton, 159.
  and the cotton-gin, 160.
  gradually freed at the North, 236.
  their condition unchanged at the South, 236.
  feeling at the South about, 237.
  feeling at the North about, 237.
  question of holding, divides the states, 236, 237.
  Lincoln in regard to increasing number of, 237.
  and the Civil War, 236, 237.
  freed by President Lincoln, 238.
  effect of emancipation of, on the Union, 238.
Smith, John, early life and adventures of, 25.
  sold as a slave, 25.
  starts for Virginia, 26.
  arrested on the voyage on a false charge, 26.
  is tried and acquitted, 27.
  court grants him damages, 27.
  what he hoped to do in Virginia, 26, 27.
  what he did for the sick, 27.
  prevents desertion, 28.
  goes in search of the Pacific, 29.
  is captured by Indians, 29.
  how he used his pocket compass, 29.
  brought before Powhatan, 30.
  Pocahontas saves his life, 30.
  made governor of Jamestown, 31.
  his opinion of the gold-diggers, 31.
  compels Indians to let settlers have corn, 31.
  makes all the settlers work, 31, 32.
  his cold-water cure for swearing, 32.
  meets with a terrible accident, 32.
  goes back to England, 32.
  returns and explores country north of Virginia, 32, 33.
  names it New England, 33.
  death and burial of, 33.
  what he did for Virginia, 33.
  his books and maps, 33.
  is called the "Father of Virginia," 33.
  writes Captain Henry Hudson, 37.
  summary of, 35.
"Sons of Liberty" in the Revolution, 41.
South, the, in the Civil War, 237, 238.
  great progress of, since the war, 240.

Spain, great possessions once held by, in America, 242.
  the war with, 241-254.
  peace made with, 251.
  we pay $20,000,000 to, for the Philippines (note), 253.
Spaniards settle Florida, 20.
  are kept out of Georgia, 88.
Squanto (Skwon'to) and the Pilgrims, 48, 49, 50.
Squaws (note), 137.
Standish, Myles, an English soldier in Holland, 45.
  goes to America with the Pilgrims, 45.
  explores Cape Cod, 46.
  lands at Plymouth Rock, 47.
  was nurse as well as soldier, 48.
  goes to meet Massasoit, 49.
  escorts the Pilgrims to church, 51.
  has a fight with the Indians, 51, 52.
  saves Plymouth from attack by Indians, 52.
  what else he did for the Pilgrims, 53.
  what he left at his death, 53.
  his monument, 53.
  summary of, 54.
Star-Spangled Banner, song of the, 161 and note.
Steamboat, Fulton's, on the Hudson, 175.
  first at the west, 176-178.
  effect of, on emigration, 178.
"Stoop! stoop!" Franklin learns its meaning, 95.
Story of Pocahontas, 30.
  "Corn, or your life!" 31.
  Smith's cold-water cure, 32.
  Colonel Goffe, 71.
  the woman and the Indians, 71.
  "Stoop! stoop!" 95.
  Franklin's "sawdust pudding," 97.
  Franklin's electrical picture, 98.
  Franklin's kite, 99.
  Washington and the colt, 104.
  Continental sharpshooters, 118.
  General Gage's nose, 118.
  how the British marched out of Yorktown, 127, 128.
  "Cornwallis is taken!" 128.
  Indian tricks, 134.
  Boone's escape from the Indians, 138.
  Clark takes Kaskaskia, 145.
  Clark wading to victory, 147.
  Eli Whitney's fiddle, 157.
  the Star-Spangled Banner (note), 161.
  Jefferson and his slaves, 165.
  Fulton's paddle-wheel boat, 173.

Story of Fulton's diving-boat, 174.
the negro and the steamboat on the Mississippi, 177.
"Move on, won't you?" 179.
the "Prophet's" corn and pumpkins, 181.
his "sacred beans," 181, 183.
Jackson and the gun, 185.
the bees and the "red-coats," 187.
playing at battle, 188.
"clean those boots," 188.
seeing a battle through a knot-hole, 189.
Tecumseh's earthquake, 191.
Morse's telegraph, 197-199.
Morse and Annie Ellsworth, 202, 203.
Marshall finds gold, 214-216, 218.
Lincoln's fire-shovel, 226.
"Honest Abe," 230.
the Armstrong murder trial, 232.
Lincoln and the pig, 233.
the frog and the ox (note), 226.
Hobson and Cervera, 248.
Submarine, the, invented, 174, 284.
Survey (note), 106.
Sutter (Süt'er), John A., his fort in California, 213.
founds Sacramento, 213.
lives like a king, 213.
begins to build saw-mill at Coloma, 214.
Marshall finds some gold-dust, 214.
Marshall brings him gold-dust to test, 215.
is convinced that gold has been found, 216.
how he felt at the discovery, 216.
loses his property, 218.
is pensioned by California, 218.
summary of, 221.
Swansea (Swon'ze), Indians attack, 68.
Swordfish (note), 174.

Taft, William H., 262.
"Tanks" in the Great War, 274-275.
Tarleton (Tarl'ton), cruelty of, 186, 187.
his soldiers and the bees, 187.
is beaten at Cowpens, 188.
what he hears from the children, 188.
Taxation of America by George III, 112.
chief cause of the Revolution, 112, 113.
Tea, taxed, sent to America, 113.
destruction of, 114.
"Boston tea-party," 114.
Tecumseh (Te-kum'seh) excites the Indians to war, 180.
takes the "Prophet" by the hair, 183.

Tecumseh (Te-kum'seh) fights for the British in Canada, 183.
is killed, 183.
Telegraph, meaning of the word (note), 198.
what it is, 198, 199, 203.
electric, invented by Morse, 198-200.
Vail's work on, 200, 201.
patented by Morse, 201.
Congress grants money to build line, 201, 202.
first message over, 203.
business of, in 1845, 203.
business of, to-day, 203.
how messages are sent by (note), 203.
Atlantic, 203.
See Morse, Samuel F. B.
Telephone, meaning of the word (note), 202.
what it is, 204.
when invented (note), 202, 289.
use of, to-day, 204, 290.
Tennessee, first settlement of, 141, 142.
Houston in, 205.
See James Robertson, John Sevier.
Terrier (note), 183.
Territory added to the United States during the Revolution, 149.
Louisiana (1803), 169, 219.
Florida (1819), 220.
Texas (1845), 207; 220.
Oregon (1846), 212, 220.
California (1848), 217, 220.
New Mexico (1848), 220.
Gadsden Purchase (1853), 220.
Alaska (1867), 219, 220.
Hawaii (1898), 220, 252.
Porto Rico (1899), 252.
Guam (1899), 253.
Philippines (1899), 252.
maps showing acquisition of territory by the United States, see Maps.
summary of ("Brother Jonathan's" seven steps), 221.
See United States, Maps.
Tests (note), 216.
Texas, forms part of Mexico, 206.
we try to buy it, 206.
Houston goes to, 205, 206.
massacre of Americans at Fort Alamo, 207.
war of independence, 207.
flag of, 207.
annexed, 207.
dispute with Mexico about boundary, 217.

Texas, Mexican war and, 217.
   and the Civil War, 208.
   summary of, 209.
Thanksgiving, the first in America, 49.
Tippecanoe, battle of, 181, 182.
"Tippecanoe! and Tyler too!" (note), 184.
Tobacco sent from Virginia to Sir Walter
   Raleigh, 23.
   Raleigh plants it in Ireland, 23.
   value of, to Virginia, 34.
Torpedo (note), 174, 284.
   Fulton's experiments with torpedoes,
   174.
Tow cloth (note), 229.
Travis (Tra'vis), Colonel, in Texas, 206.
Treaty, Indian, with Pilgrims, 49.
   with William Penn, 81.
   of peace with Spain, 251.
"Treaty Elm," at Philadelphia (note), 80.
Trumbull, Governor ("Brother Jona-
   than") and General Washington,
   221.
Tryon, Governor, in North Carolina, 140.
   oppression by, 140, 141.
   the "Great Wolf of Carolina," 140.
   at battle of Alamance, 140.
Typewriter, the, invented, 296.

Union (note), 236.
   the South resolves to withdraw from
   the, 236.
   strengthened by results of the Civil
   War, 238, 239.
United States, independence of, declared,
   120, 167.
   War of the Revolution, see Revolution.
   more perfect union formed (note), 236.
   extent of, at the close of the Revolution, 219.
   acquires Louisiana (1803), 169, 170, 219.
   acquires Florida (1819), 194, 220.
   acquires Texas (1845), 207, 220.
   acquires Oregon (1846), 212, 220.
   acquires California and New Mexico
   (1848), 217, 220.
   acquires Gadsden Purchase (1853), 218,
   220.
   acquires Alaska (1867), 219, 220.
   acquires Guam, 253.
   acquires Hawaii, 220, 252.
   acquires Porto Rico, 252.
   acquires the Philippines, 252 and
   (note), 253.
   extent of, to-day, 221.
   "Brother Jonathan's" seven steps,
   221.

United States, maps showing acquisition
   of territory, see Maps.
   War of 1812, 161, 193.
   war of, with Mexico, 207, 217.
   the Civil War, 236–239.
   growth since the Civil War, 252, 253.
   and Columbian Exhibition, 241.
   war with Spain, 243–253.
   Pan-American Exhibition, 254.
   and the Great War, 263.
   and "Victory Day," 276.
   great seal of, 278.
   what we can do for, 279.

Vail, Alfred, and Morse's telegraph, 200.
Venison (note), 22.
Vespucci, Amerigo (A-ma-ree'go Ves-poot'-
   chee), 18, 19; and "America," 18.
"Victory Day" (November 11, 1918), 276.
Vigo (Vee'go) helps Clark, 146, 147.
Vincennes (Vin-senz'), Fort, 147–149.
Virginia, Raleigh's expedition to, 22.
   named by Elizabeth, 23.
   first settlement in, 23.
   first English child in America born in,
   23.
   failure of first settlement, 23, 24.
   tobacco and potatoes sent from, 23.
   permanently settled at Jamestown,
   26.
   first English church in, 27.
   first jury trial in, 27.
   Captain Smith made governor of, 31.
   Smith's books about, 33.
   slaves sent to, 33, 34.
   tobacco, cultivation of, 34.
   prosperity of, 34.
   Berkeley and Bacon's war in, 34.
   Jamestown burned, 34.
   growth of, 34.
   makes ready to fight for its rights
   (note), 114.
   first demands the independence of
   America, 35.
   in the Revolution, see Revolution.
   owned extensive western possessions,
   144.
   George Washington and, 35.
   the "Mother of Presidents," 35.
   in the Civil War, 238.
   summary of, 35.
   See John Smith, George Washington,
   Thomas Jefferson, George Rogers
   Clark.
Virginia Dare, birth of, 23.
Voted (note), 202.

Wamsutta, death of, 66.

War, Bacon's, in Virginia, 34.
  King Philip's, in New England, 68.
  of the Revolution, see Revolution.
  with the British in the west, 143–150.
  with Indians in the west, 144.
  with Indians in Ohio, 153–155.
  with Indians in Indiana, 181–183.
  with Indians in Illinois, 231.
  the Black Hawk, 231.
  with Indians in Alabama, 191, 192.
  with Indians in Florida, 194.
  of 1812, 161 and note, 183, 193.
  cause of, of 1812, 183.
  of Texan independence, 206, 207.
  with Mexico, 207, 217.
  cause of Mexican, 217.
  the Civil, 236–239.
  cause of the Civil, 236, 237.
  with Spain, 241–254.
  cause of Spanish, 242–244.
  the Great (1914–1918), 263–278.

Washington, George, birth and boyhood of, 103–105.
  at school, 104.
  playing at war, 104.
  battle with the colt, 104, 105.
  what he owed to his mother, 103.
  visits Mount Vernon, 106.
  makes acquaintance of Lord Fairfax, 106.
  surveys Lord Fairfax's land, 106–108.
  life in the woods, 106–108.
  sees an Indian war-dance, 108.
  is made public surveyor, 108.
  appearance of, at twenty-one, 108.
  receives title of major, 109.
  governor of Virginia sends him to order off the French, 109.
  journey through the wilderness, 109, 110.
  narrow escape of, 109, 110, 112.
  receives title of colonel, 110.
  goes with Braddock's expedition, 111.
  tries to hold Fort Necessity, 110.
  goes to Mount Vernon to live, 117.
  his slaves, 117.
  fasts when the king closes the port of Boston (note), 114.
  made commander-in-chief in the Revolution, 118.
  takes command of the Continental Army, 118.
  raises first American flag, 118, (note), 126.

Washington, George, drives British from Boston, 119, 120, 150, 151, 152.
  goes to New York, 120.
  chased by Cornwallis, 121.
  retreats across the Delaware, 121.
  victory of Trenton, 121.
  victory of Princeton, 122.
  at Valley Forge, 122.
  enters Philadelphia, 122.
  marches against Yorktown, 126.
  takes Yorktown, 127, 128.
  his coat of arms (note), 126.
  goes back to Mount Vernon, 129.
  elected President, 130.
  takes oath of office, 130.
  Lafayette visits his tomb, 130.
  summary of, 130, 131.

Washington, Lawrence, at Mount Vernon, 106.
  death of, 117.
  Colonel William, 188 and note.

Washington, the Capitol at, burned, 183.
  rebuilt, 183.

Watauga (Wa-taw'ga), settlement of, 141, 142.

Wayne, General, in Ohio, 155.

Weathersford and General Jackson, 192.

West, the, in the Revolution, 143.
  conquest of the, 143–149.
  French in the southwest, 167–169.
  at treaty of peace with England, 149.
  settlement of, 135, 136, 139, 141, 142, 143, 144, 152, 155, 171, 172, 178, 179, 180, 190, 195, 196, 205, 206, 218, 223, 228, 240, 241.
  acquisition of country west of the Mississippi, see United States, and see Territory and Maps.
  once called the "Wilderness," 135, 143.
  the, a hundred years ago, 172.
  emigration to the, in early times, 172.
  effects of steamboat navigation on, 176–178.
  effects of railroads on, 195, 196.
  rapid growth of, 240, 241.
  See Boone, Clark, Putnam, Robertson, Sevier, Jefferson, Houston, Gray, Sutter, Fulton, Lincoln.

West Indies, Columbus discovers and names the, 10.

Weymouth, Standish fights Indians at, 51, 52.

What Cheer Rock, Providence, 64.

White, Father, in Maryland, 58, 59.

Whitney, Eli, birth and boyhood of, 156.

Whitney, Eli, cuts his name on a door, 156.
    makes a fiddle, 157.
    makes nails, 157.
    goes to Yale College, 157.
    his skill with tools, 157.
    goes to Georgia, 157, 158.
    stops with Mrs. General Greene, 158.
    makes her an embroidery frame, 158.
    has a talk about cotton and cotton seeds, 159.
    invents the cotton-gin, 159–161.
    effect of his invention, 161, 163.
    builds a gun-factory, 161.
    makes muskets for War of 1812, 161.
    summary of, 162.
Wilderness, the great, 143.
"Wilderness Road," Boone makes the, 135.
Williams, Roger, comes to Boston, 60.
    preaches in Salem and Plymouth, 60.
    is very friendly to the Indians, 60, 61.
    declares that they own the land, 61.
    Boston authorities attempt to arrest, 62.

Williams, Roger, escapes and goes to Massasoit, 62, 63.
    journey through wilderness, 62, 63.
    reception by Massasoit, 63.
    builds a cabin at Seekonk, 63.
    leaves Seekonk, 63, 64.
    greeted by the Indians, 64.
    Canonicus lets him have land, 64.
    settles Providence, 64.
    grants religious liberty to all settlers, 64.
    summary of, 65.
Wilson, Woodrow, 263, 266, 267.
Winthrop, Governor John, settles Boston, 53.
Woman drives off Indians, 71.
Women, services of, in the war with Spain, 251, 252.
    in the Great War, 269–270.
Wool-comber (note), 1.
World, knowledge of, before Columbus, 3.
Wright brothers, inventors of Airships, 293.

Yorktown taken, 127.
    news of its capture sent to Philadelphia, 128.